Evolution of Gestalt Series
Volume I

Deborah Ullman and
Gordon Wheeler, Editors

CoCreating the Field

••••••••••••

Intention and Practice in the Age of Complexity

A GestaltPress Book

published and distributed by
Routledge, Taylor & Francis Group
New York

All rights reserved. No part of this publication may be reproduced, stored in a retrieval system, or transmitted, in any form or by any means, electronic, mechanical, photocopying, recording, or otherwise without the prior written permission of the publisher:

Copyright 2009 by: GestaltPress
127 Abby Court
Santa Cruz, CA 95062

and   165 Route 6A
Orleans, MA 02653

Email: gestaltpress@aol.com, gestaltpress@comcast.net

Distributed by: **Routledge, Taylor & Francis Group**
270 Madison Avenue
New York, NY 10016

Library of Congress Cataloging-in-Publishing Data
1. Gestalt therapy, 2. psychology, 3. field theory,
4. relational process, 5. intersubjectivity, 6. Deborah Ullman, 7. Gordon Wheeler

ISBN: 978-0-415-87259-1

for Dan,
whose music and poems
take me to higher and deeper places
and for
Danielle, Saille, Holly, Alder and Athen George
with the intention of cocreating a more humane world!

and for Nancy,
with love.

Contents

◆◆◆◆◆◆

Foreword
Deborah Ullman xi

Prologue – Notes from Big Sur
Deborah Ullman xxvii

Acknowledgments xl

The Editors xliv

The Contributors xlvi

Chapters

1. New Directions in Gestalt Theory and Practice: Psychology and Psychotherapy in the Age of Complexity
   Gordon Wheeler 3

2. Relationality: Foundational Assumptions
   Lynne Jacobs 45

3. On Macaque Monkeys, Players, and Clairvoyants: Some Ideas for a Gestalt Therapeutic Concept of Empathy
   Frank-M. Staemmler 73

4. Cocreation and the Contact Boundary
   in the Therapeutic Situation
   Margherita Spagnuolo Lobb 101

5. Embodying Field Theory in How We Work
   with Groups and Organizations
   Catherine Carlson & Robert Kolodny 133

6. Have We Been Missing Something?
   Catherine Carlson & Robert Kolodny 177

7. Digital Storytelling with Tibetan Adolescents
   in Dharamsala, India
   Iris Fodor 211

8. Mindfulness, Magic, and Metaphysics
   Deborah Ullman 225

9. A Larger Field
   Judith Hemming 261

10. A Part of the Whole, a Part to Play
    Malcolm Parlett 295

Afterword
   Gordon Wheeler 343

Foreword

❖❖❖❖❖❖❖❖❖

I. What Matters?

With every sort of scintillating idea and fancy trinket in our world today, with such beautiful skies and mundane exigencies, with so much to read and do, all vying for our time and attention – why, indeed, might a new book on Gestalt theory and practice matter? Employing our figure/ground construct of awareness, we are all either managing multiple figures against the background of living in a complex world or we are becoming overwhelmed by life's urgent necessities and tuning out. Lots of us are doing both, that is, we are managing a lot and also at times subject to feelings of being overwhelmed and then we tune out. In defending ourselves from the complex demands of an active contemporary life, we often fail to attend to things that really matter such as painful sensations in our bodies or screaming indecencies in our body politic.

What then do we do to address the stresses some of us and many of our clients feel ongoingly? And what sorts of intention and practice will actually support us to make the changes we want in our lives and in the world? What does an evolving Gestalt psychology have to offer that we may have been missing? Because psychology is a kind of story about how humans tick, this book on Gestalt theory and practice suggests an importantly new story to help us understand ourselves in these complicated times. Western civilization has brought many gifts of creativity and empowerment to humankind but it has also bequeathed to us an overarching ideology of individualism. This, among other damaging side-effects, leaves a great weight of loneliness on the shoulders of those of us who do feel deep responsibility for the ways of our world. To shift and share that weight we need a new story of who we are and how we relate to one another. This story, here to be told, can shift our perception of who we are as humans from a focus on our separate individual natures to a focus on our essential relationality. This small shift changes everything. It generates a new set of expectations for our shared life experience as mutually involved forces of intention and meaning. This sense of our selves runs counter to the linguistic, economic, cultural, political and ethical assumptions of a civilization run amok in many ways. Yet, this different sense of ourselves shows us a natural way to a functional future, shows us that living together on this planet with all our differences can represent the flowering of our evolutionary nature.

It is for Gestalt people to tell this story because the roots of this shifting perception, this heightened awareness of our irreducible relationality lie deep in the soil of our Gestalt theory. A field-theoretical Gestalt as described by Kurt Lewin, (and advanced by Malcolm Parlett, Gordon Wheeler, Lynne Jacobs and Robert Lee among many others now) draws our attention to how our behavior is always being affected by the dynamic complexity of our own life experience and our relationship with the world around us, including, importantly, other people.

Our new story can offer some coherence in the midst of the chaos of our contemporary world. This book is offered as a tool to help us through. It presents a narrative with great capacity to contribute to a movement toward transformation. This evolving Gestalt view of who we are as people radically interdependent in every sense, can help us understand ourselves in a way that allows for healthy integration of important demands on our attention with a sustainable, responsible, and satisfactory, even joyous, way of life.

The story of how Gestalt informs our life and work as (paradoxical) agents of change in the world must help us address urgent concerns. Our old story is holding us back. The idea that heightening awareness with individual clients, couples, groups and leaders can enhance both the achievement of shared goals and individual quality of life, while true and important, is not enough. Laura Perls spoke of how her therapy work with individuals was political work (1992, p. 17). This is a provocative and bold insight! We need to build on that. These are critical times on the planet and Gestalt theory offers a coherent, comprehensive, and revolutionary/evolutionary understanding of who we are as interdependent beings. Building on our wisdom about contact experiences and how growth and learning happen, we can tell this new story that deals with the world today, with how we meet the fears and hatreds, greed and waste, hopelessness and fatigue around and within us.

We know these things — somehow we need to reclaim, reintegrate them into a new Gestalt. This is a story of what can happen when deep and authentic connecting is valued. This is, of course, an understanding that vitalizes and emboldens our therapy, coaching and consulting work. And it has to do more than that. It is a story of the myriad ways we are affected by all that's within and around us. It tells of the impact we have on greenhouse gasses and climate change, on other people and nations. It addresses race relations, gender relations, and cross-cultural contacts of all sorts, and how we deal with issues of justice and economic equity as well as religious, philosophical and spiritual differences, as we move through the world. Most of us have an instinct for this. We are appalled by the ways many politicians, banks, corporations, and nation-states behave. We have a sense of the ways we must become more conscious of the consequences of our own behaviors. And when we are among others who live with awareness, we ourselves are able to find the pleasures of consuming more mindfully and acting with greater sensitivity. When we hop into our cars to go one quarter mile, sop up spills with wads of paper towel, buy bottled water shipped from the South Pacific to the USA or Europe, race through our days wastefully and exhaustingly, we know these are habits we can change.

This list of unsatisfying and unsustainable behaviors is infinitely long and always changing. But real change, Gestalt teaches us, comes not out of some moralistic "should" introjected or added on to our already full lives and beliefs but rather out of a shift in the meanings we make from the ground of our experience. In other words, again, it comes from a change in our basic story. Knowing these stories and the ones about how much richer we feel when we take time to observe the beauty around us, noticing the effects our empathy can have in passing encounters with lonely elders and children in the market, practicing consideration instead of irritation in traffic, we remember how we want to be living. In intentional meetings with clients, friends and colleagues, we are able to apply our grounded skills and understanding of working across our human differences. Understanding our profound interdependence helps us lead and support others in our personal lives and in our professional and political lives as well. A *gestalt* is a configuration. The way we use the term as students and practitioners of Gestalt is as a holistic understanding which implies assumptions about our complex human nature, that we are vitally embodied, sense-making creatures who are

Foreword ... xv

intimately and strategically, caringly, and always, involved in the contexts of our lives. It is an optimistic theory of our human condition that presumes people's experiences will be the best they can be with the circumstances that present themselves (for more on *pragnanz* see Nevis, 1987, p. 9). Change agents engaging this approach of radical participatory dialogue offer situational supports that facilitate growth, discovery, healing, connections, problem-solving and peace-making skills. To emphasize the point, in our sense of the evolution of Gestalt, here, we are thinking of this *gestalt*, this configuration of awareness, as a story. This story must creatively adjust to the changing situations surrounding us. To generate greater inclusivity and a more truly democratic world requires more humility and curiosity on the part of people holding power. Leadership in this age requires alignment with the intentions of service to the greater good. We are all now engaged in an interdependent story of who we are in this age of complex global interrelationships. There exists also an urgent press for us to behave with ever greater self-awareness of our role as planetary citizens. This includes attention to the consequences of our own actions on every front with a sense that we are actually cocreating the world we inhabit. And to realize these grand expectations, we are wise to surround ourselves with loving, supportive others.

Gestalt's foundational principles involve us in our context. Even in 1951, Paul Goodman described the self as emerging at the contact boundary between the organism and the environment (PHG, 1951). Gordon Wheeler added some more meat to these bones in 2000, when he identified the self as "our basic process activity and tool for integrating the whole field" of our experiences (p. 162). Given this assertion of our inherent relatedness (with our own histories and the surrounding situation), we can assume we are either learning to creatively adjust to our environment including other people, or not, all the time. And if not, we might ask what is missing to give this fundamental adjusting process a chance to happen? This is about reconfiguring, constructing a more context-sensitive picture of who we are as human beings. What we find is how hapless and dangerous we can be as "cowboys/cowgirls" trying to go it alone, without certain kinds of feedback or support. And how strong we can be when we learn how to engage and develop the kind of supports we need for ourselves and our visions. A Gestalt lens lets us ask — what skills do we need to adapt to today's quickly changing world? This is our work, of course, less as dust in the wind, more as butterflies flapping our wings with all the implications of worldwide impact that image now carries. If this is so, if a new story is emerging about all this, it is, and must always be, affected by the changing terrain.

The purpose of this book is to wrestle with this "moving target," this complexity that includes our changing interior sense of things along with shifts in the exterior world. One of Paul Goodman's "false splits" is interior/exterior. This is a false dichotomy which current research findings in neuroscience help us understand. We are neurologically impacted by empathic others (or hostile others) (see chapters 1,3, 4 and 9). We explore all this that some call relational theory and others refer to as a field relational approach to working or a field-based, interdependent way, of understanding experience. Lynne Jacobs, in Chapter Two, identifies a double helix of relationality and field theory, as she honors our Gestalt understanding of how "our phenomenal fields emerge from our lived contexts." Consider now how our theory and practice have creatively adjusted to our 21st century context. This was the intention of the November, 2005 study conference at Esalen Institute, the Evolution of

Gestalt I, sponsored in part by Esalen's Center for Theory and Research, from which the ideas and the chapters that follow, emerged.

II. Edges

A book about how we cocreate the field and the evolution of Gestalt is a book about edges. It's about the developmental edges of a beloved theory of human nature and process, how we understand who we are and how we do what we do. It is also about how the practices of Gestalt, like the lives of Gestalt's practitioners, are evolving over time. And about how our elegant theory can support this evolving process.

The big idea, the meta-narrative, is that different areas of concern are stretching our Gestalt practices and applications, even our insights about human process, much as the New York study group that developed around Fritz and Laura Perls and Paul Goodman (and others) stretched the Gestalt research psychologists' ideas of perceptual whole-making to apply to psychotherapy back in the 1950's. And then in the 1960's a group of Gestalt trainees in Cleveland began to adapt these principles, including Kurt Lewin's insights about group dynamics, to apply Gestalt in organizational settings.

This story here told about the evolution of Gestalt starts when eighty curious Gestalt practitioners gathered at Esalen, in California, in 2005. The participants for this gathering were invited to look back on 40 years of Gestalt at Esalen since Fritz Perls was in residence. They were also looking at how our theory has developed different emphases over the years and what ways we can grow to meet the challenges of our current times. Finally, these Gestaltists, from many corners of the globe, were looking out at the vast Pacific Ocean, sparkling under the xviii ... CoCreating the Field

November sun, and at each other, listening to individual stories, and discovering together ways to build a satisfying learning community for the week and beyond.

As all of us who have been involved in conferencing, helping to organize gatherings over the years, know the story of the event begins at least a year and a half before the actual occurence. And within that organizing effort lay many interpersonal opportunities for growth. It could also be said that this conference idea was hatched out of a smaller group of visionary Gestaltists who met for three years, twice in Cambridge, once at Esalen, as a field circle study group and explored how we could live together, share ideas, practices, papers, and engage this radically different mode of being, sprouting from an interdependent, or field-based way of being in the world, attending to our impact as well as how we are impacted. And if we could learn lots from these small groups about how to cultivate curiosity and deep belonging, we figured, what might this experiment be like if we invited another sixty-five folks to experiment with us.

An experiential exploration of our community's growth over time, our creative adjustments in practice and theory, is an ambitious undertaking. What that Esalen event and this book are about are how change is cocreated and can be evolutionary. Gordon Wheeler, in his introductory chapter speaks of placing "the evolution of our Gestalt model in its context...." He proceeds to run through some of the concerns that generated each contributing force to our emergent theory over time. "Gestalt teaches us that meaningful development is not just any change; rather it is new creation based on capacities and potentials that are already present in our ground — in interaction with new conditions in the field" (p. 7). We have been informed by complexity theory, general systems theory, chaos theory, critical theory, self-in-relation ideas, intersubjectivity and self theory, neuropsychology, evolutionary theory, race studies, feminism, social justice initiatives, evolutionary metaphysics, and transpersonal practices, to name just a few current academic, therapeutic, and populist inquiries that bear important contributions to, and are clearly supported by, our Gestalt view.

III. Janus-Faced Experiment

What is facing you as you open this book is some of what unfolded at that edgy and very heartful event in Big Sur, California, in November of 2005, and some of what it pointed us to since that gathering. Presentations have been rewritten as chapters. Others have been added in the time since. Know, reader, that you are the intended audience. And know that the ideas between these covers are fresh in our community, ideas still formulating and expressing themselves as we develop ways of practicing and teaching both with individuals of various populations, and with organizations and larger systems. This project represents a fresh look into how we organize meaning over and over again as we traipse along, sometimes clumsily, sometimes mindfully and with grace, often with great empathy, on our way through our contemporary lives, trying to make sense and feel as if we matter and can do something in a troubled world, not as hyper-individuated forces but as relational beings at our core. Each thinker represented here, each presenter at the 2005 conference, each chapter contribution, is an effort to grapple with the lively relevance of Gestalt on this adventure at this edge of experience that exists today. If we are successful this journey may reveal ways our understandings, as students of Gestalt approaches, are crucial in today's world full of challenges, challenges that are quite unlike those of the founding theorists, 50 and more years ago.

As Gordon Wheeler describes in Chapter One, our "fundamental constructivist nature is our ceaseless human activity of making a whole picture, a meaning, an implication, a story, out of the equally ceaseless buzz of 'stimuli' that we are bathed in at every moment" (p. 9). We don't start each day with a clean slate. We are creatures of the narrative, we are living within a global meta-narrative. This book is an offering to our collective human struggle to awaken, to learn, to heal, to teach, to thrive. Storying, then, is our basic human drive. Unless we can change the dominant story from one of fear and greed, separation and suspicion, scarcity and excess, intolerance and exploitation and cocreate one of self-understanding and curiosity, generosity and energized connecting, gratitude and service, we may be stuck in spirals of increasing the suffering and rage of all the world's people ... and possibly ending this human evolutionary journey in this century.

IV. The Road Ahead

Co-editor and friend, Gordon Wheeler, begins our story with some propositions that were first presented as his keynote address to a large conference in Queretaro, Mexico in the spring of 2005. A version of this address was later published in the International Gestalt Journal (2006). Here it is our Chapter One, "New Directions in Gestalt Theory and Practice: Psychology and Psychotherapy in the Age of Complexity." Wheeler sets out seven crucial arenas for applying our Gestalt model that give us a working frame for addressing urgent concerns. The extensions or applications he considers are: 1) self and relational theory; 2) intersubjectivity and intimacy; 3) the field itself as a source of healing; 4) neuropsychology and cognitive science; 5) the revisioning of evolutionary psychology; 6) politics, economics, and culture; and 7) the values of our shared human existence, including ethics and life of the spirit. The chapters that follow flesh out some of Wheeler's key points about the life-like and evolving qualities of our Gestalt theory.

Following Wheeler's introductory chapter the first part of the book looks at issues of self and relational theory, including empathy, intersubjectivity, and intimacy. Lynne Jacobs offers in Chapter Two Relationality: Foundational Assumptions," some clarifying principles about our irreducible relationality, how we are "wired for relatedness," how our unique individuality also points to our shared humanity. She unpacks Kohut's "self-objects" and presents interventions and the intentions behind how she uses herself in therapeutic dialogue. Nobody writes casework better for me in our Gestalt clinical world than Jacobs who here, turns the tables, opening with a case in which she is the client. Later she offers the case of Jerry that highlights her points about relational practice, how at certain times, a client "may need access to the therapist's experiencing." This journey, which takes her into some deep reflections, and extraordinary generosity, exemplifies the value of a case description that can open us to new ways of feeling responsible in our dyadic work. Similarly, later, Catherine Carlson and Robert Kolodny show us ways to hold a greater responsibility for the impact of how we use ourselves in work consulting with organizations. But I'm jumping ahead of myself.

For Chapter Three, Frank Staemmler redeems the concept of "empathy" from Fritz Perls' garbage heap, where it was seen as fostering confluence, one of the early "resistances to contact." Since Wheeler's 1991 *Gestalt Reconsidered: a New Approach to Contact and Resistance*, we have come to regard these resistances as "contact functions" or "contact styles." Frank's stimulating chapter is called "On Macaque Monkeys, Players, and Clairvoyants: Some New Ideas for a Gestalt Therapeutic Concept of Empathy." Staemmler offers much to chew on and digest, from the kitchen table of intimate domestic attuning to his reflections on social referencing and motor neurons, all the way to a new non-individualistic definition of *empathy*. Staemmler's chapter, based on the material he shared at Esalen, first appeared in print in the spring issue of Studies in Gestalt: Dialogic Bridges, 2008.

In "Cocreation at the Contact Boundary," Chapter Four, Italian Gestalt psychotherapist and writer/editor, Margherita Spagnuolo Lobb, brings us deftly from infant research and neuroscience, through implicit interrelating in the clinical situation, to improvisational cocreation and relational confirmation. She suggests that we stay with the procedural aspects of the actual situation as a whole — then shows us what that looks like with sensitive and clear case descriptions.

The next section on the evolution of Gestalt in this Age of Complexity takes up Gestalt applications involving the field itself as a source of healing. Here, our authors deal specifically with how we can use ourselves in our diverse practices with individual, organizational, and community systems, in ways that might impact our larger world situation. Two chapters are coauthored by Catherine Carlson and Robert Kolodny. Chapter Five is "Embodying Field Theory in How We Work with Groups and Organizations" and is drawn directly from emergent group experiences that unfolded in the course of the Esalen study conference in 2005. Cathe and Bob walk us through the stages of designing a learning experience to fit that community as it unfolded in its process over the five days we were together. As with Jacob's earlier chapter, the reflective insights, the willing-

Foreword ... xxiii

ness to share vulnerable learning process by the authors creates a very rich resource for all of us who are figuring out how to be ever more mindful of our impact on those we work with.

Chapter Six takes us even more deeply into the subtle ways we might be impacting the organizations we work with, or in, with "Have We Been Missing Something Fundamental to Our Work?," again by Carlson and Kolodny. Here they explore how shame issues infest organizations and using the Gestalt lens on shame and belonging developed by Robert Lee and Gordon Wheeler (also drawing on Gary Yontef's and Lynne Jacob's work and others) they discover tools for shifting stuck dynamics in larger systems with regard to access to power. This is the first published exploration of this arena with this lens and reminds us of how much we have to offer the larger world of consulting, coaching and counseling when we embrace how universal are issues of shame in our world culture. This culture celebrates individualism, and values of competition in the face of scarcity (of time and resources), at the expense of connection and cooperation. The paradigmatic shift to building organizational cultures that value support and belonging allows us to situate our roles smack dab in the center of larger societal transformations.

With Iris Fodor's Chapter Seven we find a very different way to use ourselves to impact the field. Here Iris uses her apprenticeship studies with photojournalist Phil Borges and shares her exciting work with kids, in a quite different culture from her own. In "Digital Storytelling with Tibetan Adolescents in Dharamsala, India," Fodor shows young people how to use photographs and film to tell their critical life stories as refugees. She walks us through the training process and shares the new sense of resilience and curiosity that the children reveal from sharing their experiences.

In Chapter Eight, "Mindfulness, Magic and Metaphysics" we turn to my own reflections on why issues of spirit, spiritual practice, and beliefs, have an important place for consideration in our Gestalt literature. For this I draw from personal narrative from a career in music broadcasting that spanned three decades, my own experiences with Buddhist world views, panpsychism, evolutionary metaphysics, mystical inspirations and more. The chapter draws together some ideas from a lifetime of eclectic spiritual questing and training, extending our evolving Gestalt explorations into the area of ethics and life of the spirit.

Chapter Nine extends our discovery in these outer reaches of Gestalt that embrace questing and practicing with a piece by Britain's great lady of phenomenological Gestalt, Judith Hemming. Here Judith shares personal and inspiring reflections, writing on the systemic work she now finds so transformational for her own path, and for clinical and organizational clients. This chapter was derived from a lecture in honor of Marianne Fry, the late founder of the UK's Gestalt Psychotherapy Training Institute (GPTI). Judith's work is described as constellating family, couple, individual and organizational issues, and is derived from German family therapist Bert Hellinger's controversial Orders of Love work. In addition, Judith introduces the Ridwhan teaching of the Diamond Heart School.

This brings us to Malcolm Parlett's Chapter Ten, "A Part of the Whole, A Part to Play," which integrates three very moving talks, one of which was Malcolm's closing plenary session at the Esalen conference, 2005. The other two addresses were keynotes to the European Association of Gestalt Therapy conference in Prague in 2004, and for the GPTI, London conference in 2007, "The Social, Political, and Ecological Field: Facing the Future." Malcolm sends us off with a story that inspires and motivates us to apply our deep insights about human nature and process into ever more immediately compelling areas of our shared lives and to take action.

Finally, we close with some fresh and freshly urgent insights on the new story we are telling, offered by Gordon Wheeler in the Afterword. Gordon unpacks some of the dilemmas of our times, our collective struggles, and suggests ways to understand ourselves we can carry with us into our day. These perspectives can help us address these chronic challenges, as he reflects on where we have been in this journey and where we might be going. Before we begin this newly emerging story about how we cocreate the field with our intention and practice for addressing all this, we begin with our Prologue which is a backward glance at the first Esalen Evolution of Gestalt conference, called "Notes from Big Sur." This retrospective was written only days after the event and captures this participant's experiences while they were fresh. This was edited for inclusion in The Journal for Constructivism in the Human Sciences (vol II, issues 1 & 2, 2006) by leading cognitive behaviorist author Michael Mahoney only weeks before he died suddenly in the spring of 2006. The dialogues which led to the finished article were engaging and fun for this writer, making Mahoney's tragic death a significant and personal loss, although I had not known him long.

We the co-editors, dedicate our work in bringing you this collection, to the memory of Michael Mahoney. He took a leading role in the original gathering and in the rich ground of writing and thinking in the larger world of psychotherapy and consulting theories. His life and work contributed to the constructivist interplay that led to this book.

January, 2009

Deborah Ullman
Orleans, Massachusetts

Prologue

◆◆◆◆◆◆◆◆◆◆◆◆◆◆◆◆◆

Notes from Big Sur: The Evolution of Gestalt Conference at Esalen, 2005

Our human capacity for productive relationships is at the core of much contemporary philosophical inquiry, research in neuropsychology, visionary politics and many forms of the healing arts. Gestalt provides a holistic theory for understanding human relational process. It posits that we are innately relational, meaning-making beings. In 1965 Fritz Perls began leading Gestalt groups at Esalen Institute in California. In the forty years since that time Gestalt therapy has evolved with the world around it. In 1991 Gordon Wheeler, (CEO at Esalen at the time of the conference), highlighted Kurt Lewin's contribution to Gestalt as an interdependent and relational theory.

Wheeler closes *Gestalt Reconsidered* by asking if there is a connection between Gestalt's elegant theory of human process and a viable living ethics for the world today. The Esalen conference I tell about here was, from one perspective, an experiential investigation of that question.

On November 13 to 18, 2005 eighty intrepid Gestaltists (and related others), gathered from around the world at Esalen Institute in Big Sur, California. They gathered to explore, experiment, and experience themselves, touched by this stunning stretch of Pacific coast. The underlying question was how might our freshly evolving, constructed understanding of our human life experiences offer a more empowered and deeply fulfilling story about who we are ... and importantly provide an ethical model for leading the world out of so many crises that surround us today. By coming together with attention to the fundamental intersubjectivity of our life experiences we might find new and ever more mindful ways to wonder about each other because, as Lynne Jacobs said on the opening morning of this five day session, "we are all more alike than not."

This was billed as a study conference on the evolution of Gestalt designed to celebrate Gestalt at Esalen over the 40 years since Fritz Perls was in residence. Some attendees brought amusing and touching stories of their personal work done with Fritz on site during the 1960's.

Those stories and the sense of shared history they imparted contributed to building a complex human community. An evening meeting of the full community at mid-week featured a presentation by long-time Esalen resident Barclay James (Eric) Erickson on the late Dick Price who was cofounder with Michael Murphy of Esalen Institute and Gestalt heir-in-residence to Fritz Perls (Kripal and Shuck, 2005). Price's own work was called Gestalt practice, not therapy, and he integrated qualities of Buddhist practice, other Eastern teachings, and the wisdom of Native peoples into his workshops. His widow, Christine Price, carries on work out of this tradition at Esalen today. She wove a few of her stories deeply into the fabric of our week in smaller group settings.

It was clear from the conference materials and from the plenary panel topics that this conference was about more than shared history. It was an experiment in how to develop learning communities, in cultivating life supports and developing visionary skills that include greater empathy for one another in the interest of generating a more just world community. This was a chance to explore ways of living that embrace embodied self-care, meditative and reflective inquiry, interdependent identity in praxis, and interventions for change in large systems in a complex world. This was an inspiring endeavor, undertaken with much gusto by the conference convener, Gordon Wheeler, assisted by a several membered planning committee. The event was entered into with apparent trust, curiosity and excitement by everyone who came. The shared experiences that emerged, while wildly varied, seemed to encourage further adventures in meeting across our differences.

After welcoming introductions that followed a delicious dinner on the opening night, we moved around the room to discover some of the different ways we identify ourselves. Because people had arrived from such great distances as Melbourne and Moscow, from Sicily, Northern Italy, and Southern Mexico, from England, Portugal and many points across the U.S., we broke up early. Many chose to soak their travel-wearied bodies in the mineral hot baths overlooking the Pacific Ocean. The ocean was, itself, bathed in the nearly full moonlight.

The next morning was sunny and warmed quickly into a cozy 60 something degrees F. The first morning's panel hit the ground running, addressing Intersubjectivity and Process. This panel introduced the premise that all our experiences are coemergent phenomena of intersecting subjectivities. Frank

Staemmler demonstrated what this means as he described the work of Gestalt therapy that moves from the confessional to an improvisational dance. He was the first of several to introduce the discovery of "mirror neurons" and how neuropsychology reflects that we are wired for confluence, wired for what he calls "a dyadically expanded state of onsciousness."

He defended confluence (once known in the Gestalt literature as a resistance to contact), emphasizing that empathy must be a two-way street when we speak of intersubjectivity.

Margherita Spagnuolo Lobb, up next, further extended the importance of intersubjective thinking at the core of evolutionary Gestalt, by describing research that shows children imitating not only the behaviors of influential adults, but importantly, their intentions as well. She focused in on the element of timing in therapy, the ever-unfolding "now" that must be developed in order for clients to experience an alternative to their devitalized and repetitive relational patterns of behavior. Psychotherapy and cultural life in general deal with aesthetic values and the cocreation of spontaneous relational dances, Margherita suggested. This was all pretty heady material for all of us and especially many "old school" Gestaltists in attendance who later indicated they had come expecting less of a thought-provoking experience and more of an emotional one. But Lynne Jacobs reeled us in describing the essential moral vision that is Gestalt. She expanded by saying that Gestalt therapy worked initially in part because the founding folks, who were cultural outsiders, really cared. "We are all speaking from our cares" and "we are wired to resonate and respond to the fields we are part of in order to learn." "Our emotions express what matters to us. In light of all this, I must ask myself what kind of human being do I want to be? What kind of human community do I want to create?"

These questions continued to resonate across the campus throughout the afternoon and the week. Several smaller, simultaneous afternoon workshops were offered covering Gestalt research; the secret language of intimacy (by *Voice of Shame, Values of Connection* and more recently *Secret Language of Intimacy* author Robert Lee); photographic self-portraits for developing awareness with Dorothy Charles; and the evolution of mother-daughter relationships with Marlene Blumenthal. The whole group reconvened in the evening to examine how we were going to build our learning community for the week. Mark Fairfield and Gordon Wheeler asked — What voices are empowered here and which may be less so? How do we support felt experiences of belonging? We wondered these things together. The group experimented with sitting in large circle (in the dance dome), sitting mostly on the floor, many felt concerned about the limited opportunities to be heard. Finally it was decided to innovate small process groups to meet in the evenings before the plenary programs to allow more interaction and more expression of differences among us. This decision unfolded within the larger living community and supported the needs and interests of many members. Issues of the distribution of power continued to be explored along with other larger world issues, throughout the week in workshops, plenary sessions, over lunch and dinner, in strolls across the beautiful Esalen gardens overlooking the sea, and, of course, in the world famous luxurious hot baths.

By Tuesday the outdoor temperatures were headed for the 70's F, the sun was still shining. Jim Kepner reminded us in the morning plenary on Energy and Embodiment that our embodied sensing capacity may be greater than our inherited models of therapy allow. If we can develop support for integrating awareness of our own embodiment as a tool of exploration and relational understanding, we can sharpen our sense of energetic dynamics with our clients and of the boundaries of the particular interpersonal fields we move through. Michael Clemmens spoke of the giants whose shoulders we stand on, mentioning specifically his teacher, Laura Perls.

Together Michael and Jim led the group deftly through some experiences to heighten awareness of the field as a source of energy, suggesting ways we can learn to tap into it for therapeutic and life enhancing value. The afternoon included demonstrations of intersubjective therapy; a group met with Leanne O'Shea to explore accessing erotic aspects of the field with awareness. Simultaneously, this author offered a different way to understand and find healthy supports for alleviating stress in today's fast-paced world. The particular model for stress reduction is firmly based in contemporary Gestalt's shame and belonging model, on understanding that our most urgent solutions to stress are often the self-destructive habits we do not like in our repertoire of behavior. The now strong neurobiological evidence that stress contributes to many sorts of disease provides new impetus for attending to this. The interdependent field-based model of human behavior of contemporary Gestalt stresses that when we want to make a change, we need to build in more supports, This can help us cultivate more sustainable solutions to emphasize as a lifelong practice. Another workshop provided further opportunities to encounter intersubjective theory and practice.

By evening of this second day, many were ready for a playful gathering. Gordon Wheeler and Peter Mortola provided this by introducing some experiential play around our life stories. Telling our stories is how we make meaning out of our experiences. We cannot *not* make stories. This involved the use of drawing and sharing.

Gordon ended the evening with two bedtime stories as guided visualizations, one about our hyper-individualized, separate selves, the other about our felt interrelationships with the rest of our world.

Wednesday morning took off with Bert Moore, Dean of the School of Development at the University of Texas, summarizing some up-to-the minute brain research that supported his title for the talk: "All Affect All the Time." We can now measure how our brains respond to our connections with others. He described the neurocircuitry of links between our metaphoric hearts and minds, our feelings and our thoughts. He referenced some telling research with school kids who give twice as much small change after happy thoughts are induced (and take twice as much self-reward); kids who have been saddened give less but still take more than kids in the control group. He stressed that as infants there is good evidence that we are all the time downloading emotional information about the world around us empathically.

Bert was followed by Michael J. Mahoney (since deceased), professor of psychology at Salve Regina University, a leading psychologist of the cognitive revolution, and a prominent figure in sports medicine. Michael introduced the role of contrasting polarities in perception and in knowing, and therefore in the very act of attending to our human experiences. He defined attention as "knowing what to hold on to, what to let go of, and knowing what to do when." He offered an abbreviated history of the cognitive revolution leading us right up to the Stage Three we are now in, characterized as Constructivism. The attributes of this evolutionary phase are: meaning-making is more important than previously (when prepackaged information was the gold standard); relational complexities are acknowledged; most knowing is tacit knowing and emotional (our limbic systems allow us to face ourselves inwardly and outwardly simultaneously, like a Janus-faced god); intentionality matters as much as feedback from previous experiences; and the dynamics of systems are always at play, meaning there are coalitional controls, rather than hierarchical ones, evolving today.

Michael identified other nonlinear geneologies that are constructivist by nature such as Buddhism, Taoism, the pre-Socratics, Vicco, Kant, James, Wertheimer, Bergson, Frankl, Kuhn, Bruner, Bateson and others. He finished by describing some research on meditative states conducted at UC at Berkeley which documented what was previously considered as impossible attentional skills practiced by a monk and friend of H.H. the Dalai Lama.

Gordon Wheeler finished off the rich morning buffet of offerings with a presentation on how we humans got to be the way we are. This was a summary of research on apes and the evolutionary effects of social complexity on human brain architecture, on how our brains tripled in size in only the last one to two million years. Chimpanzees can manage social organizations of only up to 40 other chimps. Humans managed to develop language and syntax over the last 250,000 years (a relatively short time in evolutionary theory). This is explained by the fact that our brains are reorganizing ongoingly to cope with rapidly increasing social demands. Our band of "apes" now includes around 8 billion people. Gordon affirmed with his fellow presenters that we are wired for relationships.

Afternoon workshops demonstrated how we work with all this complexity in different ways. Mark Nicolson focused in on coaching and cultural leadership, including the explicit use of ritual; another presenter, Iris Fodor, graduate psychology professor at NYU, presented from her new passion, digital storytelling with children in India and Peru. She taught kids to make video and other visual narratives to give voice to their cultural experiences. In the same time slot there was a demonstration workshop on working with body process and another small group workshop addressed retrieving access to support.

Thursday morning's plenary started by reviewing where we had been together so far in this learning community. The morning was designed to offer experiences of "the unavoidable impact of our interdependency," as expressed by panel chair Mark Fairfield. The endeavor was about investigating the promise of our learning communities to increase participation and expand leadership potential, an urgently felt challenge in the larger world. Next, Robert Lee summarized some shared Gestalt values and the question of whether these imply a Gestalt ethics. He generated a list of similarities and differences between the assumptions of the individualistic model of human experience and therapy and the relational perspective being advanced this week.

A whole group experiment followed, conducted by Cathe Carlson, which involved breaking into first small groups to discuss our expectations and longings for this week at Esalen. I was fortunate to be grouped with Natasha Kedrova and Daniel Khlomov, who had traveled here from Russia. They shared some of what a week at Esalen meant for them, coming from across the world; some curiosities they had about access to the mountains that towered to our west; questions regarding theory and practice here versus how they teach at their Moscow Center. We three spoke slowly to bridge the language difficulties and encourage understanding. We all then moved into slightly larger discussion groups, sharing some moving moments here as we organized around selecting discussants for a fish bowl conversation in the whole group which followed. With volunteers assembled in an eighteen person fish bowl, the rest of us were instructed to pay attention to our experiences while listening to the conversation, again about expectations and yearnings for this conference week. One group member opened the discussion by leading a moment of silence, other members described their longings, expectations, and struggles. Several now shared difficult feelings. The learning experiment was cut short by insufficient time to review the teaching points, heightening all our awareness of the tradeoffs we experience in our busy lives. The twin experiences of connection and loss were described by several in the group. The unfinished gestalt, the interrupted task, continued working its way into conversations across the campus throughout the day.

This afternoon of the last full day offered four more workshop presentations: one from my friends of the Russian Gestalt Institute on personality; the founder of the Existential Therapy Studies Circle in Mexico City, Yaqui Andres, explored different dimensions of the therapeutic relationship; a workshop was also offered by Israeli author Talia Levine Bar-Yosef, whose new book *the bridge: Dialogues Across Cultures* (2005) was just pub-lished in time for the conference. A workshop on Gestalt and spiritual experience became quite moving and experiential when the large group went outside to watch their last glorious sunset of the week, over the Pacific Ocean.

All of these offerings led up to the final evening gathering at the dance dome. We gave thanks and celebration with our bodies, dancing our dreams and our embodied community, all led with a special flare by Ellen Watson, dressed in green sequines. This dancing continued for over two hours of world beat, and the best of popular music from the last four decades, a little bit of jazz, all played while we scarved our bodies brightly or stripped partially, finally blessing one another with awareness, then rolling on the floor and landing in quite a heap of sweaty Gestalt bodies!

The following morning Malcolm Parlett reconvened us for our last gathering of this profound and playful event. Fiona Coffey, an organizational consultant, who consults to prisons, the British Home Office, and to large blue chip private sector organizations, spoke of how Laura Perls considered her individual therapy work a political act.

The honored guest of the conference, Philip Lichtenberg, spoke on the subject of citizenship and awareness, addressing how awareness gets closed down in polarizing political situations. He invited some of us to reflect on dealing with the politics of our own families around the upcoming US holiday gatherings for Thanksgiving. How do we lean into the differences we feel when someone in a social get-together puts someone else down with a dismissive or bigoted remark? Do we let it pass? Do we challenge the other in a way that will shame that person into holding that prejudice more rigidly? Or might we learn to be curious about that other person's experience, meet him or her while establishing our different viewpoint, explaining that we haven't had the same experience of whatever group is being dismissed (see *Encountering Bigotry*, Lichtenberg, van Beusekom, and Gibbons, 1997). He was heartily applauded for his presentation after naming our urgent responsibilities to converse politically, be socially active, and maintain awareness of our own impacts on the world around us.

Malcolm Parlett shared his sense of urgency for us all to heighten our awareness of our common ground, build on our alliances, remember the embodied presence and excitement we can bring to the bigger world field. "The world is ruled by institutions that depend for their power on our forgetfulness. Waking up is a revolutionary act" Malcolm reminded us, quoting David Korten (1999). He closed by pointing out that we can find innovative ways to do meaningful work. If necessary for promoting ourselves, we might represent our tradition in a variety of other ways — in effect "multi-branding," so that some (for instance) might find it advantageous to introduce what they do as phenomenological, dialogic, and experimental therapy, or "PDE therapy," not as a replacement for Gestalt but simply as another way of describing it.

Malcolm then opened the floor to members of the community who built on the directions suggested by the three panelists, while passing around the mike. Giuliana Ratti was applauded for suggesting that we must not be dominated by the "narcissism of small differences" in our Gestalt communities. She also described sitting down at a café for "green shirts," the radically conservative movement in Italy, and being jokingly offered green coffee. She differentiated herself warmly, explaining that she would have her coffee in the familiar way, not green. Then she showed up the next day: an example of building bridges. Giuliana also acknowledged a distinct pleasure in branding herself a Gestalt therapist. Many others contributed at this point: Frank Rubenfeld offered some fresh discoveries; someone discussed starting to do some writing; one person brought Thomas Jefferson into the room, boldly differentiating himself from anti-war views that had been offered repeatedly throughout the week; someone else spoke of our connections to the humanistic psychology movement; another of how we have been offering coaching all along. Kenny Hallstone offered one last rousing "sermon-from-the-heart" on how much this way of being together could mean in the larger world. Many others spoke, Sara Garcia from her background as a college professor of literature, Enrique Mercadillo offered to help spread the word on the website Jim Kepner was setting up ... all voices supporting the sense of living kindness generated by the panelists and the convener, Gordon Wheeler, and then, the entire group. Many celebrated a felt sense of expansive connection in the room ... what someone called "quite a buzz."

After lunch the dynamic learning community we created went our separate ways, perhaps carrying some of the resonant empathy and curiosity we valued together so highly back into our various communities around the world. This week was surely a successful experiment in what Gordon once sought (in print) as an integration between (Gestalt's) "valid descriptive model of human process and a humane way of life." It was another stupendously beautiful day for gazing off into the sea, smelling the blooming flowers in the Esalen gardens, and being alive on this small interdependent and struggling planet we love.

January, 2009   Deborah Ullman
                                               Orleans, Massachusetts

References

Bar-Joseph, T. (2005). *the bridge: Dialogues Across Cultures.* New Orleans: Gestalt Institute Press.
Korten, D. (1999). *When Corporations Rule the World.* San Fransisco: Berrett-Koehler.
Kripal, J. J. and Shuck, G. W. (Eds). (2005). *On the Edge of the Future.* Bloomington, Indianna: University Press.
Lee, R. G. (2004). *The Values of Connection.* Cambridge: GestaltPress/ The Analytic Press.
Lee, R. G. and Wheeler, G. (Eds). (1996). *The Voice of Shame: Silence and Connection in Psychotherapy.* San Fransisco: Jossey-Bass.
Lichtenberg P. van Beusekom, J., and Gibbons, D. (1997). *Encountering Bigotry: Befriending Projecting Persons in Everyday Life.* Cambridge: GestaltPress.
Wheeler, G. (1991). *Gestalt Reconsidered.* New York: Gardner Press.

Acknowledgments

◆◆◆◆◆◆◆◆◆◆◆◆

A conference that was over a year in the planning and a book about it, more than three years in the publishing — has a mountain of people to be acknowledged.

I, Deborah, would like to start with Buckminster Fuller who offered two notions that have been with me since my early 20's. First is the suggestion that if you don't know what to do to make the world more to your liking, start by doing something about whatever you see needs doing that no one else seems to see. The second point of Bucky's that has motivated my life is that at any time there are cutting edge ideas. If they are too ahead of their time, no one will understand or support the direction of the vision. In Gestaltese, this speaks to the prerequisite ground features necessary to support developing a shared figure. The other side of this is that if the ideas are not far enough ahead, the idea-maker must deal with being celebrated and gets distracted by all the hoop-la. Now this is not to say that the authors in this collection fear too much celebrity or that the ideas put forward at the conference around these new directions in Gestalt for the Age of Complexity are inaccessable or way out ahead ... only to acknowledge the privileged position we are, all of us, in: to have some notion of what we all need to pay attention to as we participate in the massive economic, political, environmental and personal upheavals of our day — how we have a chance now to offer stealth leadership, that crystalline form around which systems organize in chaos theory, in the

xl ...

Acknowledgments ... xli

arena of how to develop a world more compatible with humane values. These are exciting times indeed.

Next I want to thank my elders and longest teachers, my parents, both gone now but I bow to them for the values they taught me including fairness, fun, attention to the neediest ones, care for the natural world, willingness to be ostracized for my beliefs, a healthy skepticism of those in power, love of words and clear thinking, and an aversion for the humorless in our midst.

Of course they also left me with much to recover from, for which I am sometimes grateful because that led me to Gestalt therapy and Esalen Institute.

Working at Esalen Institute over the past five years with the Center for Theory and Research, to deliver a series of conferences on the evolution of Gestalt (this volume represents only the first of three conferences so far) has allowed me to connect with the spirit of that place and learn about the three most important ground conditions that support rapid learning and advanced integration for me — beauty, caring people, and conscious body process! Many people in the greater Esalen community have made me feel welcome, notably Dan Bianchetta, Ilene Connelly, JJ Jeffries, Lena Axelsson, Rob Wilks, Mark Nicolson, and, of course, Nancy Lunney-Wheeler.

From my academic life I want to thank Jeanne Achterberg, Jonathan Cheek, Laurel Furumoto, Maureen O'Hara, and Eugene Taylor. Friends who have held and inspired me include Patty Ford, Dianne Gregory, Iva Liebert, Donna O'Connell-Gilmore, Jacqui Mac, and Gloria Starita among others. Clients, cousins, sisters, students and workmates have cleared the way for my Gestalt passion. I feel grateful to have them in my life.

Within the Gestalt community Deborah starts with a nod to Margaret "Pat" Korb and Alice Martin, who brought me to the well; my co-editor and colleague Gordon Wheeler who has taught me with the brilliance and generosity of his heart/mind; Sonia Nevis who teaches how to practice with insight, power, and ease; and Edwin Nevis who inspires me to a boldness that I once had as a rock n roll DJ but am only still learning as a workshop leader. Many others have been engaged with us over the years in dialogue on the evolution of Gestalt theory and practice, particularly with the emphasis on field theory that now meets our collective urgency for a global foundation of understanding across our differences. A good number of these people are wonderfully represented in this collection. There are others who helped with the Esalen conference but did not contribute to this volume. Still other Gestalt friends with whom dialogues over the years have stimulated much thought: the members of the New England Eaters and Writers' group have helped a lot with this project, Cathe Carlson, Michael Clemmens, Sally and Jim Denham-Vaughn, Mark Fairfield, Rob and Bridget Farrands, Ty Francis, Judith Hemming, Jim Kepner, Bob Kolodny, Mary Ann Kraus, Phillip Lichtenberg, Joe Melnick, Spencer Melnick, Christine and Peter Mullen, Melanie Nevis, Malcolm Parlett, Roy Partridge, Archie Roberts, Carol Swanson, Denise Tervo, George Wollants, and Joseph and Sandra Zinker, are only a few who come to mind. I also want to thank Ruella Frank, Sylvia Crocker and Gonzague Masquelier whose GestaltPress books I found great pleasure in editing. I continue to go back and re-read!

As for this collected volume, it was Mark Fairfield who was miraculously available for some skillful 11th hour editing and Robert Lee who's extraordinary ability to handcraft attractive books is the secret to GestaltPress's continued productivity during these very hectic times in all our lives! I cannot thank Robert enough for his attention to detail, unswerving encour-

Acknowledgments ... xliii

agement, technical prowess, and friendship. I also want to thank Elena Siderova for developing the artwork for the cover of this book from the extraordinary photograph of Daniel Bianchetta.

The most sincere thank you's I offer to the beautiful authors in this collection who have written such ground-breaking and provocative material, each in an accessable voice, and each author shining forth off these pages as a guide for navigating these startling times. We are so relieved, after many delays, to deliver this collection to the hands of you, the reader!

March 4, 2009   Deborah Ullman
Orleans, Cape Cod

And to this may I also add a special thanks to my dear and longtime colleagues, inspirations, and co-conspirators in Gestalt: Marlene Blumenthal, Michael Clemmens, Mark Fairfield, Lynne Jacobs, Jim Kepner, Mary Ann Kraus, Robert Lee, Mark McConville, Malcolm Parlett, Archie Roberts, and the gifted and indefatigable Lead Editor of this volume, Deborah Ullman — as well as my mentor teachers Sonia and Edwin Nevis.

March 4, 2009   Gordon Wheeler
Big Sur, California

The Editors

♦♦♦♦♦♦♦♦♦♦♦♦

Deborah Ullman, MA, is a clinician, coach, trainer, and somatics-based practitioner, working with adults and teens in Orleans, MA on Cape Cod, USA. Her Gestalt grounded work focuses on consciousness and healing, with particular emphasis on cultivation of the healing field. She has authored a number of articles and is co-editor of the collection The Gendered Field. She hosts a TV talk show exploring interdependence and a transformational world view. Deborah is co-director and senior editor of the GestaltPress logo, published and distributed by Routledge, Taylor & Francis Group, featuring books that use a Gestalt theoretical perspective to integrate psychotherapy, relational development, somatics, spiritual and ethical practice, and political visioning work. Deb travels and lectures widely, and cochairs the CTR Psychology Council conference series "Evolution of Gestalt" at Esalen Institute.

Correspondence address: gestaltpress@comcast.net

Gordon Wheeler PhD, is a licensed clinical psychologist with over thirty years of practice, teaching and training widely around the world. He is noted for his work using the Gestalt model to integrate relational, developmental, self, narrative, and evolutionary psychology, and his related work in integral education. As author or editor of some dozen books and over 100 articles in the field, he has focused on themes of co-construction of experience, lifelong relational development, intimacy and intersubjectivity, dynamics of support and shame, gender, narrative, values and culture, multicultural work and post-Holocaust studies. His edited works include a number of translations, and his own work has been translated into more than a dozen other languages. As Editor and Co-Director of GestaltPress (publishing with Routledge, Taylor & Francis Group), he has brought work by over 100 other Gestalt authors to print. Gordon serves as President and CEO of Esalen Institute in Big Sur, CA, which offers some 500 public and intern programs to 15,000 students each year, and hosts the world's largest and longest-running Gestalt-based residential community, now nearing its 50th year. Gordon and his wife Nancy Lunney-Wheeler have eight children, and make their home at Esalen and in Santa Cruz, CA.

Correspondence address: gestaltpress@aol.com

The Contributors

❖❖❖❖❖❖❖❖❖❖❖❖❖❖❖

Catherine Carlson is a principle with Key Partners, an international consulting firm specializing in leadership and organization development. She brings over 25 years experience working with a broad range of executives in diverse industries in both public and private sectors, many of them Global 500 and Fortune 100 companies. Her background reflects a synthesis of insights and experience from a variety of disciplines: business management, applied behavioral sciences, and organization development. She is a member of the professional teaching staffs of the Gestalt Institute of Cleveland, the Gestalt International Study Center on Cape Cod, and The Relational Center in Los Angeles.

Correspondence address: cathecarlson@msn.com

Iris Fodor, Ph.D., is a Professor in the Department of Applied Psychology at New York University and a Gestalt therapist in New York City where she works with people in the arts. She has written about the integration of Gestalt and Cognitive Therapy, women's body image and feminist therapy. Recent work focuses on mindfulness and Gestalt Therapy. Iris is also a photographer whose work has focused on digital storytelling and narrative process in working with indigenous and immigrant children from diverse cultures.

Correspondence address: ief1@nyu.edu

Judith Hemming has had extensive experience as a Gestalt therapist and trainer in Britain, and as a teacher in broader education. Since 1991 she has been learning about constellations work from its founder, Bert Hellinger, and many others. She has since become a leading expert in systemic approaches, pioneering work in organisations, communities and governments, as well as individual therapy. Judith is co-founder and trainer of the research and training organisation CSISS (formerly Hellinger Institute of Britain). In 1996 she began studying in the Diamond Heart spiritual school, founded by AH Almaas.

Correspondence address: judith.hemming@btinternet.com

Lynne Jacobs, Ph.D, is co-founder of the Pacific Gestalt Institute. She is also training and supervising analyst at the Institute of Contemporary Psychoanalysis. She has written for publication in both of her therapy worlds. Lynne's newest book, *Relational Approaches in Gestalt Therapy*, is scheduled for 2009 publication by GestaltPress/Routledge, Taylor and Francis Group.

Correspondence address: Lmjacobs@mac.com

Robert Kolodny, PhD, is an organization development consultant working with a wide range of human systems in the US and abroad. For more than 20 years, he has had the chance to work closely with people in business, government and the non-profit sector in organizations of many shapes and sizes and to regularly experience the uniquely supportive and creative possibilities inherent in a Gestalt perspective. Bob has been on the faculty at Columbia University and at the New School

University in New York City, and he is a member of the professional teaching staffs of the Gestalt Institute of Cleveland, the Gestalt International Study Center on Cape Cod, the Gestalt Academy in Scandinavia and the NTL Institute.

Correspondence address: RK@kolodnyassoc.com

Malcolm Parlett Ph.D., has recently retired from his psychotherapy practice and now focuses on his coaching, organizational work, lecturing, and writing. He is a former editor of the British Gestalt Journal. Following doctoral work as an experimental psychologist, he became an educational researcher. After studying at the Gestalt Institute of Cleveland, his work moved in the direction of therapy, but his interests have always encompassed wider than therapeutic issues. His main publications have been about field theory and meta-competencies that are needed in the contemporary era. In 2008 he delivered the Marianne Frye Lecture on 'Living beyond limits: hubris, collapse, and the embodied return.'

Correspondence address: malcolmparlett@virgin.net

Margherita Spagnuolo Lobb, a Licensed Psychologist Psychotherapist, gestalt therapy trainer since 1979, is also founder and director of the Instituto di Gestalt HCC Italy, and is an invited trainer and conference presenter internationally. She is Full Member of the New York Institute for Gestalt Therapy. She is the first Honorary Member of the European Association for Gestalt Therapy (EAGT) which she has served as president for six years. She is past-president of the Italian Umbrella Association for Psychotherapy (FIAP), and of the Italian Association for Gestalt Therapy (SIPG), which she founded and now serves as Honorary President. She founded the European Conference of Gestalt Therapy writers, has written many articles and chapters, edited several collected books including co-editing "Creative License: The Art of Gestalt Therapy," with N. Amendt-Lyon (Springer, 2003) translated into German, French, and Italian (Angeli, 2007). She is the editor of the Italian journal "Quaderni di Gestalt " (since 1985) and, together with Dan Bloom and Frank Staemmler, of the international journal "Studies in Gestalt Therapy. Dialogical Bridges" (since 2007).

Correspondence address: margherita.spagnuolo@gestalt.it

Frank-M. Staemmler, Dr. Dipl.-Psych., lives in Wuerzburg, Germany. He has been working as a gestalt therapist in private practice since 1976, and as a supervisor and trainer since 1981. He has written numerous articles, book chapters and books, and has edited other books; he has also served as (co-)editor of several journals. His first English language book will be published in spring, 2009, by the GestaltPress logo of Routledge, Taylor & Francis Group: *Aggression, Time and Understanding.*

Correspondence address: z.f.g@t-online.de

CoCreating the Field:
Intention and Practice in the Age of Complexity

1

New Directions in Gestalt Theory: Psychology and Psychotherapy in the Age of Complexity
Gordon Wheeler

Some sixty years ago in New York City Paul Goodman sat down to "edit" a reportedly brief and rather sketchy monograph by Fritz Perls, outlining a new approach to psychotherapy and, more generally, a deep understanding of human process and the nature and construction of human experience. The result was the founding text of Gestalt therapy (Perls et al., 1951), the founding of a school, a methodology, and the beginnings at least of a new paradigm in understanding of ourselves, our experience, and our world.

Today the influence of the Gestalt therapy model is found all over the world, including thousands of practitioners, scores of training centers, dozens of journals and books, and of course tens of thousands of practitioners of other schools, who do not necessarily identify with Gestalt therapy, yet have trained with us, read Gestalt therapy writings, or just been influenced more indirectly by the transformations the Gestalt model has stood for.

Now a theory, a method is either a relic, a mummy of itself, or it is a living thing. Like all living things, it *evolves*. Where is our Gestalt model heading today, and tomorrow? What new applications and understandings are the natural next steps for our theory and method, not reversals or "add-ons," but growing organically out of the core premises and evolution of Gestalt therapy in its first fifty years in meaningful interaction with the felt needs and conditions of today's world?

Our world today, after all, is a *radically different field* from the post-war world of 1950, when Paul Goodman sat down to write the pioneering founding text, in some sort of uneasy collaboration with *emigré* psychoanalyst Fritz Perls (renegade psychoanalyst, to be sure, yet still an analyst in good standing, as he was to remain for the rest of his colorful life). And our world is unrecognizably different from the world of 1905, when the early founders of Gestalt psychology first began thinking about the problems of unified, meaningful perception that launched the Gestalt revolution in psychology: a revolution so profound that there really is no cognitive, affective, or interpersonal psychology or cognitive neuroscience today which is not fundamentally Gestalt in its precepts and approach — just as there is no major school of psychotherapy today which is not marked by Gestalt therapy's longtime emphasis on affect, relationship, and present process in inducing important personal change.

Parts of that original model were timeless, and as useful and inspiring today as they were then. Other parts, naturally, were time-bound, limited (as our work necessarily is today) by the horizons of the culture and the times — everything that was not yet ready for deconstruction and revisioning, which are ongoing, living tasks. Which parts are which? Which are basic and fundamental to the model, and which ones contradict that basic model, when we look at them with our perspective today, fifty years on?

Today, in a world of a unified global information network, a globalizing marketplace, constant intercultural contact, and unprecedented risks of environmental catastrophe, the *core* Gestalt model offers a theoretical and pragmatic frame for addressing urgent concerns in a wide range of crucial arenas. In this discussion, we will be focusing on seven broad areas of new growth and application of our basic, core model — and new challenge in our world.

New Directions in Extension/Application of Core Gestalt Principles

The seven areas to be considered here are:

1) self and relational theory;
2) intersubjectivity and intimacy;
3) the field itself as a source of healing;
4) neuropsychology and cognitive science;
5) the revisioning of evolutionary psychology;
6) politics, economics and culture; and
7) ethics and the life of the spirit, the values of our shared human existence.

Each of these is itself a field in transition, with a plurality of competing voices, all bidding to be the new organizers of that domain. In each case we stand at a choice point in world culture: between, on the one hand, an old polarization which is itself a fixed gestalt, and on the other hand, an evolutionary step "up," to a new level of complexity of thought, and a new understanding of our shared human nature. In each case the Gestalt model has the basic understanding of human nature and process, relationship and experience, to support and inspire this necessary evolution in human culture. But in each case the Gestalt model itself has to evolve — which is to say, to articulate new organic growth out of our richly fertile and most fundamental ground.

The nourishing roots for this evolution live in an ever-fertile ground of *radical constructivism, radical belonging, and a radically relational understanding of self and experience.* To open a dialogue on these urgent issues here, we will first look briefly at each of these seven domains — separately and in their interaction — in order to articulate the cultural challenge, the theoretical problem and potential in each area, and the necessary clarification and new growth in our own model that can take us where we need to go. From there we will move to discussion of these issues, which include the largest and most urgent of our field and our times.

This chapter — any paper — is in the end, always, a work in progress, provoked and stimulated in advance by the anticipation of your reception, and then your responses and ideas. This means that the essay itself is only the first half of this presentation, one element in an ongoing conversation. The other half is the exchange itself, as all of us struggle to make the best articulation of these problematic issues that our conversational field conditions support and allow. Note too that the lifetimes of heart, mind, and experience each of us brings to the conversation are themselves part of that living field. Each of us is a vital part of this shared field of contact — which, in the way of all contact, will then shape and influence my own ideas, and perhaps yours. If our conditions of contact are good enough, we will all experience some change. Welcome to the conversation.

Ground and Context

Now first of all, a few words of history, to place the evolution of our Gestalt model in its context. Gestalt teaches us that meaningful development is not just any change; rather, it is new creation based on capacities and potentials that are already present in our ground — in interaction with new conditions in the field. These patterns in our ground are themselves the pattern trace of earlier experience. Where does our model come from, out of what ground, of beliefs, assumptions, needs and possibilities? And then what are those patterns and potentials of ground in our model today, after a century of Gestalt research and a half century of Gestalt therapy, which can serve us to take our next organic, evolutionary steps, in the contact with our changing world and our felt needs today?

Well, to begin with, every psychological model, every organized picture of human nature and process, arises out of some felt concern; this too is a lesson of our Gestalt perspective. Those new concerns are always some sense that the available pictures and models are missing the point of the world around and its urgencies, in some important way; thus those inherited pictures and models are inadequate to our needs for understanding and for a guide to action, under the conditions of the world today.

The Gestalt psychology movement, which is our parent discipline and our intellectual ground, was born out of dissatisfactions of this kind. The inherited models of perception and cognition of the time, a century and more ago now, were positivist/materialist and objectivist/reductionist to a simplistic degree. That is, these models viewed the world as just *there*, given as we see it — and then our perception is a matter of just passively registering what is "out there," one "stimulus" at a time (rather like that still-new invention of the day, the camera).

Like some of the reductionist/materialist models of consciousness today (which explain everything about the brain except consciousness itself) these old models seemed to explain everything about the perceiving, thinking subject — *except* perception, cognition, and subjectivity themselves. Once these materialistic/scientific models had reduced vision to photons, music to atmospheric pulsation, neural activity to electrical charge — how would they ever get back up to the kind of coherent, meaningful whole pictures and pattern relationships that seem to orient us and serve us in actual situations of living and dealing with each other and our worlds?

In other words, the old associationist model seemed to miss the point of experience and subjectivity altogether. In the familiar Gestalt example, when we recognize a piece of music, we are not "remembering" notes; we are registering and recognizing a *pattern*, a relationship among notes. That relationship itself does not seem to have any direct, material, physical existence: It cannot be reduced to photons and sound waves and decibels from the outside, that would somehow each correspond in a one-to-one, linear way with a specific nerve firing in the brain. So where is the perception, the melody, and what is it, beyond a kind of pattern-propensity in the brain? That is the kind of question the old models of that day seemed completely unable to address and explain.

And so the Gestalt psychology model was born, out of a need to understand our human process of recognizing pattern, relationship, intention, discrimination, interpretation, feeling, misinterpretation, context, and the way we make and use whole pictures of meaning, or gestalten — all those things that necessarily characterize our human process and our lives.

It is important to note here that these early founders of the model — for all that they were dissatisfied with the inadequate models of awareness and cognition they had inherited — did *not* actually set out to found a movement that would lead to replacing positivism with constructivism in cognitive and self psychology, localism with holism in brain/mind research, and reductive, linear causality with field models of complexity and multivariant field conditions in the study of relationship, behavior, and experience. All these were the radical, transformational effects and influences of the Gestalt psychology model, on the fields of psychology, social psychology, art, philosophy, and psychotherapy, among others. But all of them were unintended consequences of that early research, and the light it shone on the constructivist, meaning-making nature of the human mind and the human self. This fundamental constructivist nature is our ceaseless human activity of making a whole picture, a meaning, an implication, a story, out of the equally ceaseless buzz of "stimuli" that we are bathed in at every moment.

Even meditation — which generally involves trying to suspend this integrative, holistic functioning in favor of something more purely receptive, more dispassionately open to the flow around us — even then, we're still registering *images*, not photons. The whole discipline is to disconnect from our inherent tendency to turn those images into thoughts, plans, ideas, with all their associated emotions, and relax instead into a state that is deeply refreshing but not that deeply natural. It has to be learned; the other way does not. Only in certain radical, extreme meditative states — and then generally only in interaction with psychedelic substances — do we get beyond meaningful whole images, at times, to something like direct perception of physical stimuli. And even then, the effect is to transform our understanding of our world and our own nature — but still not to change that whole-making nature, which is both our evolutionary survival equipment, and the ground of our relationships and meanings in life. (After all, you do not meditate when your children are in immediate danger; you act).

Now, all this is an impressive, transformational history, and one not always fully appreciated in the sometimes narrow world of psychology and psychotherapy. But what does it have to do with our Gestalt therapy model today, and the new and next evolutionary developments of that model?

Well, when we talk about "constructivist nature," whole pictures, the integration of experience into living scenarios and even stories — as Gestaltists, of course we immediately think of the Gestalt therapy understanding of *self*, which is not a "fixed thing" in Gestalt, but a fluid function of the person (or more properly, and perhaps less naturally to us in Western culture) a function of the field. Not something fixed and given, but a process. Self is the integrator of the field, we say (but even that language, like all language in the end, has reifying tendencies built into it). In other words, the Gestalt self is that constructivist process itself.

But what is "the field?" It is a characteristic of our shared human field that in addition to being unified, it is also organized into semi-distinct points of view. These points of view, which are agents or persons — in other words, us, — are fluid, interpenetrating, ultimately inseparable — and yet experientially distinct, at least at times. We can experience the field either way — differentiated, or undifferentiated. If you like, try it right now:

After reading this or if you can have someone read this to you then close your eyes, and let the sharp edges of things soften and blur. Let boundaries dissolve. Feel the breath going in and out of you, in and out of anyone around you, no boundary. Draw the breath all the way up from the floor, from the earth under the floor, and let it pass through you and out through the top of the room, and into the sky and the universe. Let that keep happening, for as long as you like, there's no time, no boundaries ...

When you are ready, open your eyes. What does the world around you look like? Sharper, more vivid in outline and color? Softer, more blurred and relaxed? Now, what was that like for you? Was it refreshing? Anxious-making? Relaxing? Irritating? Exhilarating? Erotic? Did you have a sense of a difference from your state before? If so, did you come back reluctantly? Gladly?

Now, ready for another one? If you are, then again close your eyes — or leave them open, as you like — and let yourself sense how different you are from people who come to mind: different size, different shape, different temperature, different physical state right now, different tiny aches or discomforts or stiff places in your body, different memories, tastes, desires. And there are so many people to consider — most of them wearing clothes, just as you are, which are quite distinct from their bodies, their skin — your body, your skin. And you can open your eyes. If there are people around you see them, or close your eyes and make the sight of them go away. And blur your vision or sharpen it. You can move around in your chair — or not. You are so different, so individual, such a creature of whims and choices and tastes and needs and feelings, right here, right now.

Well, most of us are quite familiar with the range of our self experience like that — its moods and what we might call its modes. The point here we need to be clear about as we go forward is that these are the range and the modes and the inflections of contact. All experience, all the time, rests on a ground comprising *both* these poles, both these potentials of the field: the one, and the many. If we were not fundamentally one with a unified field, there would be no such thing as contact, interaction, relationship, communication, communion. And if we were not many, individuated, we would never *register* the world or the contact. We would not experience it — we would just *be* it. There would be no such thing as experience. The idea of contact, experience, self (which are very close to the same concepts in Gestalt) presumes both these realities — the one and the many — both these are the necessary field conditions for life itself. An "organism" is distinct, by definition. But if it is actually separate, cut off, it dies — or never exists in the first place.

Now all this may seem trivial and obvious. But note how it completely contradicts the whole 3000-year tradition of our mainstream Western culture and thinking. The most fundamental assumption of this mainstream tradition, after all, is that self, the individual, is primary — it exists first, it is "more real" than connection, relationship, identification, which come later, and have a sort of secondary reality. You can see this vividly in Freud — and also in Perls. And this is to say nothing of feeling, transcendence, metaphysical union, or love — all of which to Freud were illusions (built on regressions), while to Perls they were at best uneasy, precarious states, which he regarded, according to some who knew him, with something like a phobic reaction.

You can see this discomfort as well in Sartre, and much of mid-century existentialism in general, which had a great influence on Goodman and his particular articulation of Gestalt therapy: this idea that even though our existence here, our *Dasein* as Heidegger said, is by definition with other people, still those other people always represent a *loss of self,* a threat to our autonomy and our authenticity. Steeped as he is in Western philosophy, it does not seem to occur to Sartre that while living only for others might be a pitfall, even a path to fascism, there might also be such a thing as living *in* others, being *one with* others, relaxing that self-boundary sort of like we just did — not as an "avoidance of contact" or a loss of contact, but as an *inflection of our self-experience* that could be energizing, clarifying, and a *source* of greater authenticity and richer, fuller contact itself.

This kind of narrowness of vision sometimes crept into our Gestalt model as well. Even though the model claimed to give theoretical priority to "the field," it sometimes has seemed that if you were actually experiencing that unified field, you might be told you were "out of contact," or you were "being confluent" — which was not a mode, an inflection of contact experience, but a "resistance." (On the other hand, feeling absolutely separate and bounded — "I'm me and you're you and that's the end of it" — was not resistance, in these hyperindividualistic [mis]-interpretations of Gestalt therapy but was more like the ideal of the healthy person! Lonely, you might say — but healthy!) Instead of that "separateness" being a capacity, an inflection of contact and experience that some of us might indeed need to develop, as part of our full human potential, it seemed at times to become an end it itself, an ideal, even reality itself. How Western!

Meanwhile, many of us, in Gestalt therapy and in general in the West in our day, have turned to the traditions of the East — or to the shamanism and traditional societies of the Americas — to help us break out of the narrow cultural assumptions of the Western self-model. This has been a great gift, but sometimes it seemed that the great yogic systems of the East had lost sight in turn of the other pole of our experience — our sense of the individuality of ourselves and others.

What the Gestalt model offers us — alone I believe of the major psychological models and systems available to us today — *is the integration of both these poles of experience, "the West" and "the East,"* if I may use those terms loosely in that way. That is, the Gestalt model represents a step up to greater *complexity* — beyond the reductionist poles of a caricatured "Eastern" or "Western" worldview. This greater *complexity of vision* can hold and experience the whole of the *mysterium universum* — the mystery and meaning of life, instead of simplifying the field to only one pole.

I would also venture to say that this complexity of experience — this holding in one and the same breath that I am me and I am you, and you are you and you are me, the one and the many — is the actual experience of love. We all know it, we all want more of it, and I dare say, we all want a world organized around the ability to hold and operate out of that greater complexity of experience, that ground of love. To realize that vision — in our wider world, in our work, in our relationships, in our selves — requires that we take this step, up to a greater complexity of understanding. That step — growth in the direction of greater complexity, greater potential for complex articulation and action — is evolution itself, the unfolding of the inherent tendency of life toward creativity and growth, which is another fundamental tenet of our Gestalt model. In this sense —

and we will come back to this point at the end — the Gestalt model offers, as no other system does, the necessary ground for the evolution of culture and consciousness in our shared world, which so desperately needs it today.

After all, *greater complexity of vision* — holding a fuller whole picture, studying how we organize complexity, and (in psychotherapy) deconstructing those complex pictures and sequences in the interests of freeing them up — all that is what the Gestalt model was about in the first place, and still is about today, in all its many rich variations. Best of all the available psychological systems, the various worldviews of human nature and human process, Gestalt offers us a way forward through all the regressive, reactionary, oversimplifying tendencies of our world situation — all the fundamentalisms around us today. (And note how a fundamentalism — any fundamentalism, — by definition, is a reaction against complexity, against the stress of evolutionary growth itself).

We will return to these larger issues in a moment, at the end of this part of our discussion. But first, let us take a look, briefly in each case, at a limited number of specific areas where that growth in vision, those more complex approaches are needed in the world today. In each case we will look at, it is the Gestalt model which offers the theoretical ground and the practical interventions to support and guide that growth. And in each case, we need to do some clarifying and regrounding of our own Gestalt model itself — shedding some of the extra baggage we picked up over the last fifty years, and drawing anew on the creative potential of those original Gestalt precepts, the principles of our constructivist, meaning-making, evolving human nature itself. The seven topic areas we will focus on here (and there could be others) again, are

1) self and relationship;
2) intimacy and intersubjectivity;
3) energy and healing;
4) neuropsychology and cognitive science;
5) evolutionary psychology;
6) politics and ecology; and
7) ethics and spirit.

We will turn — again briefly — to each of those now.

Self and Relationship

We have covered a lot of this one already, in talking about how the implications of the Gestalt psychology model contradicted the most basic assumptions of the Western cultural tradition — and especially the assumptions of what I have called the individualist paradigm, that meta-ideology in the West that has organized so many of the other ideologies that have come along, even when those systems seemed to contradict each other deeply. I wrote a book about this a few years back, *Beyond Individualism* (Wheeler, 2000) which tries to develop all these ideas out of direct experience, through a series of exercises and discussions that lead the reader through the book. The idea of the book is for the reader to develop the theory for her/himself — your own version of it — out of your own experience, and that of others.

Maybe I can illustrate this paradigm, and the problems with it, with a remark from the late Isadore From, a very influential and beloved Gestalt trainer of an earlier generation. Isadore was fond of saying, "Gestalt therapy has *nothing to do with relationship*. Relationship is very important in life — but it has nothing to do with Gestalt therapy, which is a therapy of *contact*" (personal communication, 1992, and further occasions). In other words, *first* you have (implicitly, if unspoken as an assumption) the individual person, the individual self, who is just *here*. Then you have something called contact, which takes place "at the boundary" between that preexistent person and the preexistent world, or other person. And then when you add up, or somehow get enough contact episodes, you come out with relationship — but that is later, it is a sort of side-effect.

The therapy then consists of sitting in a room with another person — but that is not what you start with either, in your analysis and methodology. That is presumed to be a neutral background, which does not affect the experiment. You do not then focus on studying or deconstructing the co-construction of the meaningful relational situation between these two people, right here and now, *as the therapy*. What you study is only or chiefly what one person "walked in with," his/her contact problems, often around people who are not there at the moment, and so on.

Ironically, this is called "present-centered." But actually, it is hard to get to the actual present under this model — you tend to be dealing with the just-past — not the real, relational situation you are actually in. It is easy to see, in retrospect, how close this is in some ways to the classical Freudian model Perls in particular came out of. It lends itself to being an "expert model," in the same way that early psychoanalysis did, by claiming that the present relational situation is out of bounds, as a real subject for question. To be sure, these models — the early psychoanalytic and the more Perlsian Gestalt therapy — do have necessarily to deal with the client's feelings and beliefs about the relationship in the room: But they do not deal with them *relationally,* as a real thing (they deal with those things "transferentially" — or deflect them to other relationships, or make them a case study in correcting the client's contacting process [which may be a perfectly good, choiceful one, given the relationship the client is co-experiencing with the therapist — but then that is made hard to talk about]).

And then the goal of the therapy — early psychoanalytic or Perlsian Gestalt therapy either one — comes out of these same individualist assumptions: If our nature is to be separate individuals first, relational second, then the ideal of the system will be the maximum achievement of that nature. Maximum autonomy — meaning independence, freedom from the influence of others — is the more or less explicit goal of both systems.

As Erikson and others have observed, a theory always contains the pathology of the founders, raised to a normative level. Some of that was in our early model, true, but still Gestalt therapy — including Perlsian Gestalt therapy — is much more than just that. The premises of constructivism — holism, field theory, phenomenology, subject as active organizer of meaning in the experiential field — are inherently relational, even beyond what most of the pioneers of the Gestalt psychology movement or the Gestalt therapy movement could fully appreciate at the time.

An early rich exception to this limitation was Kurt Lewin, the most fertile, the widest-ranging, and doubtless the most influential of all the Gestaltists of the 20th century. Lewin did see the radical relational implications of the model — as you might expect from the man who is most credited with founding group dynamics, organizational dynamics, T-groups and encounter groups, action research, and social psychology itself as a discipline.

As Lewin remarked toward the end of his brief life: "The American [meaning United States] cultural ideal of a self-made man, of everyone standing on his own feet, is as tragic a picture as the initiative-destroying dependence on a benevolent despot. We all need each other. This type of interdependence is the greatest challenge to the maturity of individual and group functioning" (Marrow, 1969, p. 226). Maturity, in other words, is not "autonomy" but *interdependence*; not simplification of the relational field, but an ever-growing capacity to experence its complexity.

It seems to me that we know this. We know it in our cells, in our deepest self-experience, because that self-process, and that self-experience (and those cells) are the creative effects of a relational process — which is growth itself, most pointedly in human infancy and childhood. We are born into a pre-existent web of relationships. Our entry affects that web or field, in anticipation, even before we get there. And that field co-creates us.

Now up to that point Freud and Perls would probably agree — though in different terminologies. But here is where a radically relational Gestalt model differs: *We do not outgrow that cocreation*, with (as Freud maintained) the resolution of the Oedipal crisis. That active, relational interdependency is on-going, all the time, all through life. It *is* life. It cocreates us — we interpenetrate and cocreate each other and our field, reciprocally, all the time.

Stop a moment, and take that in. You are unique, you occupy a unique, creative point in the field — *and* you interpenetrate the people around you, the people next to you. Breathe into it. How does it feel to breathe into and out of the other person — and let them do the same? Anxious? Invasive? Shaky? Less alone? Excited? Erotic? Frightened? In our culture we have to get used to this idea. We are more accustomed to the idea — the words anyway — that we are not "really separated" from the atmospheres, say, the molecules, the environment around us. Note how carefully non-personal those words are!

This interpenetrative process with other people never stops. That is not "regression," it is what life *is* — flexing and melting that individual boundary, which is a living muscle, an experience, not a thing. If we can *only* flex it into differentiation — or *only* dissolve it into union — we are in trouble, of one kind or another. We cannot live a full life — we cannot realize our gifts, and give them to life, to others, to the world — which is after all the point, the most satisfying thing, by the terms of our nature.

Now again, in Gestalt therapy we have often emphasized the flexing, not the melting. Sometimes we have even pathologized the melting, the belonging, the relational — just as Freud sometimes did. Now please understand, I am not putting down the liberating work that went on — and still goes on — to develop our sense of agency, our own birthright of uniqueness, in Gestalt. If you are as old as I am, you know how essential that was, forty years ago, and still is. But it is not the whole story.

The whole story — the real story of Gestalt, when we are consistent with our basic beliefs and our own phenomenology — is a *paradigm of radical belonging*. We are relational before, beneath, and around our individuality. And the goal of life is not to outgrow that interdependency — but to enrich it, enliven *both poles*, and make their interplay more complex, and thus more fertile.

This shift is theoretical, but it is also directly practical: Again, it was Kurt Lewin who said that the most practical tool you can have is a good theory. But to make this shift, to realize the potential of the Gestalt model, Gestalt itself has to evolve — and that evolution begins with clearing up some of our own contradictions, and some of the contamination that necessarily clung to the early founders of the model, from the individualism and dualism of their times.

The irony is that other schools of therapy — psychoanalytic, cognitive-behavioral, Ericksonian, somatic, constellations work, and many others — have begun to see the implications and the importance of this radical Gestalt/constructivist shift toward truly present, truly relational work, and have adopted it and taken it further — even while parts of our Gestalt world were still clinging to a mid-century Perlsian hyper-individualism! Psychoanalysis in particular has reinvented and renewed itself (at least in its most forward-looking branches) with the kind of intersubjective perspective I will talk about next.

A radical relational perspective — one that is freed of the old individualist, expert, Cartesian/dualist assumptions — *is* the cutting edge of evolution in Gestalt psychotherapy. We invented it (in psychology, that is): Now we have to clean up our own act and own it. I will say more about that in the next section. And it is key to all the other new directions and evolutionary developments I will talk about below.

Intersubjectivity, Intimacy, and Development

When you take the Gestalt field model seriously — the hereand-now, ongoing cocreation of a field of meaning, with those meanings and the present dynamic self as field-effects — what you have done is to move from the old, more individualistic constructivism of a century ago, toward a perspective known today as co-constructionism (in the work of Gergen, for example, which has become so important in anthropology and cross-cultural work). Co-constructionism is this recognition we have been talking about, that we do not create our meanings, our behaviors, our unique selves, alone. Our cultural and relational surround — both in our past and also right now — are cocreating us at every moment.

Again, in radical psychotherapy this perspective leads us to the school known as intersubjectivity — the way our subjecttivity, our self experience, is a product of the present, relational field dynamic. Intersubjective therapy as a movement grew out of psychoanalysis and self-psychology, with the work of Stolorow, Atwood, and their associates. But its real philosophical, methodological home is in Gestalt. I have written elsewhere about this (e.g. Wheeler, 2000), but I think you can find the very best exposition of this work in the writings and training of Lynne Jacobs. Her radical, impeccable assumption at every moment that you and I are creating this situation together — with neither one of us having a privileged point of view on it; her *radical attunement*, which supports people to move to areas of self experience they did not even know were there (or did not yet sense as missing) — is enormously clarifying and inspiring, and can renew your work, and your relationships.

This kind of work also opens up our understanding of *intimacy*, and its role in development. If you work with couples, you know that "intimacy" is a tricky word, generally not defined, or not very well. Often it is used to mean sex (which we all know can be very intimate *or* can be a terrific defense against intimacy). Nevis and Melnick define it in terms of a harmony of contact cycles, goals, pacing, etc. All that seems important to me, but it seems to miss the central Gestalt point.

Intimacy, in Gestalt perspective, is the shift of focus of our interest, from figure to ground. Instead of focusing just on what a person is doing — behavior, figure — we shift the focus to "where they are coming from." What is *their experience,* that is producing this behavior, and making it make sense to them. And from there we can broaden out, to the relational ground of their experience in the moment. In psychotherapy — or in life — this shift can take the form of "What am *I* doing, right here and now, that might contribute to your seeing things that way. What meaning are you making of *my* behavior, what are you imagining about *my* experience, that makes you choose to react in this way?" After all, we almost never react to each other's *behavior*. What we react to, in all but the most dire physical emergencies, is our *interpretation* of their behavior.

Imagine that I am pacing back and forth in front of you and you have got your legs stretched out, and I stumble over them. How will you react? Well, you will say, it depends. First of all, how violent was the kick? Because if it was startling enough to the physical organism, then the physical organism will respond from lower brain centers, or directly from spinal cord centers. We do not have to think about it and interpret it to draw our hand out of the fire; our spinal centers take care of that for us.

But in the more ordinary case, there is higher cortical processing going on. This is a part of the brain that does not communicate directly with the "outside world" at all: It communicates with other parts of the brain. It synthesizes, coordinates a judgment, integrates the situation and adjusts the response in the light of our own intention or interest, and of perceived context.

In other words, we *interpret*. That is what the higher brain is *for*, that is why we have it, why it evolved — basically, to synthesize the complex interpretations required to *predict others' behavior*, in an incredibly complex social field. After all, the figure — the behavior, the kick — has no meaning, except in relation to a relevant ground: This is one of the most fundamental principles of our Gestalt model. And the relevant ground here has to include my intentions, my own "inner world." And since you cannot see that directly, you have to imagine it, construct it, make the best picture you can, and predict my *future* behavior on that basis. Trust, after all, is an assumption about the future, not the present.

But this means that interpretation — specifically interprettation of others' motivations and feelings — is our basic nature, our basic human equipment, our basic tool kit for navigating the world of people. So if we tell our clients, "Don't interpret," we are telling them something that goes utterly against our Gestalt model and is utterly useless in their lives. But if we tell them, "Let's unpack those interpretations, see if they're fixed and rigid, see if you're taking in all the available data, using all the dialogic means you might have here to learn more, test out, hold your prediction as an idea, not a certainty," then we are empowering them, to take their own assumptions apart, when they need to, and, well, interpret more effectively.

To repeat, short of a physical emergency, your reaction will be not to my behavior, but to my imagined — interpreted, projected — intent. That is how we work, how we survive and function in an interpersonal field: We estimate and predict how others will behave, based on what we understand/imagine about their *motivational state and system*. We are born — evolved — to do this. We emphasize deconstructing projection in therapy, after all, not because projection is inherently pathological, but because it is so utterly natural that we have to learn the skill of taking it apart, when it is not serving us. (And note here that a trauma reaction is the activation of a physical emergency response, in an atypical way — i.e., when no immediate physical emergency appears to others to be present, yet the person and the brain pattern react as if it were).

Now what does this mean for intimacy? Well, intimacy is that dialogic process of exploring, deconstructing someone's ground in this way. What are you basing that on? What do you hope? What do you fear, in this interaction? Where do those hopes and ideas and beliefs come from? Are they flexible or rigid? Most of all, where am I in all that? What am I doing that might support your interpreting me one way, as opposed to some other way? What would support you to feel more able to ask me about it, about myself?

That is an intimate exploration; and it is also the Gestalt definition of dialogue. Dialogue is a particular kind of conversation focused not on your positions, our behaviors only, but on why those positions, those behaviors make sense to us: a conversation, in our terms, about personal ground. That is where dialogue differs from debate. In dialogue your goal is to listen and inquire, and to support your partner to express him/herself. In debate you are focusing on expression, maybe persuasion, probably on winning, but not on listening or clarifying why those positions draw you (or the other person), personally. You are not concerned in debate with what seems more appealing to you or him/her, out of concerns that are more than just logical reasons.

Now therapy is obviously one type of intimate relationship, in this definition. But it is a one-way intimate relationship for the most part. That is the integrity of the transaction: you are taking my money, basically, in exchange for setting aside your agenda, your ground, in favor of just concentrating on mine. You do share enough of it, at times, to clarify my world, but not in the interests of clarifying yours (or at least not on my time). In a friendship, eventually this would get lopsided. What are *you* getting out of this, a person may come to feel, maybe with some mistrust, maybe with a feeling of shame or inferiority (how come you never share *your* problems?). Or alternatively, what am I getting out of this, if it is always only about you? That is why the payment is so essential in therapy; it works to remove some of the question of a hidden agenda (of course, it leaves me with the question that you may be doing it "just for the money," and many clients do come to us with that feeling).

Parenting is another kind of intimacy which, if not just oneway, is still asymmetrical. The parent is, and should be, more interested in the child's inner life than *vice versa* (including their need for zones of privacy and autonomy!). If it is the other way around, then we get what we sometimes call a "parentified" child, a codependent structure, where the person may become way more skilled at taking care of the others' needs, than of their own.

And then there's *instrumental intimacy,* where we do try to understand the other person, but it is in order to influence them or manipulate them — not necessarily a bad thing. This could be sales, or supervision, or training, or some other goal of influence. But we are not taking an interest in them for the sake of their own growth, or the growth of that kind of relationship between us.

An *intimate relationship,* in the full sense, is one which has shifted — at least part of the time, at least potentially — to that kind of intimate contact as a goal in its own right. These are the relationships we treasure, the ones we turn to when we really need it, really need that *intimate witness,* in order to deal with everything life is throwing at us.

Full, flexible, healthy personal growth takes place in a context which includes, at least at significant times, that intersubjective gaze, the particular kind of support we feel when someone else sees something of our world, from our point of view; sees what we are up against, knows how it feels, understands why we do what we do, even if it is not "the best thing." We do not have to have that, to make creative adjustments and develop: It is a condition of growth, not necessarily of life. But the creative adjustments we make and the growth we achieve in a field without that intersubjective presence, that intimate witness to our lives, will tend to be rigid, not adaptable, functional only in the impoverished, low-support field where it was formed.

Those adjustments tend to become our stuck places. We all know this, in our clients and in ourselves. Those parts of us that were unseen, unreceived, unsupported in this way when we were young and very dependent, stay with us as rigid places — fixed gestalts — later on. The intimate witness — it might be a parent, a grandparent, a teacher, an early friend, a lover, a partner, or a life friend later on — is, all through life, the key to *healthy* growth. We never outgrow our need for it. And this of course is why therapy takes place in relationship — because with that support, that seeing, we can relax the rigid, too-alone adjustment, deconstruct it, and start to explore something new. It is not impossible to do that at times on your own, but it is way more difficult.

Thus the intersubjective perspective changes our understanding of both development and therapy — tying development and growth much more closely to a Gestalt understanding of intimacy and support. I teach workshops on working with shame — another topic that is completely transformed by a Gestalt relational/intersubjective perspective. And sometimes I like to do a little exercise with my groups. Here is how it goes: First you are asked to think about a part of your life that just *does not seem to change*, no matter how much you come back to it and worry about it and try to do something about it. We sort of get beyond it, but even in ourselves, it has not really changed.

So that is one thing, and then we do a great deal of work on that. Then for the second part: Think about something in your life you feel *too alone with*. Most of us have some places like that — an old failed relationship, a sibling, a lover, a parent you feel too alone with. A fear, a regret, a goal you know is important, but somehow it is just a little too out of reach, it does not seem to happen. And then we do some work around that.

And then the third part: Think of a place in your life that is tinged, colored with *shame*. And no surprise — but it often comes as a surprise to the participants, when you are in it: These three generally turn out to be the same. The thing we are too alone with turns out to be the thing that does not change; *and* there's shame in it somewhere, because (and only the Gestalt model really clarifies this experiential reality for us) *shame* is *the feeling of being too alone, unseen, unreceived, unaccompanied,* in our development as children, and in our living and growing today. It is our Gestalt relational field model, with its appreciation of our *irreducible immersion in an intersubjective field,* that gives us this transformed understanding of shame and support.

All these areas — intimacy, development, support, shame, therapy itself — are transformed, both in theory and in practice, by a radical Gestalt relational/intersubjective field perspective, on ourselves and our process. All of them take off in new directions with new energy, as fields of exploration, once we apply that Gestalt understanding. Gestalt is the natural base of new directions in each of these areas. But again, to do that — to exploit Gestalt's potential to go on transforming these areas of work — we have to clarify and reground our own model, in its own fundamental principles.

Sensitivity to Field: The Healing Field

The next topic, the next developmental area is less clearly developed and articulated in our theory and in our culture than these first issues, but no less important, and directly related to the others. This is the whole area of *direct apprehension of the field itself as a whole,* and direct intervention in/on that field. As social animals we are in fact exquisitely sensitive to the human, intersubjective, energetic field. We all know this, and we use it all the time in our work. We are constantly drawing on and being guided by knowledge that we cannot explain or justify — often may find it hard even to put into words at all.

Like all social mammals, all we have to do is arrive in a group of our fellow species members, to "get a feel" of the mood of the group. Part of this may be pheromones. Part may be exquisitely subtle postural and muscular signals from others. The point is, we know far more than we think we know — much more than we can put into words. This is part of our radically social/relational nature, of deep belonging, in the world of people and in the natural world. (Think about dowsing for water. Some people are extremely sensitive to the presence of water. This sensitivity is of course in them, not in the dowsing rod. The rod is just the way they manifest (to themselves as well as to others) a subtle change in tension in their hands, which they themselves could not pick up without this indicator. I imagine something very much like that is involved in certain gifted people's use of traditional "psychic" tools for reading character and making predictions about a person's field: the pendulum, the cowrie shells, even the enneagram or astrological table, in certain sensitive hands — all that functions as a way for them to exteriorize the knowledge that they hold organismically, and get it into words where we can use it.

Now you may say that this is far afield from Gestalt, but if you're at all familiar with the work known as "Orders of Love," or Constellation work, the field-constellating methodology pioneered by Bert Hellinger, then you find a use of this kind of field-reading that is highly social, relational and phenomenological — especially in the hands of certain deep Gestalt practitioners such as Judith Hemming in London, or Hunter Beaumont in Germany. The work can look almost mystical or "spooky" at first glance, for its power to suggest clarifying perspectives on long-embedded, cross-generational issues and blocks to growth. Look deeper, and you see a sophisticated methodology for exteriorizing the field sensitivities we are naturally equipped with. Again, understanding this work depends on a Gestalt perspective on how we co-construct a field of meaning, and then relate to each other, ourselves, and our worlds in terms of that interpreted field.

Ty Francis and Malcolm Parlett call this kind of thing "fieldsmithing" — learning to use and operate in and on our living human field — and our living natural field in general. We will come back to this in a minute, when we talk about politics and participatory world citizenship. Meanwhile, in this regard I refer you to the healing energy work of Jim Kepner, an amazing practitioner, or to the interpersonal somatic process work of Michael Clemmens. These are only a couple of the many, many gifted practitioners and therapists — we all know some — who through their work in Gestalt, have been led to other field sensitive methods and practices, which they sometimes practice "with the left hand." With the tools of an evolving Gestalt theory, we don't have to be afraid to bring this work into the light, for want of any theoretical way to approach it and make it understandable to others.

Neuropsychology and Cognitive Science

With the hot current topics of neuropsychology and the new field of cognitive science, we come to a place where the Gestalt model of the brain/mind is coming fully into its own. Basically the story here is that the new technology of brain imaging is revolutionizing our understanding of brain and mind in a number of directions. In each case, the new picture confirms longstanding Gestalt positions and perspectives, in contradiction to traditional views in this field. Consider the following central arguments of the Gestalt model:

1) Cognition, perception, memory, and problem-solving are inseparable from affect, emotion, intention — *confirmed* (see for example the work of Damasio, and the body of work cited in his books).

2) The brain itself has to be viewed holistically; functioning always depends on a coordination of multiple areas — confirmed. Chomsky's model of the brain as a set of selfcontained "modules" or relatively separate sub-organs, which is in line with the old thinking, has been largely disconfirmed, and Chomsky and his followers have modified their position. The Gestalt position, that it is the connections that matter, not just the elements in isolation, is much closer to the current view.

3) Perception, attention, and memory are organized in a figure-ground way; the currently active focus of attention draws and uses energy, while context and memory are lightly energized in support — *confirmed*. A good image here is a series of over-lapping concentric rings, like the active and long-

term memory on your computer — only with many more than two levels.

4) Mind-body unity — *confirmed*. The old brain/body distinction — the captain and the crew, — the new technology confirms, is not meaningful and cannot describe how we actually function. Intelligence is all over our body, and functions in an integrated, holistic way.

5) The old nature-nurture debate. Goodman regarded this old debate as one of those "false dichotomies" he wrote about — simplistic reductions of a complex, integrated phenomenon. We now know that the actual physical brain itself is only partly organized at birth, and will be patterned, physically organized and networked, by *experience* — largely *relational experience* — in the early months of extra-uterine life. We will say a little more bout this in the next section.

6) Perception is a kind of constructive problem-solving, not a passive, camera-like activity — *confirmed*. We are born to be scenario-planners, to look for a pattern fit, a solution, a prediction, as a basis for action. When you think about it, this is why we are the story-telling animal. A narrative, after all, is a *gestalt over time* — first this, then this, then this: And then the whole thing is the unit of meaning, it works as a whole. This is why kids (and adults) love a story — and why they do not want you to stop in the middle! It is also why fairy tales and parables are readily understood cross-culturally. We are problem-solving scenario planners by our evolved, neurological, gestalt nature — narrative beings through and through. The structure of ground — everything that supports and gives meaning to our figure-forming process — *is narrative.*

7) Finally, lifelong development — *confirmed*. Goodman argued that the best image of healthy adult personality was not the old Victorian patriarch of the Freudian tradition, but its very

opposite — the artist, growing and changing and experimenting all through life. As a metaphor, this too is confirmed: We now know that the actual, physical brain is still growing, renewing itself, changing its actual neurological pattern structure, all through life — *if you use it that way!* And is not "using it that way" that Gestalt therapy is all about, in all its different subschools and applications?

Now how did this happen? How can it be that a particular school of psychology and psychotherapy could turn out to be so right about so many things, in the fields of neuroscience and cognitive psychology that really did not even exist in their contemporary forms fifty and a hundred years ago? I think the answer has to be in the fact that we were based on a good idea in the first place. That good idea was the principle of starting with *experience,* and trying to understand the phenomena from that point of view rather than from some preconceived idea, and trying to reduce the phenomena to fit that idea.

Not — and this is important — that we ever free ourselves completely of our cultural, ideological, and personal beliefs and assumptions. That would be the "phenomenological error" — the position that since I am "being phenomenological," therefore I have "bracketed" all my own ground! That would be a meaningless claim, in the Gestalt model. Without my ground of assumptions, I would not perceive anything at all. A smart client will never believe that claim, which is really just the old "objectivism," the old expert position in new language. All that really happens if I do try to take that false position is that my assumptions, my beliefs or prejudices, are just taken "off the table," so the client has no support to question them. The intersubjective, dialogic perspective we talked about just now guards us against that error.

Still, we can say that our Gestalt *intentionality*, our commitment to understanding experience, to trying to follow closely how our client's own experience is put together, makes us more open to new ideas and insights than some of the other models. The secret to the success of the human animal in the world is the capacity to learn, our evolutionary capacity to go on evolving. A really useful theory is like that — it contains the tools for deconstructing itself, and therefore for learning and growing as a model.

A New Evolutionary Psychology

If we are the story-telling animal, narrative-spinners by nature, then our most fundamental stories, those that define and inform the contours of our consciousness, are the creation myths of our cultures. Every human culture has one — or several. Who are we, where do we come from? How did we get here — and then what does that say about the *kind* of creatures we are, what is our basic nature, what is important and right and good in human living, and where can we go from here?

Our own Western culture has contributed an enormously rich and fertile story to this mythic collection, which is the theory of evolution. We are not going to go deeply into that now, but it is important to note that evolution — and closer to home, evolutionary psychology — have been captured, hijacked I would say, by hyper-individualist ideology, in direct contradiction to everything the Gestalt model stands for — and everything we know about human behavior, lived experience, social relations, culture — and now the brain itself.

In that popular model — but it also permeates much of lab science (I call it the "selfish gene model," after the work of Dawkins, 1989) — it's a dog-eat-dog world, the survival of the most dominant *individuals* — and the survival, into the 21st century, of the old Victorian social Darwinism of what the poet Tennyson called "nature red in tooth and claw."

None of that fits with current research in primatology, anthropology, paleontology, ecology, genetic biology (where context and gene activation — turning the genes on and off, which is an environmental effect — are everything). For an intensely social species like ours, where individual survival and reproduction were and are impossible as a model, the most dominant individuals are by no means the most genetically fit — i.e., they do not pass on the most genes. If you think about it, common sense should have told the evolutionary biologists this long ago: If they did, then wouldn't the species just go on getting more and more aggressive, more and more dominance oriented, with every generation? And in spite of the desperate shape of the world today (and the aggressive bullying in the world by some of the developed nations, so-called), that is manifestly not the case.

This story — the myth of the selfish gene, the survival of social Darwinist individualist ideology long, long after its discrediting in science and in social policy — has to be deconstructed, if we are to move ahead with our joint dream of building a humane world. Gestalt, with its close attention to how the organism functions in its niche, its evolutionary ground, offers a natural correction to this narrow reductionism. Our "environment," after all, our evolutionary niche, is the social world — the intersubjective field. Let me say that again, because it radically contradicts the dominant thinking in this field: The econiche of the human species is the intersubjective world of other human beings, the complex interpenetrating dynamic of interacting, mutually interpretive systems of intention and meaning. That ecological evolutionary niche/

environment cannot be meaningfully reduced to its not-social components (like food, water, etc.), no matter how essential those physical elements are as well.

The complexity demands of that social environment — far, far more complex and cognitively challenging than tools, hunting, aggressive display, etc. — were what drove the explosive growth in brain size in our species, over the past million years.

We have to retell that story, for our times. Gestalt shows us the way.

And note here too that nothing in evolutionary theory or a true evolutionary psychology contradicts a spiritual perspective on our being and our lives. It does not even contradict traditional religion and creationism unless you take a heavy, fundamentalist reading of certain folk myths of Hebraic or some other ancient cultures. The evolutionary adventure, the advent or permeation of the whole universe by *complexification,* which is the *evolution of consciousness,* is an exciting spiritual adventure story.

What is more, reclaiming evolutionary psychology has direct and indirect implications, for political ideology in our troubled world. Which leads me to the next section.

Politics and Culture

Nobody has to tell us that our beautiful, suffering world hangs today at a tipping point — a desperate balance, between creation and destruction, continued evolution of culture and consciousness, or regression into a new dark age, perhaps the end of human life on the planet.

As we said at the outset, a unified world culture *is emerging.* It is unstoppable, driven by technology, trade, and travel —

and germs, ecological disasters, and the reactionary politics of injustice (on both sides of the power divide).

But what kind of emergent world culture will it be? At this moment we have a world of separate parts — unequal in power, but politically separated into nation states. Against this separateness we have the pressure of global business, the International Monetary Fund, the World Bank — and military aggression. This unstable equilibrium cannot last. With our present thinking the result will be one of two things: domination by one or two superpowers (and a homogenized, flattened, consumerist world culture based on the power of the market) or a regressive catastrophe which leaves isolated communities at a more primitive level (or else no human life at all).

Or we will see the emergence of something wholly new at a world scale: a culture that is both unified *and* diverse, a richly stable world federation of some kind, built on the strength of energized, interdependent, evolving parts or cultures. In such a vision, and such a world, parts and whole support each other, and work together to hold that dynamic, creative tension, which is the condition of healthy growth.

But then this is a Gestalt problem *par excellence*: the relation of energized parts, fully creative and distinct, which are yet integrated into a living, nourishing whole. The whole nourishes and draws strength from the parts; the parts are supported, protected, and ultimately energized by each other, and by the whole. Can we imagine such a thing, on a global level? And then can we support its emergence? Chaos theory — which is Gestalt theory writ large — teaches us that at times of unstable transition from one equilibrium state to another, the power of a seed crystal, an organizing template or idea, is way out of proportion to the apparent strength of that group. Gestalt — not just our Gestalt therapy community alone of course, but

Gestalt as an idea, as an organizing perspective — has a role to play in that seeding process. The form has to be there somewhere, in microcosm at least, in discourse, in shared consciousness, for the emergent state to organize around it. Something like that happened with Christianity in Europe, in the 4th century: A tiny minority sect became the organizing template — for good and ill, as we know — of an empire, and then of half a world.

This new creative model of world-organization depends on a new approach to multi-cultural contact, intercultural relations, and intercultural conflict. Now this is a hot topic in psychotherapy and in organizational dynamics and consulting today — because it *is* one world now, because multi-culturalism is our reality.

Gestalt has a role to play here, and a unique perspective to offer. In its simplest terms, that perspective is *radical dialogue*. Dialogue, after all, (in the sense of the exploration of ground, as we described it above), is *our fundamental Gestalt intervention* — and our Gestalt contribution, to the field of multicultural study and interventions. Here I'd refer you to the 2005 book edited by Talia Levine Bar-Yoseph, called t*he bridge: Dialogues Across Cultures,* published by the Gestalt Institute Press of New Orleans (2005).

Again, the key here is the transition to greater complexity of consciousness. We know — and every point in this list supports this — that people who are traumatized, cannot think complexly. We know how this works clinically — and we even know now how this works neurologically, as the higher centers, the integration of stimulus into meaning, are "short circuited" and bypassed, as in post-traumatic stress disorder. Here we see how our clinical and other work, supporting healing and restoration of full self-and-other functioning, is of directly political use, in the support of this move to greater complexity of mind which is the ground for greater complexity of politics, economics, and culture.

Ethics and Spirit

In the end the Gestalt paradigm of radical participation, radical belonging *is* a spiritual perspective; and the practice of living and healing under that paradigm is itself a spiritual practice. Specifically, it is *relational practice,* the practice of caring for and about the whole field (including ourselves).

And that perspective contains an ethics as well: the ethics of the field, as Robert Lee (2004) writes in his beautiful, collected book. These are the ethics that flow from deep belonging, deep participation, and authentic membership in the whole field.

Maybe I can illustrate that ethics in this way: Why is it tolerable to me that children are starving in Ethiopia, enslaved in Thailand, bombed in Baghdad? If we only think about it for a focused moment, this is *not* tolerable, it is literally unbearable as an image. And yet I desensitize myself to it, to a considerable degree, much of the time. How do I do this? In the end, we can do it at all only *because they are not our children.* If they were *our* children, we would have to act.

But of course, they *are* our children. And then it is intolerable, so intolerable we can hardly bear to think about it at all, without special and deep support. (Remember that Gestalt never promised to make us feel better; it promises, or it threatens, to support us to *feel more,* and then from there we take our chances. As the Tin Man says in The Wizard of Oz: "Now I know I have a heart, because it's breaking.")

Conclusions

There you have it — some thoughts about the creative, growing edges of Gestalt theory and practice, in a troubled, even darkening world. And yet our world is a field of possibility, of new creative solutions, of evolution. It is no news to say we live in unprecedented times, one of those grand transitional inflections in the evolution of human culture — there have been only three or four of them at this level, in the last 10,000 years. The cultural evolutionist Robert Wright cites the transition from scavenging bands to herder-gardeners; the shift from there to field agriculture, which first permitted surplus population, and with its towns, increased trade, and civic culture, but also greater hierarchy of roles, greater gender divides, and land armies; the Industrial Revolution, with all its explosive dislocations, and all the horrors of 19th century European cities, now echoed around the world; and now the post-industrial transformation to a unified world culture. The stakes, the challenges are unprecedented, at a whole-earth level. Where are our tools, our guiding beliefs and methods, to empower us and support our imagination for these new challenges in this new world?

From our Gestalt relational field theory we take the conviction that that emerging world, our world, is not working for anybody really *until it works for everybody*. In our model, the idea of a healthy individual, a healthy single human life without a *healthy shared human field of living* is a contradiction in terms, an impossibility, and makes no sense.

From intersubjectivity and the study of intimacy we take the ideas that that relational world is intersubjective through and through. We live in a world of *interpenetrating minds*, co-constructive selves, dynamically interacting self-experience. Therapy, or social policy, which tries to deny this basic, Gestalt principle, can only be destructive in the end, no matter how good our intentions.

In other words (and this is crucial, only Gestalt supports this essential, transformative insight): For the human animal, the most fundamental organ of perception is dialogue. That is, the capacity to communicate and understand, to imagine and create, is never something "wired in us," individually, the old "lonely genius" model, in isolation from the corrupting crowd. Rather, it is something *constructed and shared*, found everywhere and nowhere, in what Winnicott called "the space between."

From "fieldsmithing," the direct apprehension/ mobilization of our shared field of living, we come away with the conclusion that the greatest healing, the most useful insights derive from our deep, often intuitive sense of the field conditions, especially the social field conditions, that are our ocean of life, and our source of creativity and empowerment for change. From a radically new evolutionary theory, informed and guided by a Gestalt understanding of all the new research, the emerging story, we take a new world myth, one that can join and empower us — synergizing with our diverse spiritual traditions and perspectives, not in conflict with them. From cognitive neuroscience we see how the power of shared narrative is embedded in the structure of our cognition, as are affect, relationship, and the transformative potential of this new selfstory.

From a Gestalt understanding of politics we are empowered to revision the current political struggles of the world, as part of a great transition from the world-scale feudalism of separate nation-states (and remember, the basic nature of the nation state is war) to some form of whole-world organization, whether for good or ill, from a human point of view. And we take as well the beginnings of a model of world citizenship, based on duality or multiplicity of belonging — first to the earth, to all humanity and to life as a whole — and yet no less to our own richly different local or chosen traditions and identities. And all of it held in rich, creative tension with the other dimensions and with each other, all at the same time. Again — greater complexity, requiring greater support.

Part of that support, for many of us, comes from the rich spiritual traditions we grow from or rediscover, many of which explicitly tell a tale of our world as a locus of evolving consciousness, growing awareness of our radical belonging, *both* to the whole *and* to the vibrant parts. Again, a Gestalt field perspective of radical belonging is a spiritual perspective and yields a unifying ethics as well. Not an ethics of memorized rules and thou-shalt-nots: an ethics based in experience and participation, and heightened sensitization to our own diminishment, individually as well as collectively, when our shared field does not flourish.

In each of these areas, the challenge is to move up to a new level of complexity or else fall back into the oversimplifications, the fundamentalisms, and the fascisms that call out to our fears and our sense of lonely vulnerability. Our world is moving, inevitably, unpredictably, toward a new whole-world organization (or a radical devolution, into surviving, postcataclysmic enclaves). What kind of organization will it be: a new complexity of vision and understanding? Or the old familiar reductions, to the old familiar politics of separateness and fear (which are the same thing). Our strength and our hope lie in our connections — not as a mindless mass, but as living members of a dynamic, richly-textured whole.

And in each area, Gestalt shows us the way, supports us to make the necessary transition up from past simplifying categories including some past categories in our received Gestalt therapy tradition itself.

New complexity *requires* new support for a new, more complex consciousness. But let us not forget that new consciousness in turn must be supported by a reorganization at the material, world-economic level, the transition to a political *economics* of belonging, of justice, and of care. The currently dominant world powers — especially the United States of America — have to step up to that challenge with new imagination or else go the way of all empires of the past. (An empire after all, is programmed by definition for competition and death, not evolution and learning).

Abraham Lincoln, the great emancipator in United States history, said, "a house divided against itself cannot stand." Our house today is the world. That world, divided into a small camp of "haves," and a vast, agonizing camp of "have-nots" — two billion people who survive (or rather, do not survive) on a dollar or less a day — cannot stand. Our consciousness will evolve — is evolving — to support these new directions of thinking, *or* the long evolutionary adventure of our human species will come to an end.

The world we can have is the world we can imagine. Each of us has some role to play in that great transformative work, liberating the human imagination, healing and empowering the weak and the damaged, holding and growing this greater vision. Gestalt offers the support, the compass directions, and significant parts at least of the map for getting there. In the familar, treasured words of the wise Rabbi Hillel, contemporary of Jesus of Nazareth:

> If I am not for myself — who will be?
> If I am for myself alone — what am I?
> If not now — when?

References

Bar-Yoseph, T. L. (Ed.). (2005). T*he Bridge: Dialogues Across Cultures*. New Orleans: Gestalt Institute Press.

Dawkins, R. (1989). *The Selfish Gene*. Oxford: The Oxford University Press.

Lee, R. G. (Ed.). (2004). *The Values of Connection: A Relational Approach to Ethics*. Hillsdale, NJ: The Analytic Press/GestaltPress

Marrow, A. J. (1969). *The Practical Theorist: The Life and Work of Kurt Lewin*. New York: Basic Books.

Nevis, S. M. & Melnick, J (1994). Intimacy and power in long-term relationships: A Gestalt therapy-systems perspective. In G. Wheeler & S. Bachman (Eds.). *On Intimate Ground: A Gestalt Approach to Working with Couples*. San Fransisco: Jossey-Bass.

Perls, F., Hefferline, R. & Goodman, P. (1951). *Gestalt Therapy: Excitement and Growth in the Human Personality*. New York: Julian Press.

Wheeler, G. (2000). *Beyond Individualism: Toward a New Understanding of Self,Rrelationship & Experience*. Hillsdale, NJ: The Analytic Press/ GestaltPress.

2

Relationality: Foundational Assumptions
Lynne Jacobs

Introductory Story

My first therapy experience, begun in the year preceding my discovery of Fritz Perls and Gestalt therapy, was with a gentle, kind, and respectful if somewhat reserved psychiatric resident. His kind and respectful attitude, for which I am grateful to this day, helped me to begin to believe that my exeriences, perceptions and world of meanings were worthy of attention and articulation.

A particular moment with him helped to point me in the direction of the direct engagement proffered in Gestalt therapy, although he himself was psychoanalytically oriented. We had been meeting for about a year, twice weekly. I was a "good patient," appreciative, eager to explore, but also painfully shy and skeptical of my own thoughts and feelings. We were exploring the impact on me of his planned move to a different residency setting. He had told me he would be leaving the current clinic a few months hence. When I first heard him say

... 45

those words my heart just plummeted, because although I rarely spoke of it, I was deeply attached to him and to the experience of being listened to with such kindness. He offered me the chance to move along with him, and continue our work together.

It emerged as we talked, that his next residency was a family and child placement, and that having me transfer along with him was not usual policy for either of the involved clinics. I was in a quandary. I very much wanted to continue seeing him, had become lethargic and depressed at the thought of ending prematurely, and yet I could not bear the prospect of creating difficulty for him, or being a burden to him. I imagined that he felt trapped by my fragility, so that although he might rather be free to start with a clean slate at the new clinic, he saw me as too fragile to handle a transition to a new therapist. I also imagined that the authorities at the two clinics were annoyed and might create strain for my therapist. I tried haltingly to raise my concerns with my therapist, and I could barely speak. He said, "It sounds like you think our relationship is so tenuous it cannot bear any strain or difficulty." I was stunned. Actually, I had the sensation of a bomb going off suddenly under my chair. Did he say, "relationship?"

It had never occurred to me that he would consider us as being in a relationship together! I did move with him to his new setting, and we met for about 16 more months, until I moved away to attend graduate school. In one of our last meetings, as I was detailing my fears and insecurities about graduate school, and said I was full of doubt regarding my ability to learn clinical psychology, he burst out with "I have no doubt at all that you will be a fine psychologist!" Again, I was surprised that he had formed a personal opinion of me, rather than just a clinical opinion. I carried his confidence with me like a talisman as I left on my new adventure.

More importantly, that sensation of being stunned by the bomb under my chair because he said we had a relationship remains a touchstone for me. It always brings me back to one of the core themes that animates my personal and professional development: relationality[1].

The Double Helix of Field Theory and Relationality

When I moderated the first panel at the Evolution of Gestalt conference in 2005, at which Frank M-Staemmler and Margherita Spagnolo Lobb gave papers, I suggested that overall, the evolution of Gestalt can be characterized in two ways: as a radicalization of our field theory roots, and a radicalization of a relational perspective on the Gestalt approach. The field theory emphasis and the relational turn stand in reciprocal relationship to each other, deriving from and expanding each other.

While some at the conference focused on our field theory, others of us focused on our relational turn. The word in the title of the conference, "evolution," reflects I believe, that from the very beginnings of the development of Gestalt theory there has been an understanding that our phenomenal fields emerge from our lived contexts. Although some of our practice and clinical-level theory did not always reflect this understanding, as we have matured we have embraced this notion more viscerally, more comprehensively. While all clinical theories of which I am aware have made what can be called, "the relational turn,"

---

[1] I first told this story in "Pathways to a relational worldview," in M. Goldfriend, (Ed.), (2001), *How Therapists Change*, Washington, DC: American Psychological Association Press.

Gestalt theory, while not the most systematic in its application, was one of the earliest. Perhaps the fact that all of our founders were cultural outsiders in one way or another provided a vantage point from which they could observe and challenge the Cartesian, individualistic orientation in which we lived at the time. Since I introduced the first panel, which focused on relationality, my paper aims to point out a few assumptions that undergird a relational sensibility.

Foundational assumptions

1. First and foremost, our relationality is irreducible. Our relatedness in our environment and with each other does not begin with us as separate selves, with relatedness being an "add-on." Our very existence is utterly, thoroughly context-dependent, and our worlds of experience are emergent from our contexts. We have no experience that is prior to relatedness. As Merleau-Ponty has demonstrated is his writings on corporeality, we are born into a world "always already there" (Taylor, 1983). I am reminded of Peter Philippson's invocation of the Escher drawing in which who is drawing whom cannot be discerned (2001). Every experience we have, including that right now, between us, is co-shaped, or co-emergent from what I bring and what you bring, along with our setting, our task, and other aspects that go into comprising our situation. Your emergent subjectivity and mine are utterly interdependent.

2. We are all more alike than not. We come into being in the shared context of being human: of using meaningful language, of physicality, of even a neuronal readiness and capacity to resonate and respond to each other and to new emotional experiences (recent research on mirror neurons points to our

being "wired for relatedness," a term I have used metaphorically for many years)[2].

I wrote the following words in a chapter in *The Values of Connection: a Relational Approach to Ethics* (Jacobs in Lee, 2004)*:*

> We swim in contexts... Our phenomenological fields are emergent from these contexts, and are shaped by them. ..And yet it is a bit misleading to refer to "one's" phenomenological field, because that can be easily misconstrued as a solipsistic, subjectivist assertion. Actually, that is far from the case. Our phenomenological fields are also shared fields, despite their uniqueness. Our shared fields range from the most abstract communality of shared language, culture and various "forms of life," as Wittgenstein described, but also more directly, in that my being-in-your-world and your being-in-my-world yields co-constituted and broadly over-lapping fields. This is the most basic inclusion.
>
> We are born into historical, cultural, language and action practice contexts, we come into being in them and we also contribute to the shaping of these very contexts. These contexts obviously constitute our experiential worlds, albeit largely without our awareness. They are the

---

[2] I caution against a kind of biologic or neuronal reductionism. It is problematic to assume that since mirror neurons exist, the feelings I have are direct empathic access to the patient's experience. We are complex, complicated, and have no more privileged ability to read our feelings than our patients do (and vice-versa), and in fact they may sometimes read us better than we can. Also, both of our experiential worlds have been shaped by longstanding sedimented experiential history. The neurons reflect the arousal, a window to beginning meaningfulness, but our feelings are complex amalgams of arousal, history, language games, thinking, etc.

necessary precondition for the existence of our phenomenological fields. They are the "ground" that makes the "figure" of "experiential world" possible." (2004, p.41)

3. While our commonalities make connection possible, our individuality makes connecting interesting, novel and provides us a chance to learn something new, to expand our experiential horizons. What I am about to say may seem paradoxical, but our uniqueness is also an emergent configuration that points to our shared humanity. On the one hand our mutually shared human situation puts us in a more common position than otherwise, despite whatever differences of language, culture and personal narratives we have. On the other hand, each of you carries a way of being that emphasizes a different aspect of our humanity than I carry, and thus further illuminates our fundamentally overlapping ground, the ground of our shared human situation, our humanity. Anyone with whom we come into contact gives us the gift of enriching our ground. They teach us about our own humanity as well.

4. Our sense of self, including such dimensions as: sense of agency, emotional capacities, individuation and differentiation, capacity for intimacy, is contingent, dependent on our developmental and our immediate emotional contexts. This means not just that we are all interrelated, but that the quality of our self-functioning, and most importantly, our developmental possibilities, depends on what some contemporary analysts — self psychologists and intersubjective systems theorists refer to as our "selfobject surround."

> By his cumbersome term 'selfobjects' [Kohut] meant to describe a variety of relational supports that support the maintenance, restoration and transformation of positive

self-experience. Kohut was attempting to describe a variety of environmental supports that often occur at the fringes of awareness but which are, none-the-less, central to one's personal sense of wellbeing. In much the same way that oxygen, crucial to wellbeing, usually only enters awareness by virtue of its absence or depletion, (and, even then, it is more likely that distress and restorative actions will be figural to awareness than the presence or otherwise of actual oxygen molecules), we can see that variations in the availability of these relational experiences may not always figure in awareness per se, but their absence or diminution could be found implicated in processes of human distress and alienation. In other words, their presence supports and enhances both personal wellbeing and intimate relatedness. It was this discovery that started to reveal finer and finer details of how our respective resolutions of the field interact (Stawman, 2007).

So the point I make here, is that not only is the quality of our contacting a co-emergent process, but the developmental trajectory of our patients relies on the quality of the relational supports for development that inhere in the therapeutic relationship. One of the most significant relational supports is emotional availability: our emotional attunement and emotional responsiveness. We speak from, reach out from, relate to others in terms of, our cares. And our emotions tell us about the possibilities and constraints regarding these cares, in whatever situation we exist at the moment. They also tell us something of what matters to those around us. Because of this triple conjuncttion, that our emotions reflect the highly personal world of our cares, and they signal our relationship with our situation, on a moment-by-moment basis, and they are being shaped by the cares of those around us, emotions are a powerful exemplar of inescapable emergence and interrelatedness.

The Moral Thrust of Gestalt

In a way, although I am purporting to merely say that relationality is our inescapable, irreducible truth, I also think of it as amplifying the visionary sensibility that is the Gestalt approach. The visionary sensibility is that it allows us to raise the question; in what kind of human beingness do I want to participate? What kind of relational world do I want to help to co-shape? Both Margherita and Frank will, in the next chapters, contrast the relational sensibility with the isolated mind perspective that is our Cartesian, individualist legacy. From the isolated mind perspective, how can we come to know each other? We have to reach across empty space, imagine, and reconstruct the other as an image in our minds. The relational sensibility has a holistic, field orientation, and an appreciation of the notion of reciprocal mutual influence. This means that people are found and become present with us through contacting. Knowing, in the Cartesian sense, becomes less important than undergoing a process of understanding, making sense, together. Thus our question changes from how do we know each other, to how shall we meet each other? We are less interested in the question of knowing, more interested in the meeting. This is the moral stance of the Gestalt approach; what mode of approaching you will expand the chance of being most enriching for us? What mode do I prefer, what kind of being-together do I want to co-shape?

Clinical Implications: Co-implication

This is the question that each of us answers, consciously or not, by the values and attitudes we cannot help but bring into our clinical work. We answer the question by how we engage with others in our clinical work, be it in organizations, in a community, or in the consulting room. I will speak about what I know best, the consulting room.

Every utterance, every thought, feeling, sensation, every movement that happens in our consulting rooms is variably mutually influenced (and influencing). Nothing that happens arises pristinely from "within" the therapist or "within" the patient. Therefore, such thoughts as, "this is merely my countertransference, my issue," or of the patient, "this is projecting," will need to be discarded as remnants of an individualistic, non-relational sensibility. Instead, our understanding of co-emergence leads to the following idea: "something is going on between us that gives rise to the experiences the patient and I are having right now. Even if I cannot fathom it yet." My task as the therapist is to engage in a dialogue that stands the greatest chance of enabling me to understand how my patient's experiences — and mine — make perfect sense at this time in this situation together.

Hence, I will work to try to grasp how the puzzling or disturbing or contrary experiences we are having, could be so. I will have to refrain from any temptation to evaluate that it could not be so, but instead I will dialogue, wrestle, struggle to make sense, until I can say, "of course! Now I get it!" This is the horizontalism of phenomenological exploration, done in a dialogical context.

An important corollary to the co-emergence of experience is the co-implication of the therapist and the patient in everything that happens in the consulting room. It can't be said, for instance, that the patient is avoiding intimacy with me. We together have not found what will support better contacting between us. Our contacting is the best we can support at this moment. From a relational sensibility, in which patient and therapist are thoroughly implicated in each other's experiencing and behaving, it behooves us to recognize that we are participating, to whatever (possibly minimal) extent, in an emergent process that has more supports for avoidance, in that particular moment, than it has for more direct contacting. If I find myself thinking that a patient may be "avoiding," then in keeping with this theory:

> I might wonder if I too am avoiding something, thereby diminishing the possibilities for good quality contacting. For instance, I might find myself thinking that my patient is avoiding responsibility for deciding whether or not to tell me a dream. She seems to want to tell the dream, but she also seems to want me to ask about the dream so that I can be the one "responsible" for her telling the dream. Such an analysis of the situation is probably reasonable, and a situation many of us can recognize. But it leaves out my participation. If I ask what I am avoiding, I might find that I dread the possibility of being blamed by this patient, or of being poorly used. My awareness of a subtle rigidity in my posture — where I am non-verbally saying, "no, I won't take the blame!" — allows me to consider that supports for good quality contacting are lacking between us, not within her. (Jacobs, 2003, pg. 137)

Recently, in a peer supervision group with my analyst colleagues, I described difficulty working with a particular patient. The patient feels incredibly hungry for me to find a way for me to help her, and equally despairing that anyone can help her. And, in a perfect example of parallel process, I went to the group saying I did not think anyone could help me with my difficulties. I kept referring to this woman's style as like Teflon, refractory to influence. My colleagues noted that I seemed stymied and disrupted, and they asked me what my description of her (as "like Teflon"), and my disturbance, was saying about how I was organizing my experience, and how that might be influencing our sessions. I realized this woman's despair had a form similar to my mother's despair, in relation to which I felt helpless to relieve my mother's suffering. So I became Teflon-like with my patient. I worried about intruding on her, by reaching frantically to rescue her as I did with my mother, and also, I was protecting myself from the pain and frustration that I felt when I tried to engage my patient's suffering. The familiar rejection I felt when I reached for my patient was daunting to me, and so I had tamped myself down. My own "cool" demeanor then mirrored her Teflon-like manner. So, in terms of co-implication, we were creating together the quality of contacting going on in the consulting room. We co-shaped the possibilities, and we co-shaped the limits. My coolness was relevant to what was possible between us, just as hers was.

Clinical Implications: Confirmation and Attunement

Both Frank's and Margherita's chapters will address, in different ways, confirmation as a foundation for contacting that fosters development of our "becoming a person," as Carl Rogers said so many years ago. (1961). They both refer to emotional attunement and emotional responsiveness. I suggested above that emotional availability, especially in the forms of attunement and responsiveness, were key ingredients that support the emergence of development-enhancing relatedness.

I have found that in the context of a relationship where I systematically attune to the patient's experience, patients feel safer with me to explore sensitive topics, especially their painful emotional reactions to aspects of our therapy relationship. In my clinical experience, the patient is increasingly able to bring into awareness, and into the contact, more realms of previously disowned or otherwise sequestered self-experience. The more realms of experience patients can bring into our relationship, the more resilient, cohesive and integrated their emotional regulatory capacities become.

The contemporary analytic theories I mentioned earlier make a strong case for reliable affect attunement as the means whereby the affect integration necessary for self-development occurs. Gestalt therapy believes another element of relatedness is central to self-development, and that is the "interhuman meeting." In the meeting, attunement, while centrally important, is accompanied by the therapist's presence. By presence, I mean that the therapist is willing to be open to a kind of contact in which the patient can touch the therapist's subjective experience, both directly and indirectly. Quite often this occurs indirectly. But at crucial points in the therapy, for instance in efforts to address serious disruptions in the "selfobject dimension of the relationship," or at certain developmental thresholds, the patient may be intensely interested in, and require, access to the therapist's experiencing. In my view, self-development proceeds not only through the experiences gained through systematic affect attunement, but also through the experience of the attunement coming from a discernible, personal other.

I think that attunement functions at two levels. On the one hand, it is the ground from which a sense of affect validity, articulation, and integration occurs. We have seen that such integration enhances and strengthens the patient's sense of self to a great degree, expanding contacting possibilities. But the second level of communication may be even more crucial. Emotional attunement serves also as recognition of the wholeness of the patient. The therapist, in attempting to attune to the patient's emotional life, and to understand it in the context of this patient's history and present life, is recognizing a unique and yet understandable person. The therapist is also first and foremost a human being, and can only attune to the patient from the depths of her own subjectivity. I think patients often apprehend — if mostly subliminally—the significance of the fact that the therapist must process their communications through her own subjectivity, and her successes as well as her struggles to be as accurate as possible are affirming. We see signs of this awareness in our patients' struggles and hesitations as they endeavor to communicate their experiences to us, as well as their noticeable relief when we understand them deeply. In the mutual empathic engagement between patients and myself, they help me to meet them. When I meet them, they are confirmed as both a contributing and understandable other in the stream of human relatedness. This is a restoration of dignity, and the restoration of dignity is transformative confirmation.

So taken all together, emotional attunement functions first at a regulatory level, in that we regulate each other's emotional states in dialogue. Secondly, more profoundly, it operates at the level of confirmation. One who is confirmed is able to think of herself in this way: "I am somebody who can be understood, can contribute to making myself understood, and I do so in part by understanding the other enough to be able to recognize what they are not getting about me." That is how patients help us. Attunement is a mutual, reciprocal engagement. Without their ability to help us by showing us the limits of our understanding, our understanding of them (and ourselves) cannot deepen.

The Case of Jerry[3]

Jerry is a patient with whom I have wrestled with seemingly intransigent emotional difficulties, revolving around my shame, his shame, and each of our defenses against being exposed. Unfortunately, this man's characterizations of me when he is disappointed in me tended to confirm my worst fears about myself as a cold and heartless person. I reacted to what I experienced as a humiliating exposure by withdrawing psychologically, thereby compounding his sense of my destructive defectiveness. Eighteen months into treatment, this recurrent pattern brought us to a point of impasse. I had, by this point, admitted to having difficulties maintaining my emotional balance and being able to listen to him from an empathic vantage point, and I was working to lessen their impact on the therapy, although without much success. In agony, he sought a consultation with a colleague of mine. He was in an excruciating bind. He was very attached to me, and could not imagine surviving without me. On the other hand, this pattern was also "killing" him. The consultation proved useful for both of us, in underscoring his desperation. I decided to tell him more about what I knew of my particular difficulties. I told him that I felt humiliated, and dreaded that his characterizations might prove to be true of me, and my defense against the humiliation was withdrawal. That session was transformative for both of us. By articulating my experience, directly with him, I was less

---

[3] This case, with some minor changes, first appeared in, Optimal responsiveness and subject-subject relating." (1998) in Optimal Responsiveness: How Therapists Heal Their Patients. Bacal, H., ed., Jason Aronson Pub. It appears here with permission of the publisher.

dominated by my dread of humiliation. My patient was deeply moved, and relieved in that by my admission of my own agonizing self-doubts he was freed of the burden of trying to "work around" my problems. Now they could be addressed directly and empathically as they occurred.

What was crucially important for our work to continue was that I reflect on my defensiveness. Even though I was reacting with shame and defensiveness, our work could continue if I was able to recognize my defensiveness, even if I could not avoid it. Working with this patient has provided a lesson in livingthrough repeated mismeetings triggered by shame and defensiveness (on both of our parts), and then getting back on track by being able to reflect upon and reestablish contact by addressing the shame and defensiveness directly. What follows is a description of one particular watershed contacting episode in this patient's therapy.

The context of his therapy has been one of steady, persistent and disciplined attempts on my part to stay in contact with, and attuned to, the terrible demons who dominate Jerry, and the faint whispers of hope which keep him tenuously attached to his therapy. The demons and the hopes have woven themselves tightly into our relationship, so that every meeting between us is a terrifying struggle for him. Dare he trust me? From his perspective, I give him so many reasons not to.

We spend much of our time trying to understand and repair the wrenching dislocations caused by my myriad betrayals of him; a poorly chosen word which signals that I have contempt for him, a tone of voice which says that I wish to be rid of him, a subdued response at a time when he needs a firm loud sign that I am intensely engaged.

In each of these disappointments, the shadow of shame which hovers like a thick fog at the edge of our relationship sweeps over us. He feels ashamed, and then reacts to me in ways which shame me. Or, perhaps I was already being swallowed by my shame, and my poorly chosen word was a subtle defensiveness, which then shamed him. At any rate, repeatedly and often, the fog of shame permeates the air we breathe.

Jerry was sadistically beaten and sexually abused as a very young child. Both parents worked, and he was left every day in the care of a young couple who abused him. In the course of our work together we have pieced together a story which seems to fit with the body sensations, feelings and images which have long tormented Jerry, along with newly emerging sensations and memories. His babysitters left him alone in his crib for extended lengths of time. He would gaze wistfully at the door, hoping for some respite from his loneliness. But they would come in and harm him and cause him great pain, discomfort and confusion. The details, as they have emerged, have horrified and appalled both of us. Among the many legacies of this background are severe sexual inhibition, terror of intimacy, a tendency to defend himself by subtle attack, and chronic suicidality.

In our first session, Jerry told me he was desperate to hold onto a relationship with a man which had lasted now for seven years but he was afraid he was "killing" it with his enormous problems. He was pessimistic that he could be helped because he felt so "alien." He was also deeply frightened of becoming dependent on me and then being betrayed or abandoned. He felt an intense attachment to me immediately, which exacerbated his fears and sense of vulnerability. Several times he has decided he must quit because he cannot bear the pain of needing me and having me fail him so often and so thoroughly. He has also had recurring periods of intense suicidal preoccupation.

After the impasse and resolution which I described above, Jerry's trust in me increased greatly, and our work continued to deepen. Eighteen months later another impasse occurred. It seemed to follow from another deepening of trust and confidence in my abilities. The background for the "forward step" is too lengthy to describe here, but often an increase in any sense of trust, confidence or intimacy with me gives rise in him to terrible fears of betrayal, or of being flooded with unbearably intense and shameful (to him) longings for more contact and closeness with me.

We were then meeting three times weekly, for a full hour each session. In our first meeting of the week, he reported that he had spent the weekend hungrily wishing to throw himself into my arms and be gathered in. He was also convinced that, unlike the people of a group to which he belongs, I was simply too constrained and "immobile" as a person to be able to reach for him in the bold way he needed. For instance, he fervently wished I would be willing to cradle him and I was not willing to do so. He thought that in the absence of bold movement on my part he was doomed to an ice-shrouded isolated withdrawal (In the first months of his therapy he had related to me primarily through pictures and collages. One frequent drawing was of an ice cave in which he huddled, turned towards the corner, and if I was in the picture at all I was in the opposite corner and did not seem to notice him). He then moved on to talking about his love of roses. He had realized over the weekend that roses symbolized an antidote to his experience of himself as filled with garbage. He felt very sad. He began to see an image of a rose framed by purple flashes — the purple flashes he used to see when he was being beaten about his head. He said the image was a satisfying affirmation that there was a rose to be found amidst his garbage. I suggested that he needed to know that I, too, knew there was a rose in him, to be pulled from the garbage. I said I thought that together we must sift through his garbage and find his roses. At this point we were both teary. I also remembered his concern that I was too constrained, that he had not sensed from me a "permission" to go connect more deeply. I said maybe he was not sure it was worth it to me to get my hands dirty. He was moved by that statement, feeling very close to me, and he became nauseous. I suggested, based on past work together, that the experience of intimacy with me stirred up his feeling of being full of garbage. He said intently, "Wear gloves!" I said no. I said I did not expect to be permanently soiled. I wanted to be able to feel the rose with my bare hands, and I knew that we would find a way to wade through the messes created by our intimacy, that together we would find ways to untangle and clean up the messes.

He began to realize that as miserable as he had been all his life, he had still kept his worst horrors hidden away, and now they were crowding in on him. He was in agony as the session ended. He was terribly frightened over what else might emerge. As he left, so shaken, I instinctively reached out and squeezed his elbow. This was the first time I had touched him spontaneously. He had always wanted me to be freer with touch, and had to settle for the fact that at certain emotionally charged times, if he wanted to hold my hand I would do it. Those times were often packed with meaning for him, especially because he knew it was a stretch for me to do it.

He began the next session saying he did not know if he could survive the space between this session and our next. He was desperate to have me with him all the time to protect him from the horrors of his inner world. And the longings themselves were unbearably shameful and dirty. In the course of his anguished speaking I began to notice small changes in his physical state. We ended up attending to some unusual bodily sensations, and what developed was an experience that seemed to be halfway between a recovery of a memory and a flashback. The end of the memory involved lying desolate in his crib after being abused, and longing for one of his sitters to return and pick him up and soothe him. He remembered the awful confusion of wanting them to return, and yet being terrified of their return because it would lead to further abuse. Now we understood more viscerally how his longings to be gathered in by me were acts of selfbetrayal that left him prey to me, and which turned intimacy into sickness. He felt horribly trapped, both by these awful people, and also by his longings for connection. He was crying very deeply now, more than he had ever done. I reached out and held his hand while he sobbed.

In the remaining minutes of the session he sought out a cabinet in my office and said he was leaving his tortures and his longings tucked into one drawer, and reserved the rest of the cabinet space for himself.

After that, all hell broke loose. He called and left a tearful message on my machine after the session. I returned his call and left a message on his machine (a longstanding pattern between us). We spoke in person later in the day, because he was dissatisfied with my return phone message. He left several messages over the course of the next day, saying he must quit, that therapy could not possibly work for him if he felt worse after a phone contact with me than he did before the contact. His messages felt like blows to my stomach and head each time he called. He said he would return for one last session, only because it was the appropriate thing to do, but he was only coming in "to say goodbye." I reached his machine at one point and told him I was very concerned about his thoughts of quitting at this time, I offered a tentative interpretation about his need to protect himself as he became more vulnerable, and asked him to consider allowing for more than one session if need be, so that we could walk through what was happening between us slowly and carefully. I was befuddled, angry, humiliated and crushed. From my perspective, I had risked reaching out in a way he had yearned for since the beginning of our work, only to be rebuffed. The rebuff simply confirmed for me a deeply embedded shame about myself: that at my core I was a disgusting toxin, and therefore spontaneous gestures of mine poisoned people and ruined relationships.

By the time of our session the next morning, I was filled with dread of more shame and humiliation, and my chest was sore with the residue of hurt feelings which I had spent the night trying to work through. Jerry appeared willing to take whatever time was necessary to try to understand what had happened. We spent the first half of the session working out the problems that had occurred during our phone calls. We learned that I needed to make only a small adjustment in my way of handling his calls in order to permit him to feel more reassured of my availability. In the course of working out the problem, I told him that I felt pretty defensive, and that I found it difficult to listen well to him without also speaking from my point of view. There was a surpriseingly relaxed atmosphere of serious purpose and humor in our exchanges. My defensiveness was obvious to him, and we had enough prior experience to know that if I spoke from my perspective — even when I was defensive — at times, it actually led to further clarification of his perspective. So with good humor, we forged ahead. I lamented, "Why must you throw the baby out with the bathwater? Why leave our face-to-face sessions because our phone contacts are problematic?" Jerry pointed out that all our contacts were part of a whole for him. He said he had never felt closer to me than in our last few weeks, and my failings on the phone meant that I had only seduced and betrayed him. It felt as though I had come into his room, lifted him from his crib, and as he breathed a sigh of relief, I had raised him over my head and smashed him to the ground! At another point I asked rather plaintively, "Why must you threaten to leave? Why not just say you feel like leaving?" Within a minute I answered my own question. I slapped myself across my forehead and exclaimed, "Of course! If you cannot at least leave me, then you are utterly trapped! That must never happen to you again." Both of our eyes teared up at this recognition, and at the same time we both laughed gently at my plaintive plea for him to be "rational and mature." By this point, we were thoroughly settled back into our relationship. I was no longer filled with dread, although I was still quite sore from what I had been through.

    Jerry told me quietly and shyly that he loved me. We chatted for a few minutes about other parts of his life. Then in a pause, he asked how I was feeling about what had transpired. I told him I was greatly relieved that what he needed from me over the phone (a particular line of inquiry) was something I could understand and readily provide. Then my eyes filled with tears. Jerry looked at me with curiosity. I told him I was still recovering from the emotional storm, and I said I was unable to talk about my feelings further without crying. But it was already too late. I was crying. Not just a tear or two, but streams of tears. I told him that I had been deeply hurt by his need to leave the therapy, that unfortunately he had touched upon a very painful core issue of mine. I explained (while he handed me two tissues) that at the very moment when I had jumped into our relationship with all my heart and soul he had snapped back that our relationship was no good, and that he was abandoning me (shared laughter at recognition of a familiar theme for him as well)! I also said I lived with a core sense of shame, and a dread that my spontaneous touch of others, both physical and emotional touch, was destructive, and his behavior had only served to confirm that dread.

Jerry started to weep. He told me how much my touch had meant to him. For him my voluntary touch had meant there was more to him than just garbage and slime. He cried more deeply. I had touched his substance. Monday's touch had carried him through until our next meeting. He said my touch gave him life. At this point I handed him one of the tissues he had given me, and we both chuckled. He spoke tearfully of how different his experience was, compared to mine. For him, our relationship had been the most important, nourishing, positive thing in his life of more than fifty years. He wanted to protect and cherish it the only way he knew how. Since he had no hope of cleaning up the mess, his only option had been to leave in order to at least save what he had.

The session ended in what seemed to me to be a sweet, sad humility about our interwoven vulnerabilities, and a renewed sense of intimacy and optimism about our work together.

The next week he said he had experienced a massive shift in his internal world. He had decided that he could risk committing himself to his therapy. I wondered if he had felt some pressure from me to make such a commitment to rescue me from my own vulnerabilities. He laughed and said "no'" and that he thought I would in fact still get hurt in the trenches with him. I said, "because roses have thorns?" He said, "of course," and that his reasons had more to do with the fact that he had been deeply moved that his leaving would have such an impact on me. This evident impact was once again an affirmation to him that I saw beyond the slime to the rose in him. If our work together meant so much to me, then perhaps he was safe in throwing his lot in with me. What surprised both of us was that he also said his sense of being suicidal changed. By committing himself to seeing the therapy through, he no longer found himself turning to the prospect of suicide as an escape. He felt more fully embedded in life than he had ever felt.

Approximately two years have passed since this incident. There has been a profound change in our work, which endures as a new underpinning for our efforts. Jerry now has a reliable sense that I am "in his corner," no matter what might happen between us. He no longer doubts my commitment to helping him achieve his aims, nor does he doubt (except when he is buried in shame) my deep affection for him. Needless to say, these are hard fought gains for him — for us, really — which appear to have been firmly consolidated by the incident I have described, and the subsequent exploration of its meanings.

The change has affected the flavor of our work in two discernible ways. First, when there are misunderstandings or other disruptions between us, he does not question the very foundations of our relationship. In fact, at times he uses misunderstandings between us as openings for him to reflect on his own defensive organization. In the past, these misunderstandings were so threatening that he could not afford the luxury of such exploration. All of his attention was directed to merely surviving the rupture through either "fight or flight."

The second change, a poignant one to me, was in the tone of his suicidality. His suicidal wishes did not disappear for long after the "watershed" incident. In fact, he plunged into his deepest despair to date shortly after that incident. The difference now was, he seemed to be bringing his suicidal despair into the room with me as perhaps the loneliest of all of his lonely experiences, and he was asking me to get to know him "in the darkness," just as he had struggled to let me know so much else of his tormented inner world. Prior to this point, his suicidal feelings peaked largely in reaction to my misattunements. Now, his suicidal despair emerged when our bond was intact, at a time when our bond had its deepest impact on him. As he struggled to discern, articulate and identify with what it meant to love someone (me), he realized that "they got all of me." That is, no aspect of his inner world, not even his capacity for love, was unscathed by the abuse which he endured. Most recently, as we have continued to explore how alien he feels even his love to be, he has spoken of feeling a sense of integration and a sense of belonging, both new experiences for him.

We still go through rough patches where each of us, feeling ashamed and dreading greater shame and humiliation, withdraws or in some way becomes defensive with the other. The reciprocal impact, a vicious cycle of escalating shame and defensiveness between us, is at times maddening and painful, at other times laughable. With each cycle I am finding a little more ability to stay centered even when I feel ashamed. I am better able to use my own shame as a signal that Jerry and I are caught in another shame/defense cycle, instead of just mobilizing my defenses. And with each cycle, Jerry and I are finding more ways to explore, experiment, and observe the emotional processes that lead us to these tangles.

Conclusion

Our inevitable, irreducible interrelatedness leaves us necessarily humble about what we can know about how we are implicated in the experiences of our patients, and also how they are implicated in ours. I have a particular interest in the therapeutic implications of this notion, and more specifically, its implications for our understanding of the therapeutic relationship. One of the most difficult arenas for Gestalt therapy theory and practice, it seems to me, is the arena of enduring relational themes. We seem to know that any particular contacting episode emerges from a ground of sedimented learning rife with specific expectations and ideas about life and relationships. Yet little of our literature is devoted to case examples and clinical ideas about what it means to practice Gestalt therapy with this in mind.

Psychoanalysis has staked out this territory well, in its explorations of transference. But the classical notions of transference, as a transfer of mental contents from the past onto present-day circumstance, do not sit well with our ideas that all experience is emergent and contextually contingent, and is always a creative adjustment to the current situation. Our responses to our current situation include our history — how can it not? — but they reconfigure our history, put it to new use, they are never mere repetitions of our past. Over many years up until the present, attempts by various Gestalt theorists to incorporate notions of transference into Gestalt therapy have drawn upon the classical ideas of psychoanalysis, rather than learning from contemporary psychoanalytic ideas about transference.

This is an uncomfortable fit because the attempts have still been wedded to some of the Cartesian notions that inhere in classical conceptualizations of transference. These Cartesian notions include: the idea of mind as an "intrapsychic container" of representations of the world "out there", and the idea of transference as a distortion. I assert that a field theory such as ours cannot accept the idea of such a separation between inner and outer, since experience always emerges from our embeddedness, our being of a field. Nor can I accept the idea of distortion, because a field theory perspective includes the assumption that human behavior is inherently ambiguous and that reality is open to multiple perspectives. We can accept — as an alternative to the idea of distortion — that sedimented learning limits anyone's ability (including the therapist's) to understand any situation fully, and that we are constantly revising our understanding, our knowledge, with every passing minute.

Perhaps we are better served by appreciating that patient and therapist are constantly influencing each other into engagements that reflect the sedimented learning of both parties, and an exploration of the sedimented ideas and expectations of only one of the parties would fall prey to a /Cartesian separatedness that increases the isolation of both parties. In a dialogical, phenomenological exploration I hope the therapist would be keeping in mind that both parties are contributing to the range of experiences that are occurring, and that both dialogical partners are constrained by the limits of their own perspective. In so doing, they would be better prepared to learn about the advantages and limits of the perspectives of both therapist and patient. I find the notion of perspective, which "houses" expectations, emotional patterns, beliefs, etc., a more congenial notion than transference.

Reconfiguring our thinking about transference along these lines is just one example of how our clinical thinking evolves as part of the relational turn. There are many Gestalt theorists who are contributing to the evolution of relational thinking and field theory in the Gestalt approach, so many that I dare not list them, for fear of leaving someone out. Some names would be very familiar to the reader, some less so, as Gestaltists in the next generations from mine pick up the thread. I shall only say that I am pleased to be part of the tapestry that is still being woven, and heartened to find so many newer authors joining adding their threads and stitches as well.

References

Jacobs, L. (2004). Ethics of context and field: The practices of care, inclusion and openness to dialogue. In R. G. Lee (Ed.). *The Values of Connection: A Relational Approach to Ethics* (pp. 35-55). Hillsdale, NJ: GestaltPress/TheAnalytic Press.

Jacobs, L. (2003). Differing views on implications of a relational self: Book review. *International Gestalt Journal*, 26(1), 137-148.

Philippson, P. (2001). *Self in Relation*. Highland, NY: Gestalt Journal Press.

Rogers, C. (1961). *On Becoming a Person*. New York: Houghton-Mifflin.

Stawman, S. (2007) Relational Gestalt: Four waves, in relational Gestalt perspectives (in press).

Taylor, C. (1989). Embodied agency. In Pietersma, (Ed.). *Merleau-Ponty: Critical Essays*. Washington, DC: University Press of America.

3

On Macaque Monkeys, Players, and Clairvoyants: Some New Ideas for a Gestalt Therapeutic Concept of Empathy[1]

Frank-M. Staemmler

Frederick Perls's view was that empathy fosters confluence, that is, it blurs the distinctions ("boundaries") between the self and the other: "There can be no true contact in empathy. At its worst it becomes confluence" (1973, p. 106), he said in his rigorous way. Hence, "empathy" has been almost a dirty word for many gestalt therapists right up to the present. However, I am convinced that empathy cannot be relegated from gestalt therapeutic practice. It may be useful to think about a gestalt therapeutic understanding of empathy. Of course, on the one

---

[1] This paper is based on a lecture first given at the "Winter Residential" of the Pacific Gestalt Institute in Santa Barbara, California, in March 2005. It was first published in *Studies in Gestalt Therapy: Dialogical Bridges*, 1(2), 2007. I am indebted to Neil Harris who thoroughly edited this paper for language.

hand Perls's warning should be taken seriously (but not rigidly). On the other hand the danger of individualistic thinking, according to which the individual is locked in his inner world and in the end remains unreachable for the other, is to be avoided. In this paper I will offer some ideas about a notion of empathy that I think are in keeping with more recent trends in gestalt therapy (e.g., dialogue and field theory). I will also draw on sources such as phenomenology, gestalt psychology, hermeneutics, neurosciences, and others.

In order to survive, human beings need to understand each other to a high degree. Mothers empathize with their babies to find out if they need a new diaper, a hug, or some food; children empathize with their parents to spot the right moment to ask for a favor; and waitresses point the way to the bathroom when they see a customer getting up from his chair and looking around the room: Empathy is a basic human capacity without which social life would be impossible. Empathy forms the basis of any relational bond; it is a necessary precondition for prosocial attitudes and ways of behavior such as solidarity and compasssion. "The empathic understanding of the experience of other human beings is as basic an endowment of man as his vision, hearing, touch, taste and smell" (Kohut, 1997, p. 144). People who are essentially impaired in their capacity for empathy are diagnosed as "sociopaths" or "psychopaths," or as suffering from an "antisocial personality disorder" (DSM-IV code 301.7).

Hence it is no wonder that psychotherapy, which both rests on the human relationship between the people involved and aims at fostering the relational faculties of its clients, cannot proceed without empathy. Accordingly, clients expect their therapists to be empathetic — sometimes even in an idealizing (and at the same time paranoid) way when they assume that their therapists might (or should) be able to "look through" them. And some therapeutic orientations, such as Rogers' (1951) client-centered therapy or Kohut's (1971) brand of psychoanalysis, self psychology, explicitly build their approaches on their respective concepts of empathy.

I hold that, in their everyday practice with clients, not only the proponents of a "relational attitude" (see, for instance, Yontef, 2002), but *all* Gestalt therapists rely on their empathetic capacities, even if they do not call it "empathy" in their usual ways of thinking and talking about it. Some of them prefer to think of it in terms of "contact," "healthy confluence," or, in allusion to Buber (1958), "inclusion." Whatever the words may be, if our therapeutic work makes use of empathy in a significant sense, we need to look for appropriate ways of reflecting on it.

I want to share my preliminary thoughts with regard to the question of how we might conceive empathy within a Gestalt therapy framework. As I develop my thoughts it will become evident that the title of this chapter might as well have been "In Defense of Confluence" or "A Contribution to the Psychology of the 'As If.'"

In order to clarify my position I must, however, begin with a description and critique of what might be called the "traditional notions of empathy."

Traditional Notions of Empathy

Looking Back

"Empathy" was among the words included in Frederick Perls's black list — along with "interpretation" (see Staemmler, 2004;

2006a) and others. For him, "empathy [was] a kind of identification with the patient which excludes the therapist himself from the field and thus excludes half the field.[2] In empathy, the therapist's interest is centered exclusively around the patient and his reactions" (Perls, 1973, p. 104). "If the therapist withholds himself, in empathy, he deprives the field of its main instrument, his intuition and sensitivity to the patient's ongoing processes" (ibid., p. 105).

Although I doubt that "a kind of identification," which is so far-reaching that the therapist "excludes himself from the field," is possible at all, I agree that the therapist's identification (if the word is used in a strict sense) with the client is not desirable, since the client needs a recognizable other person to be with. But I think that Perls's equalization of identification with empathy is overhasty. Not in a single sentence does he discuss the possibility that if there are two different signifiers (empathy and identification) there may also be two different signified phenomena.

The opinion that empathy is not a useful concept or not a useful therapeutic attitude has been maintained by many Gestalt therapists who just like Perls have emphasized differences and clear boundaries, for instance the late Jim Simkin (Yontef, personal communication, 1993) and, recently, Peter Philippson (2001, p. 39[3]). Proponents of the relational approach to Gestalt therapy, although also attentive to the

---

[2] Which field was Perls talking about? His statement only makes sense to me if I assume that he is referring to the *phenomenal* field of the *therapist* (see Staemmler, 2006b). The therapist, who identifies with the client, may not be aware of himself anymore; but that certainly does not necessarily mean that his client is not aware of the therapist anymore.

[3] For a critique see Jacobs (2003).

differences between individuals, are not as confluence-phobic as Perls. Yontef, for instance, clearly attributes positive value to empathy: "As the therapist attends to the experience of the patient with empathy and caring, the relationship will develop" (1993, p. 447). For him, empathy means "as much as one can to see the world as the patient does, while simultaneously keeping aware of one's own separateness and remembering that it is projection — one cannot truly experience another person's experience" (1993, p. 273). And Lynne Jacobs simply defines empathy as "an attempt to comprehend, from the patient's perspective, the patient's experiential world" (2003, p. 145).

Looking Sidewards

Buber

In the literature of Gestalt therapy sometimes Buber's term "inclusion" (or "confirmation") is used as a replacement for "empathy." However, the two terms do not refer to exactly the same phenomenon. According to Friedman, "Buber distinguishes between inclusion and empathy. Empathy literally means to feel into the other. It means you leave your ground and you go over to the other" (1990, p. 22). And he goes on:

> True confirmation, in contrast, has to be bipolar: it has to be both sides simultaneously. . . . The therapist has to be there and here at the same time. Inclusion is this bold swinging, through an intense stirring of one's whole being, through which one can, to some extent, concretely imagine what the other is thinking, feeling and willing. (Friedman, 1990, p. 23)

In another publication he softens this contradistinction again when he writes:

We have also seen in Rogers' discussion of empathic understanding in his later essays that he stresses accurately seeing into the client's private world *as if* it were his own without ever losing that *as if* quality. This, too, is very close to Buber's definition of "inclusion." (Friedman, 1985, p. 199 — italics in original)

Maybe Lynne Jacobs hit the bull's eye when in a recent paper she wrote that

> the act of inclusion means entering into the experiential world of the other without judgment, while still knowing one's own being. It is a full-bodied turning-towards-the-other that includes empathy, but is more visceral than the way we usually describe empathy. (Jacobs, in press)

In summary, one may discuss whether there is in fact a difference between inclusion and empathy; I am not sure. In any case, if, as Jacobs says, inclusion includes empathy, it is useful to clarify that aspect, even if one opts for Buber's concept.

Rogers and Modern Psychoanalysis

We have already touched upon Rogers' notion of empathy in Friedman's statement. Now let us listen to Rogers himself. For him:

> The state of empathy or being empathic, is to perceive the internal frame of reference of another with accuracy, and with the emotional components and meanings which pertain thereto, as if one were the other person, but without ever losing the "as if" condition. Thus it means to sense the hurt or the pleasure of another as he senses it, and to perceive the causes thereof as he perceives them, but with-

out ever losing the recognition that it is *as if* I were hurt or pleased, etc. If this "as if" quality is lost, then the state is one of identification. (1959, p. 210f. — italics in original.)

In short, "to sense the client's private world as if it was your own, but without losing the 'as if' quality — this is empathy" (Rogers, 1961, p. 284). Please note Rogers's repeated use of the "as if"; we need to keep it in mind, since we will encounter it again later.

This "as if" can also be found hidden in Kohut's (1977) brief characterization of empathy as "vicarious introspection," and it shows up in Stolorow, Brandchaft, and Atwood's definition of empathy too, which to them "refers to the attempt to understand a person's expressions from a perspective within, rather than outside, that person's own subjective frame of reference" (1987, p. 15).

If we look at all the aforementioned traditional notions of empathy, we find that they all refer to the therapist's reconstruction of the client's given experiential world on the basis of the client's verbal and nonverbal communications. Empathy, we may say, is the therapist's imagination of how it is to perceive and experience the world in the way the client does.

This is close to that which in the philosophy of mind (see, for instance, O'Hear, 1998) is called the *theory theory*, that is, the theory that holds that people form theories about other people in order to understand them.

Critique of the Traditional Notion of Empathy

There is a common denominator in the traditional notions of empathy that can be subdivided into three aspects.

Empathy as a One-Way Street

In a way, clients are only seen as providers of information and addressees of empathetic responses by the therapists. This idea of empathy strikes me as a relic of a one-person psychology that only looks at the psyche of the client; the therapists themselves seem to remain unknown or — as they used to say in earlier psychoanalysis — "anonymous" to their client. Moreover, it reflects an elitist mentality of the therapists who seem to think of themselves as being the only empathetic human beings in the room.

This notion very much resembles the situation in a confessional; maybe it is a reflection of the pastoral discourse of power (see Foucault, 1982) in which psychotherapy is still involved to a certain degree today. And maybe it is this misconception of empathy that made it appear necessary for Buber to invent "inclusion."

However, I am certain that clients do need a lot of empathy in order to understand their therapists — just like everybody does in any conversation. Moreover, the uniqueness and peculiarity of the therapeutic situation is demanding of an extraordinary sensitivity of clients. How else would they be able to make sense of some therapeutic techniques — for instance those involving certain types of furniture such as couches and empty chairs — that at first may strike them as strange procedures?

Disembodiment

In the traditional notions of empathy there is primarily a person's *mind* that reconstructs the *mind* of another person. It is a representationalist, mentalist, or cognitivist notion, in which the fundamental fact of human embodiment is more or less left out of the picture — even if it takes into account the emotions of the person. But emotions are rather seen as *irrational cognitions* than as a *physically "felt sense"* (to use Gendlin's term).

Individualism

According to Wheeler,

> the fundamental propositions of ... [the individualistic] paradigm ... are: 1) that the individual is prior to relationship, and exists in some essential way apart from relational context and connection, and 2) that relationships themselves are therefore secondary, and in some sense less real than the individuals who enter into them.... The fundamental separation of one individual's experience from that of another... follows directly from these assumptions. (2000, p. 53).

This anthropology can also be found in the way empathy is usually seen: An individual existing in fundamental separation from the other's experience tries hard to bridge the interhuman gap by reconstructing the other's subjectivity in his own isolated mind. "This kind of subject is the master inside its own home (e. g., soul, consciousness, private inner world), but does not know how to get out of it" (Schmitz, 2003, p. 493).

This subject does not even appear to be involved in a certain situation that encompassed himself and the other person. There is no joint context, nothing that connects the one to the other; there are only scanty attempts at coping with the pervasive isolation surrounding the lonely individual.

Steps to a New Concept of Empathy

In what follows I will outline some preliminary ideas as to how these shortcomings might be overcome. This is not to say that the traditional notion of empathy is entirely misguided or even wrong. It is only to say that it represents a pretty narrow and truncated idea of what empathy can be.

Mutuality of Empathy: Social Referencing

In my experience, my clients are frequently empathetic towards me just as I am towards them. Some of them are even so empathetic that they are afraid of burdening me with their problems when they realize my compassion for their sufferings. Fortunately, in most cases they are at least empathetic enough to recognize my empathizing with them. "It takes one to know one," as the proverb has it, and if that were not so, my clients would not be able to benefit from my empathy.

In a certain sense toddlers at the age of seven to eight months already show a certain kind of empathy. The famous "visual cliff" experiment demonstrates this in an impressive manner. In this experiment the baby is placed onto one end (the "shallow" side) of a table; the mother stands at the opposite end of the table.

> The cliff table is made of clear, very hard glass and is divided into two sides. On one side (the shallow side) there is a checkered pattern immediately under the surface of the glass. On the other side, a similar checkered pattern is spaced some variable distance beneath the glass to create the illusion of a drop-off, which the solid glass prevents. (Klinnert, Campos, Sorce, Emde, and Svejda, 1983, p. 67)

As the baby begins to crawl towards the mother it approaches the visual cliff at which it hesitates and stops since it finds itself confronted with an ambiguous situation. Can it trust in the tactile information suggesting that the table-top continues at the same level? Or should it believe more in what it sees, that is, a dangerous drop-off? In other words, does it want to move on or stop? The baby typically stops, looks at its mother's face, and then makes its decision depending on what kind of feeling her face displays: "none of the infants crossed over the deep side of the cliff when the mother displayed a fearful facial expression, but 74% crossed when she smiled" (Sorce, Emde, Campos, and Klinnert, 1985, p. 197).

Obviously, both the mother and the child are empathizing with each other. Without the baby's empathy with the emotional expression of the mother and without the mother's empathy with the ambiguous situation of the baby, this process of mutual attunement could not take place. And already at that age the infant accomplishes at least three important social, affective, and cognitive tasks:

> First of all, she must understand the content of the message. Thus, if the mother provides a fearful message about the visual cliff, the infant must recognize these facial, vocal, and kinesthetic cues as reflective of fear, rather than of joy or interest. . . .
>
> Second, infants need to be in an appraisal and evaluation mode when they are processing information about cnviron-mental events. In other words, they must be constructing the reality of the situation, and not just responding to it in a prewired fashion. . . .
>
> Third, the infant must be able to identify the particular referent that is the topic of the referee's communication. (Feinman, Roberts, Hsieh, Sawyer, and Swanson, 1992, p. 31)

The subtle communicative process that includes all of these achievements is an example of what developmental and social psychologists call "social referencing." It is defined

> as a process in which one person utilizes another person's interpretation of the situation to formulate her own inter-pretation of it.... In referencing, one person serves as a base of information for another and, in so doing, facilitates the other's efforts to construct reality. (Feinman, 1992, p. 4)

Similar processes can be observed between therapists and their adult clients. Gendlin describes them wonderfully:

> My sense of you, the listener, affects my experiencing as I speak, and your response partly determines my experiencing a moment later. What occurs to me, and how I live as we speak and interact, is vitally affected by every word and motion you make, and by every facial expression and attitude you show.... Thus it is not the case that I tell you about me, and then we figure out how I should change, and then somehow I do it. Rather, I am changing as I talk and think and feel, for your responses are every moment part of my experiencing, and partly affect, produce, symbolize, and interact with it. (1962, p. 38f.)

And this, of course, applies to *each* partner in the interaction.

Embodiment

There is something happening to the empathizer herself right there and then; it is not just that she is thinking hard, or trying to figure something out. She is *physically* involved. I will demon-strate this from three points of view, academic psychology, phe-nomenological philosophy, and neuroscience.

Academic Psychology

For many years empirical researchers have investigated a phenomenon that most people know well from their everyday experience: how contagious yawning can be! You only need to watch somebody yawning and very soon you tend to yawn yourself. The same with laughter; you can easily be seduced to laugh by somebody else's laughter. Observing body postures and gestures can have a similar effect. It frequently happens that if two people sit together (not only in a therapy session) they tend to align their postures or mirror each other's gestures. If one crosses his legs, the other one will very likely soon do the same.

This phenomenon is called "mimetic synchrony":

> Psychological research demonstrates that people have a natural tendency towards mimicking the posture, gestures, expressions or movement of the people they are looking at.... Mimetic synchrony is a natural and automatic response to the experience of being with another, as opposed to a conscious and deliberate attempt at imitation. (Cooper, 2001, p. 224)

Another example can be found in Paul Ekman's research on the way emotions show in the human face. There are seven "basic" emotions that are expressed in the human face in the same way in any culture. There appear to be certain innate patterns of innervation of the muscles in the face for each of these emotions, which are sadness, anger, surprise, fear, enjoyment, disgust, and contempt. Of course there are huge intercultural differences with respect to the occasions when each of these emotions will be experienced as well as with regard to the so called "rules of display" that determine when and how one is "permitted" to express certain feelings.

However, if one of the basic emotions is experienced and its expression remains uninhibited, it will be expressed universally in the same way. That also means that people across cultures will be able to recognize each of these emotions intuitively (see Ekman, 2003).[4]

Phenomenological Philosophy

Many phenomenological philosophers have written about intersubjectivity and its various aspects. For them, empathy does not simply and only consist of the capability to grasp the feeling state of another person, but also — and much more fundamentally — in the capability to recognize another person as a person who is basically just like me: an embodied subject who has similar experiences and her own subjectivity. "One of the unique possibilities that human empathy affords is the development of nonegocentric or self-transcendent modes of consciousness" (Thompson, 2001, p. 23).

This notion forms the background of formulations that refer to more precise aspects of the mutual understanding of humans, for instance in Merleau-Ponty's writings. In the *Phenomenology of Perception* he writes:

> The communication or comprehension of gestures come about through the reciprocity of my intentions and the gestures of others, of my gestures and intentions discernible in the conduct of other people. It is as if[5] the other person's intention inhabited my body, and mine his. (1962, p. 185)

---

[4] In an interesting paper Cole (2001) describes what it means not to have a face that can express emotions.

[5] Please note, that here we encounter the "as if" again.

These phenomena have been subsumed under the notion of "*Einleibung*" by the German founder of "New Phenomenology," Hermann Schmitz (1989). "*Einleibung*" is an artificial word that is derived from "*Einfühlung,*" the German word for empathy. Both words consist of three parts, (1) "*Ein-*" which means "into" just like "em-" in empathy, (2) "*-leib-*" or "*-fühl-*" which are analogous to the center part of empathy, "-path-", and (3) "*-ung,*" which is the ending.

In other words, in order to describe the phenomena in question, Schmitz replaced the center part of em-*path*-y, "*-fühl-*" (to feel), by the German word for the "lived body," "*-leib-*". The resulting artificial term, *Einleibung*, can be roughly translated as "embodypathy," the physically based perspective taking that takes place, if, for instance, you are attending a circus performance and are fascinated by the exercises of acrobats in the circus dome: You will, again and again, become aware of your muscles performing similar movements in a subtle way.

Another example is a mother who watches her naively playing child being threatened by an advancing car, but who is too far away to be able to help directly. In this situation she will feel tied to the child by her horror, probably unable to move. She will put herself in the child's place, but not in the sense of her taking the role of the child and play naively in the street.

Pedestrians walking in a crowded shopping mall very much rely on their "embodypathy": Without any planned coordination they attune their movements to each other with surprisingly rare failures in the form of collisions. They have a pretty clear sense of the other people's movements and directions and constantly adjust and redirect their own movements accordingly. Mutual "embodypathy", then, is called "*leibliche Kommunikation,*" "lived body communication."

Mirror Neurons

Corresponding[6] to the phenomenon of "embodypathy" there is a neurological system, consisting of so-called "mirror neurons." Only a few years ago, two Italian neuroscientists, Gallese and Rizzolatti, found some interesting evidence for the existence of an observation-execution matching system in the brain of Macaque monkeys. They called the neurons involved "mirror neurons," because their activity links the *perceptive* regions of the brain with the *motor* regions in the following way:

When a monkey watches a certain movement of a fellow monkey, the visual brain sends information to the mirror neurons that transforms it and, in turn, sends it to the motor regions so that a small degree of energy is elicited in the efferent neurons that go to the muscles. The pattern of that nervous activity is exactly identical to the pattern the brain would produce with more energy, if it were to have the muscles imitate and literally perform the observed movement.

There is now strong evidence that in humans too

> several brain regions, including the premotor cortex, the posterior parietal cortex and the cerebellum, are activateed during action generation and while observing and simulating others' actions.... Particularly interesting is the demonstration that action observation activates the premotor cortex in a somatotopic manner — simply watching mouth, hand and foot movements activates the same

---

[6] I use the word "corresponding" here in order to make clear that I am not embarking in any kind of reductionism that maintains that empathetic behavior could be "traced back" to, or "explained" by, neurophysiology. Behavior belongs to a different, more complex system level, which has to be understood as "emergent" from less complex, for instance physiological, system levels (see Anderson, 1972; Bunge, 1977).

functionally specific regions of the premotor cortex as performing those movements. (Blakemore & Decety, 2001, p. 566)

"Although we do not overtly reproduce the observed action, nevertheless our motor system becomes active *as if* we were executing that very same action that we are observing." (Gallese, 2003, p. 174 — italics in original). To put it in different words, action observation implies action simulation. — Do you remember Rogers's "as if?" It now acquires an entirely different meaning.

Interestingly, evolution appears to have designed mirror neurons not only for the purpose of imitation, but rather for the purpose of *understanding*:

> In a PET study, Grèzes et al. asked humans to observe meaningful arm actions, either to understand their purpose or to imitate them. They found significantly stronger activation of premotor areas when the subjects had to understand the motor actions than when they had to imitate them. (Rizzolatti et al., 2001, p. 667).

By the way: Recent studies suggest that autistic children may suffer from an impaired development of mirror neuron areas in their brains. But normally, to a certain extent we are *wired for confluence* in order to understand each other. I will give you an everyday example:

> My wife, Barbara, and I are sitting at the breakfast table. We have already finished eating and are engaged in a conversation while having another cup of tea. My cup is empty. I grab the teapot to get some more tea. There is not much left. As I am going to put the teapot back on the teapot-warmer I realize that the tea candle is still burning.

Since the tea-warmer is about a yard away from me I spontaneously inhale a bit deeper in order to get enough air to be able to blow out the candle. Doing this I become aware that most likely my breath will not suffice to extinguish the candle. The movement of my hand, that has already been "on the way" to put the teapot back on the tea-warmer, slows down for a second. — From the moment I had finished pouring the tea and begun to put the teapot back, the time taken was maybe five seconds.

Barbara who during my dealing with the teapot had been continuing to talk to me vividly about an important experience she had had a few days before, immediately interrupts her talking, inhales and blows out the tea-candle that is much closer to her than to me ... and goes on talking. I accelerate the previously slower movement of my arm and replace the teapot on the tea-warmer.

When I discussed the process with Barbara she reported that she "somehow" saw the slowing down of my arm movement, but did not become aware of my deeper inhalation.

This is obviously an example of confluence; however, as Perls at al. say: "The distinction between the healthy and the neurotic confluences is that the former are potentially contactful.... Yet obviously immense areas of relatively permanent confluence are indispensable as the underlying unaware background of the aware backgrounds of experience" (1951, p. 451).

From what I have written so far, I conclude that a certain degree of confluence appears to be a necessary precondition for empathy. This casts a light on confluence that makes it look less "neurotic" than one may have thought after reading Perls et al.

Moreover, I dare to posit, that being confluence-phobic means being empathy-phobic. And if it is true that empathy is an important ingredient of intersubjectivity then being empathy-phobic also means being relationship-phobic.

Confluence phobia, of course, is one of the typical phobias of the individualistic self — a self that suspiciously tries to maintain the impermeability of its boundaries (see Staemmler, in press).

Embodiment of Empathy and Theory of Mind

The observations of the psychologists, phenomenologists, and neuroscientists — mimetic synchrony, "embodypathy," and mirror neurons — form a challenge to the theory theory. Obviously we do not always need a theory about others, if we want to understand them. So theory theory has been supplemented or, by some philosophers, even replaced with *simulation theory.*

> The simulation model dispenses with the requirement that an attributor knows much about his own psychology or the psychology of others. It instead postulates an ability to *use* one's own psychology as a sort of analog device to parallel the psychology of the other. It allows us to assume that the attributor is quite naive in matters of mental theory and lawful generalization. (Goldman, 1993, p. 90 — italics in original)

One might say that simulation theory is the elaborated version of the "as if" that so many authors mention. However, the discussion on whether theory theory or simulation theory is the more adequate description of what happens in human understanding appears to be off the mark to me. I hold that both theories describe a part of what happens — or better: a *phase*. It seems to me that in everyday situations our first immediate approach to another person is based on intuitive simulation. In a second step we then form hypotheses and theories about the other, when we think about her or him and when we talk to our confidants about her or him. So to me a sequential *combination* of theory theory and simulation theory makes the most sense. In short, simulation comes first and is then followed by theory.

Summing up this section of the chapter, I would like to put on record that there is ample evidence for the embodiment of empathy. Interestingly, as the examples from academic psychology, philosophy, and neuroscience show, this evidence also points at a non-individualistic notion of empathy. In other words: In empathy, there are (at least) *two* people involved, and they are *physically* involved. It is pretty much like *playing tennis* or like *dancing*.

This takes me to my next point.

Community: Joint Situation

In my account of social referencing I have already stated that empathy is based on *mutuality* (as opposed to one-sidedness). Nevertheless, although mutuality already transcends individualism to a certain extent, it can still be seen as the mere sum of two basically separated individuals that happen to direct their respective attention to each other.

However, the whole is more than, and different from, the sum of its parts. Therefore we need to find a notion that transcends the remaining individualism of mutuality. We can find it in play and dance.

In essence, play and dance are pretty much the same: The German word for play, "*Spiel*," originally meant dance. Hermeneutic philosopher Hans-Georg Gadamer, who was Heidegger's most prominent student (see Staemmler, 2002), writes:

> This linguistic observation seems to me an indirect indication that play is *not* to be understood as something a *person* does. As far as language is concerned, the actual subject of play is obviously not the subjectivity of an individual who, among other activities, also plays but is instead the *play itself*. But we are so accustomed to relating phenomena such as playing to the sphere of subjectivity and the ways it acts ... (1989, p. 104 — italics added)

Accordingly, Gadamer speaks of "the *medial* sense of the word 'playing' ... It happens, as it were, by itself.... The structure of play absorbs the player into itself" (ibid., p. 105 — italics added). From a Gestalt therapy perspective, Gadamer's hint at the "medial sense" of the word play can be seen as an allusion to what Perls et al. call the "middle mode, neither active nor passive" (1951, p. 245; see also p. 376, footnote). And it is certainly not by accident that in the sentence that follows they write about children and their play.

Hence, for Gadamer

> all playing is a being-played. The attraction of a game, the fascination it exerts, consists precisely in the fact that the game masters the players.... The real subject of the game ... is not the player but instead the game itself. (ibid., p. 106)

> This point shows the importance of defining play as a process that takes place "in between." We have seen that play does not have its being in the player's consciousness or attitude, but on the contrary play draws him into its dominion and fills him with its spirit. *The player experiences*

the game as a reality that surpasses him. (ibid., p. 109 — italics added)

This "in between" reality of the play — a reality that "surpasses the player" and that is "transpersonal" (to use the term in a rather unusual fashion) or "beyond individualism" (to quote Wheeler (2000) again) — is its *primary* reality. As Wertheimer said, "in certain situations a person is not present as an 'I' but as a characteristic part of a 'we' " (1924/1938, p. 362).[7] This primary reality, the greater whole, is the level of analysis that according to the Gestalt theorists always has to precede the analysis of its parts, because it has its own character which cannot be recognized by an elementary investigation.

In one of his compelling phenomenological analyses Hermann Schmitz (the creator of "embodypathy") coined a term that suits this primary reality very well: the "joint situation":

> Actually, whenever people are together, a *joint situation* is established from the very beginning, that cannot be fractionalized into the parts each participant contributes to it by means of her character or perspective. This can be recognized from the fact that a person, depending on which joint situation she is involved in, can become almost a *different* person. Her *individual* situation ... becomes a dependent variable by virtue of her participation in the *joint* situation: Self-determination and heteronomy are intermingled. (2002, p. 27 — italics added)

---

[7] In another paper, Wertheimer uses the metaphor of dance too: "Imagine a dance, a dance full of grace and joy. What is the situation in such a dance? Do we have a summation of physical limb movements and a psychical consciousness? No." (1925/1938, p. 9)

People who are participating in a joint situation such as being immersed in a play or dance are functioning in the middle mode: "One is engaged and carried along, not in spite of oneself, but beyond oneself" (Perls et al. 1951, p. 382). "That is, the self, aware in middle mode, bursts the compartmenting of mind, body, and external world" (ibid., p. 389).

That is, the joint situation is the *decisive* dimension. The participating individuals are *parts* of that situation. The empathizing, the social referencing that takes place, does not only take place in relation to the individual other. Rather, it takes place in the context of the whole situation, of which both the I and the other person are parts. The tennis player does not only refer to the individual intentions of the other player in order to understand his behavior. She or he also refers to the "affordances" (Gibson, 1979) or the "demand character" (Lewin, 1936) of the joint situation, of the game. The player moves within the play and, at the same time, allows himself to be moved by the play.

"Dyadically Expanded State of Consciousness"

Of course, this has an effect on the respective state of consciousness of the individuals involved. If you think back to the visual cliff experiment, you will remember that the social referencing that takes place between mother and infant implies a joint understanding and an interdependent cognitive-affective regulation. In individualistic terms, we are speaking of the capacity of each of the participants in the interaction to appreciate the meaning of the affective displays of their respective partner, and to scaffold her or his partner's actions so that they can achieve their goals. That is, the internal and external mechanisms [of each of the participants] form a single system made up of two component systems (i.e., infant and mother or therapist and client) — a dyadic system. Moreover, these regulatory processes involve communication among different components of this dyadic system. (Tronick, 1998, p. 293)

In terms of the state of mind of the participants we can now assume that the respective other's state of mind expands each person's individual horizon. "Thus, this dyadic system contains more information, is more complex ... than either the infant's (or the mother's) individual state of consciousness alone" (ibid., p. 296) — it is a "dyadically expanded state of consciousness" (ibid.).

In other words, when speaking of empathy we are talking about "a lived experience, which involves an intersubjective resonance that is irreducible to the consciousness of either participant taken alone" (Neimeyer, 2005, p. 81).

Feminist therapists have previously described this process in which the participants' attention is shifting back and forth between the parts and the wholes to which they pertain. O'Hara even speculates that dyadically expanded states of consciousness might account for phenomena such as clairvoyance or other

> seemingly magical and even paranormal breakthrough events that occur in psychotherapy, such as when the therapist and client simultaneously share the same image, when the therapist makes a statement out of the blue that proves to be profoundly appropriate, or when the therapist knows in advance that the client will soon begin to share some until-now hidden story. A sociocentric view would explain this not by suggesting that the therapist is "inside

the skin" of the client, but inside the skin of the relationship, of which he or she is a part. (1997, p. 306)

A dyadically expanded state of consciousness can only come into being through the joint situation. The state of being "inside the skin of the relationship," then, can make it possible that you know something *of* (not *about*) the other person — not because she transmitted the information to you in the sense of a simple sender-receiver model of communication, but because both she and you are integral parts of the same larger whole that encompasses the two of you. And the "container" of the information, as it were, is this whole, not the individual person.

Conclusion:
Proposal for a New Definition of Empathy

In conclusion, I would like to assemble the various theoretical concepts about which I have written, and integrate them into a proposal for a non-individualistic definition of empathy. This new definition, then, reads as follows:

Empathy is an embodied social referencing both to the joint situation and to each other by the persons involved that takes place within the frame of that joint situation. The joint situation both includes and transcends the individual situations of the participants and provides them with a dyadically expanded state of consciousness.

References

Anderson, P. W. (1972). More is different. *Science 177(4047)*, 393–396.
Blakemore, S.-J., & Decety, J. (2001). From the perception of action to the understanding of intention. *Nature Reviews: Neuroscience 2*, 561–567.
Buber, M. (1958). *I and Thou*. New York: Scribner's Sons.

Bunge, M. (1977). Emergence and the mind. *Neuroscience 2*, 501–509.
Cole, J. (2001). Empathy needs a face. *Journal of Consciousness Studies 8(5–7)*, 51–68.
Cooper, M. (2001). Embodied empathy. In S. Haugh & T. Merry (Eds.). *Empathy: Rogers' Therapeutic Conditions: Evolution, Theory and Practice* (pp. 218–229). Ross-on-Wye, UK: PCCS Books.
Ekman, P. (2003). *Emotions Revealed: Understanding Faces and Feelings*. London: Weidenfeld & Nicolson.
Feinman, S. (1992). In the broad valley: An integrative look at social referencing. In S. Feinman (Ed.). *Social Referencing and the Social Construction of Reality in Infancy* (pp. 3–13). New York & London: Plenum Press.
Feinman, S., Roberts, D., Hsieh, K.-F., Sawyer, D., & Swanson, D. (1992). A critical review of social referencing in infancy. In S. Feinman (Ed.). *Social Referencing and the Social Construction of Reality in Infancy* (pp. 15–54). New York & London: Plenum Press.
Foucault, M. (1982). The subject and power. *Critical Inquiry 8*, 777–795.
Friedman, M. (1985). *The Healing Dialogue in Psychotherapy*. New York: Jason Aronson.
Friedman, M. (1990). Dialogue, philosophical anthropology and Gestalt therapy. *The Gestalt Journal 13(1)*, 7–40.
Gadamer, H.-G. (1989). *Truth and Method* (2nd rev. ed.). New York: Crossroad.
Gallese, V. (2003). The roots of empathy: The shared manifold hypothesis and the neural basis of intersubjectivity. *Psychopathology 36*, 171–180.
Gendlin, E. T. (1962). *Experiencing and the Creation of Meaning: A Philosophical and Psychological Approach to the Subjective*. Glencoe, IL: Free Press of Glencoe.
Gibson, J. J. (1979). *The ecological approach to visual perception*. Boston: Houghton Mifflin.
Goldman, A. I. (1993). *Philosophical Applications of Cognitive Science*. Boulder, CO: Westview Press.
Jacobs, L. (2003). Differing views on implications of a relational self: Book review of P. Philippson, 2001. *International Gestalt Journal 26(1)*, 137–148.
Jacobs, L. (in press). Dialogue, confirmation and the good. *International Journal of Psychoanalytic Self Psychology*.

Klinnert, M. D., Campos, J. J., Sorce, J. F., Emde, R. N., & Svejda, M. (1983). Emotions as behavior regulators: Social referencing in infancy. In R. Plutchik & H. Kellerman (Eds.). *Emotion: Theory, Research, and Experience, Vol. 2. Emotions in Early Development* (pp. 57–86). New York: Academic Press.

Kohut, H. (1971). The Analysis of the Self: A Systematic Approach to the Psychoanalytic Treatment of Narcissistic Personality Disorders. New York: International Universities Press.

Kohut, H. (1977). *The Restoration of the Self*. New York: International Universities Press.

Lewin, K. (1936). *Principles of Topological Psychology*. New York: McGraw-Hill.

Merleau-Ponty, M. (1962). *Phenomenology of Perception: An Introduction*. London: Routledge.

Neimeyer, R. A. (2005). The construction of change: Personal reflections on the therapeutic process. *Constructivism in the Human Sciences 10*, 77–98.

O'Hara, M. (1997). Relational empathy: From egocentrism to postmodern contextualism. In A. Bohardt & L. Greenberg (Eds.). *In Empathy and Psychotherapy: New Directions in Theory, Research, and Practice*. Washington D.C.: American Psychological Association.

O'Hear, A. (Ed.). (1998). *Current Issues in Philosophy of Mind*. Cambridge: Cambridge University Press.

Perls, F. S. (1973). *The Gestalt Approach & Eye Witness to Therapy*. Palo Alto, CA: Science & Behavior Books.

Perls, F. S., Hefferline, R. F., & Goodman, P. (1951). *Gestalt Therapy: Excitement and Growth in the Human Personality*. New York: The Julian Press.

Philippson, P. (2001). *Self in Relation*. Highland, NY: Gestalt Journal Press.

Rizzolatti, G., Fogassi, L., & Gallese, V. (2001). Neurophysiological mechanisms underlying the understanding and imitation of action. *Nature Reviews: Neuroscience 2(9)*, 661–670.

Rogers, C. R. (1951). *Client-Centered Therapy: Its Current Practice, Implications, and Theory*. Boston: Houghton Mifflin.

Rogers, C. R. (1959). A theory of therapy, personality, and interpersonal relationships, as developed in the client-centered framework. In S. Koch (Ed.). *Psychology: A Study of Science: Vol. 3. Formulations of the Person and the Social Context* (pp. 184–256). New York: McGraw-Hill.
Rogers, C. R. (1961). *On Becoming a Person*. Boston: Houghton Mifflin.
Schmitz, H. (1989). *Leib und Gefühl: Materialien zu einer philosophischen Therapeutik* [Lived body and feeling: Material for a philosophical approach to therapy]. (H. Gausebeck & G. Risch, Hg.). Paderborn, Germany: Junfermann.
Schmitz, H. (2002). *Begriffene Erfahrung: Beiträge zur antireduktionistischen Phänomenologie* [Experience comprehended: Contributions to an antireductionist phenomenology]. Rostock, Germany: Koch.
Schmitz, H. (2003). The "new phenomenology". In A. T. Tymieniecka (Ed.). *Phenomenology World-Wide* (pp. 491–494). Durdrecht, The Netherlands: Kluwer Academic Publishers.
Scorce, J. F., Emde, R. N., Campos, J., & Klinnert, M. D. (1985). Maternal emotional signaling: Its effect on the visual cliff behavior of 1-year-olds. *Developmental Psychology 21(1)*, 195–200.
Staemmler, F.-M. (2002). Hans-Georg Gadamer: An obituary. *International Gestalt Journal 25(1)*, 129–131.
Staemmler, F.-M. (2004). Dialogue and interpretation in Gestalt therapy: Making sense together. *International Gestalt Journal 27(2)*, 33–57.
Staemmler, F.-M. (2006a). The willingness to be uncertain: Preliminary thoughts about interpretation and understanding in Gestalt therapy. *International Gestalt Journal 29(2)*, 9–40.
Staemmler, F.-M. (2006b). A Babylonian confusion?: On the uses and meanings of the term "field". *British Gestalt Journal 15(2)*, 64–83.
Staemmler, F.-M. (in press). On metaphors, myths, and minds: Boundary disturbances in Gestalt therapy theory. In G. Wheeler (Ed.), *Reading Paul Goodman*. Cambridge, MA: GestaltPress.
Stolorow, R. D., Brandchaft, B., & Atwood, G. E. (1987). *Psychoanalytic Treatment: An Intersubjective Approach*. Hillsdale, NJ: The Analytic Press.
Thompson, E. (2001). Empathy and consciousness. *Journal of Consciousness Studies 8(5–7)*, 1–32.

Tronick, E. Z. (1998). Dyadically expanded states of consciousness and the process of therapeutic change. *Infant Mental Health Journal 19(3)*, 290–299.

Wertheimer, M. (1924/1938). An approach to a Gestalt theory of paranoic phenomena. In W. D. Ellis (Ed.), *A Source Book of Gestalt Psychology* (pp. 362–369). London & New York: Kegan Paul & Harcourt, Brace & Company.

Wertheimer, M. (1925/1938). Gestalt theory. In W. D. Ellis (Ed.). *A Source Book of Gestalt Psychology* (pp. 1–11). London & New York: Kegan Paul & Harcourt, Brace & Company.

Wheeler, G. (2000). *Beyond Individualism: Toward a New Understanding of Self, Relationship & Experience*. Hillsdale, NJ: the Analytic Press.

Yontef, G. M. (1993). *Awareness Dialogue and Process: Essays on Gestalt Therapy*. Gouldsboro, Me.: The Gestalt Journal Press.

Yontef, G. M. (2002). The relational attitude in Gestalt therapy theory and practice. *International Gestalt Journal 25(1)*, 15–35.

4

CoCreation of the Contact Boundary in the Therapeutic Situation
Margherita Spagnuolo Lobb

An Overview

In this chapter we will explore the concept of cocreation of contact boundary from a contemporary point of view. After discussing some findings of infant research as they have been applied to psychotherapy I will critique the traditional aim of psychotherapy to make "sayable" what has been "unsayable" — lamenting a lack of criticism even within the Gestalt therapy literature. I will then offer an alternative concept of the therapeutic situation as emerging from a phenomenological field where intentionalities for contact cocreate contact boundaries. Clinical examples of how this perspective changes our way of looking at therapeutic intervention will be provided. I will conclude by showing how in our contemporary focus on interconnection we support what our founders identified as the primary aim of psychotherapy: to recover the patient's spontaneity in contacting his/her environment.

Co-Construction of the Contact Boundary: from the Intrapsychic Paradigm to the Experience of Between-ness

In contemporary thought, "interconnectedness" is taken more and more as the basic paradigm of human nature, and thus as the leit motif of any scientific or philosophical inquiry. Not only in the field of neuroscience with the discovery of mirror neurons, and in the field of human development with the observation of mother-infant mutual-regulating patterns of behavior, but also in the field of physics, the interest has been in what happens between two persons or elements (instead of in just one) and in fields rather than in intrapsychic systems. From the paradigm of self-regulating subjectivity of the 1950's, we have moved to a paradigm of reality that is no longer construed as external to what is happening, but as arising from a context of relationships from which it cannot be separated. In the field of arts, where we can usually find the very first emergence of cultural trends, we can see new interactive forms of art: for instance, in exhibitions of contemporary art, a masterpiece can be a jacket made of fresh meat, the aim of which is not to linger in time (it will be thrown away after a couple of days), but to stimulate a fresh reaction in those who look at it: it seems that even a masterpiece is made of the here-and-now of the relationship between the artwork and the person, rather than by the artist in isolation.

The so-called "narcissistic society" (Lasch, 1978) has given way to a "technological society" (Galimberti, 1999), which has by now developed into what has been called the "liquid society"

(Bauman, 2000). The social feeling is becoming increasingly "liquid:" it may take on many forms and at the same time has neither containment nor structure. For example, children cannot stay still at school, they have to keep moving all the time (sometimes, with their enormous bodies, they look like rolling mountains), they are incapable of concentrating and breathing: their breath has no container, there is no experience of an entire body that contains the emotions.

In our present society — where "liquidity" seems to replace the principle of non contradiction previously in force and progressively demolished in post-modern society — a new trend is emerging that helps us to overcome the technological reasoning and the corresponding mentality of solving instability through the "sure" functioning of the machine. I'm referring to the polyphonic perspective on interactions, where, like in the chorus of Greek classical tragedies, individual meanings derive from an evolving field of experiences.

We can say that there is a new perspective on human nature: social sharing is no longer considered as based on the logic system or the ethics system — in other words on an a priori system — but on a connate condition, that of self-regulation of the relational situation (see figure 1). I say "situation" to refer to a phenomenological consideration of the relationship, as an event happening in a given situation, rather than an intra-psychic reality that evolves on its own.

Psychotherapy is confronted with the task of providing new perspectives and tools to support our being interconnected with therapy's nourishing possibilities. In this frame of reference, Gestalt therapy is rediscovering its original intuition of the experience that occurs at the contact boundary, "between" the I and the you. From an undifferentiated field (or situation), some excitements emerge and create boundaries. Boundaries function both to share parts of the field and to differentiate one-self from non-self. We see human relations as a process, a development of figure-ground dynamics of the field as a unit, and this view makes a difference and has consequences in our clinical intervention.

Figure 1. From the Intrapsychic Perspective to the Perspective of Contact Boundary

Intrapsychic Perspective	Contact Boundary
Separation between: wo/man – culture and also nature – culture	Unit of evolutionary process: wo/man – nature – culture
Human relations need to be regulated by external rules	Human relations self-regulate
Aggression is a destructive force	Aggression is a necessary force for survival

The cocreated contact boundary, as I call it, represents a new perspective on the client-therapist contact event. For example, when a client tells us: "I couldn't sleep tonight", he is not only telling us about an experience of his "inside", he is also telling us something about our relationship. Therefore our question might be: how am I contributing to this event, to his choice of telling me this sentence? What is the shared field between him and me and what is the intentionality of contact that supports his statement? What is the process by which he is differentiating himself in the shared field? What does his differentiating process aim to in our relationship? Maybe he intends to tell us about an anxiety that looms from our previous session or that anticipates the session about to begin (Müller, 1993). He might want to tell us: "During the last session something happened that caused some anxiety in me. I hope you will be able to see that today and to protect me from its negative consequences."

This perspective allows us to step outside the intrapsychic viewpoint that sees treatment as a process linked to the satisfaction (or sublimation) of needs, and to enter fully into the post-modern perspective in which the power of truth has been replaced by the truth of the relationship (Salonia, 2006).

Infant Research, Neuroscience and Implicit Regulative Strategies in Psychotherapy

As I have described elsewhere (Spagnuolo Lobb, 2006), in the last fifteen or twenty years, psychological studies have gone through a revolution: from a one-person psychology, where everything is assumed to happen in one brain, to a different mentality, where things are understood to be happening between people. In neuroscience, the discovery of mirror neurons (Gallese, 1995) as well as of neurons which work as "adaptive oscillators" (Port & van Gelder, 1995; Torras, 1985), and the observation that a feature of the mirror neurons system is to detect goal-directed actions (Blakemore & Decety, 2001), have been the fundamental evidence for this shift in perspective and the inspired support for many other related researchers, especially in the realm of infant research (Beebe & Lachmann, 2001).

The outcomes of this relatively recent research confirm and develop in some way what our founders had sensed more than fifty years ago but did not yet have the support to adequately develop. That is, all the evidence now points to interrelatedness: what can be experienced is that which is "between", the contact boundary, what Buber called Zwischenheit ("between-ness") and, more recently, what our intersubjective colleagues have referred to as the space where "I know that you know that I know".

An important epistemological novelty that Gestalt therapy introduced and that is now reemerging as a "new trend" in psychotherapy is the consideration of a procedural theory of self, the conception of the self as an ability to make contact with the environment (Spagnuolo Lobb, 2001a; 2001b; 2001c; 2005), rather than as a one-person system of perceptions, emotions, thoughts, etc. If the self is a process, we have to understand it with the language of music and of mathematics, rather than with verbal categories. Infant researchers have observed early competencies in babies that enable them to take part — in procedural terms — in the experience of contact with care-givers. Trevarthen (1974) claims that the newborn begins his life with an innate capacity to separate his own mind from the other's. Afterwards these primary intersubjective experiences can be shared with others, reaching what is called "primary intersubjectivity." He has pointed out for instance an early synchronicity of rhythms between newborns and caregivers, both in body and vocal communications (Trevarthen, 1988).

In brief, infant research has shown evidence of crucial procedural features of human nature: First, babies know what others feel; they can represent in their experience (at the level of non-verbal, implicit knowledge) what others feel, and they are able to synchronize with others. Second, babies imitate not just the actions of caregivers, but their intentions (Stern, 2001). Babies wish to carry forward their caregivers' desires. Increasingly using a phenomenological language, those researchers who have built on infant research and neuroscience, outline the ability of babies to cocreate a relational field with their caregivers, something that they do from birth, as a basic feature of human nature. They consider that good contact implies empathy for others' intentions or, to use a phenomenological concept, the sharing of an intentionality.

Following these various scientific voices, we are led to a new perspective on human nature and relations based on a concept of cooperative relational self-regulation, or, in proper phenomenological terms, self-regulation of the situation (Robine, 2001; 2003). This concept definitely replaces the old concept of organismic self-regulation (dear to the humanistic movement). The self-regulation of the field/situation becomes the new way of looking at human nature. In the words of Perls et alia:

> The question may quite seriously be asked, by what criterion does one prefer to regard "human nature" as what is actual in the spontaneity of children, in the works of heroes, the culture of classic eras, the community of simple folk, the feeling of lovers, the sharp awareness and miraculous skill of some people in emergencies? Neurosis is also a response of human nature and is now epidemic and normal, and perhaps has a viable social future. (1951, p. 319)

When we look at human sharing as a self-regulating flow, we also look differently at a whole series of events, for instance at divergent behaviors. We will see madness as well as adolescents' rebellion as a striving to bring forward an intentionality for contact; as psychotherapists we can try to support that intentionality. To see human relations as self-regulating will also challenge our capacity to integrate diversity in a shared space that is cocreated. I doubt that this concept is well assimilated in our contemporary culture, despite many cultural movements that have supported it, such as the anti-psychiatric movement of the 1980's and any activism that supports the rights of minorities.

I offer a brief example of a moment in my work that gives a sense of how much we can understand and support when we stay with the procedural aspects of the actual situation as a whole. A female patient with whom I am working is quite moved while telling me positive things she has never told her mother. Then she says that since moving to a different town she finds herself shut off from her mother. On the other hand she also admits that she deliberately chose to move to a safe distance from her mother, one that would guarantee that she would not be overwhelmed with emotions. As she tells me this, she lifts her feet from the floor. I suggest to her that perhaps in breaking the contact her feet have with the floor she is now removing the possibility of a bodily support for her emotions, and that in this way she is "taking her distance" from me, as she does from her mother. What emotions might she now be avoiding with me? Is it possible that when she takes her distance from the ground, this is precisely one of those moments she had described before in which she is overwhelmed by her emotions? At my invitation she returns her feet to the ground, looks at me, breathes and, feeling moved, manages to tell me how important I am to her. With more support, she has the resilience she needs to feel her powerful emotions. By discovering this together, we have begun a new story at the boundary of our contact, a story that will influence her relational patterns outside therapy too.

Overcoming the Paradigm of "Making the Unsay-able Say-able"

Any model of psychotherapy, from a specific anthropological perspective to one based on a reading of healthy (developmental theory) and suffering (theory of psychopathology) development, must be capable of "growing" with society, and treating new pathologies.

In the cultural climate to which Freud belonged, and in which, consequently, psychoanalysis originated, the idea of treatment was linked to the concept of bringing to reason every aspect of the pathology. The novelty of Freud's approach lay not so much in the idea of making rational all that was not so, but rather in suggesting an unconscious, an irrational level, which actually determined human behavior. Freud's saying "Whatever is Id must become Ego" was based on what was at the time a normal Enlightenment faith in reason. Interpretation as a treatment mechanism is the consistent methodological application of this faith. In the intervening hundred years, notwithstanding the cultural changes that psychotherapy has undergone, this idea of making conscious what is not, in fact, conscious, persists as the core — variously applied according to the theory of self and theories on normality and pathology adopted by all methods — of all psychotherapies. Some approaches speak of conscious and unconscious, others of rational and irrational, yet others of aware and unaware, but in the last analysis the spoken, theorized aim of psychotherapy remains that of making the unsay-able say-able.

Gestalt therapy, which as everyone knows works on process, mainly observes those relational patterns with which an individual makes contact with the environment, from breathing and all bodily processes to the relational meaning of the dreams recounted to the therapist. Yet even this kind of psychotherapy — though it has the merit of having overcome the dualism between healthy and sick, individual and society, body and mind, in favor of a holistic perspective on the organism-environment relationship and on the harmonious integration of personal experiences (bodily, affective, intellectual, spiritual) — has not sufficiently developed a methodology based on the unsay-able, and continues to use techniques based on making explicit what is implicit, as though treatment consisted exclusively of the explicit knowledge of the processes of relationship.

What, in fact, is the say-able? It is an experience that can be recounted. Making the unsay-able say-able implies socializing an experience. The theory of treatment as "say-ability", as narration, is based on the presupposition that the disorder lies in what is not said, in what remains locked in the isolation of the heart. But is this the only "unsay-able" with which the therapeutic relationship is concerned? Or is it also a whole series of experiences and communications that keep us in contact with each other and which are not say-able? Take, for example, panic attacks. Part of this experience is say-able, but the person recounting it, however appropriate and refined her/his words, never feels that s/he has said everything that could be said.

Patients define panic attacks as an unsay-able ill (Francesetti, 2007). "You can't understand them if you've never had one", is the typical disarming remark that we hear. This unsay-ability seems to be the core of the experience of a panic attack, its essence. Everything else belongs to logic: the patient knows that objectively s/he is not dying, but continues to be afraid of death; s/he knows that palpitations are not a sign of a heart attack, but is still afraid that her/his heart is going to explode any moment; s/he knows that the feeling of suffocating is due to a psychological mechanism, but fears that this is not the case. And so the sense of the mystery, of unsay-ability typical of this experience depends not on the lack of verbal categories to express it, but in the type of experience in itself. In the therapeutic relationship, for instance, therapist and patient "sniff" each other to find out whether they are "made for each other"

(Stern, 2004) and the success of treatment seems to depend more on this kind of communication than on verbal statements.

The question, then, is this: does the possibility of psychological treatment always lie in the say-ability of the disturbing experience? For it is precisely the ineffectiveness of psychotherapy in some disorders, such as panic attacks, that calls this treatment approach into question. In other words, the question for psychotherapy is: can a constitutionally unsay-able experience be treated? Is it possible to remain within the therapeutic parameter of making say-able what is not so, or must psychotherapy find other categories that explain a therapeutic path within the channels of unsay-ability? (Spagnuolo Lobb, 2007)

Is the sense of redemption that accompanies the psychotherapeutic experiences of those patients who succeed in recounting their experience to the therapist the experience of treatment par excellence, or in some cases do we need to seek a therapeutic dimension beyond say-ability?

Daniel Stern, who has always worked on the interface between research and psychotherapy, between child observation and working clinically with adults, has reached the conclusion that implicit knowledge — the knowledge that will never be verbalized — plays a huge role in the context and the change of people in psychotherapy. Explicit knowledge is verbal, symbolic, explicatory; it is what makes up narration. All interpretations are by definition explicit. Implicit knowledge is non-verbal, non-symbolic; it is unconscious but not repressed; it has simply never been in awareness (Stern et al., 1998a; 1998b; Stern et al., 2003, 21ff.). The new theories of development and the neurosciences (briefly outlined in the previous paragraph) come some way towards resolving our difficulties by asserting that some experiences are preverbal and cannot be say-able because they belong to a wordless language. This non-verbal awareness has its own development in relational life, and its maturing has nothing to do with transformation into verbalized or verbalizable knowledge.

Much therapeutic change is nowadays attributed to this implicit interrelating. This theme of the "say-able" and "unsayable" is consequently the subject of much debate in contemporary psychotherapy (Spagnuolo Lobb, 2006a), both because some researchers, such as Stern himself (2004), are reviewing the concept of conscious and unconscious in the psychoanalytic method, and because some new disorders, such as panic attacks, no longer respond positively to psychotherapies based on making the unsay-able say-able. It appears that what creates a positive change is not words, or the therapeutic technique that, in various ways, makes the unsay-able say-able, but rather what happens in the sphere of the unsay-able (Stern et al., 1998a; 1998b), of perceptions at the contact boundary (Spagnuolo Lobb, 2003).

A hundred years after the foundation of psychotherapy, we wonder whether its success depends on the control the individual succeeds in having over experiences, or on a sort of relational confirmation we seek in the other. The answers to this question from the various psychotherapeutic methods make it possible to define a common ground on which to build theoretical reflections and clinical perspectives that are better adapted to the new challenges of the post-modern age.

A radical change of perspective is being imposed not only on psychotherapy but on culture in general and on the agencies of socialization: what heals is not rational understanding and hence control of the disorder, much less the acceptance *ob torto collo* of a limit, but rather something that has to do with procedural and aesthetic aspects. "Treatment" does not consist in helping the patient to understand and control, but to live fully respecting her/his innate ability to regulate her/himself in the relationship, and this not only at the verbal level, but above all at the level of spontaneous activation of the neuro-corporeal structures that manage the life of the relationship.

All this, as psychotherapists well know, is an art, in which the say-able and the unsay-able interweave in the encounter between therapist and patient. Like in a dance, they together discover the possibility of fulfilling interrupted intentionalities. The therapist, with all her/his special knowledge and humanity, and the patient, with all her/his suffering and desire to recover, create the ground on which the sense of security in the world and in the other — and thus the letting go in intimacy — dwell.

Psychotherapy as a Phenomenological Field Where Intentionality for Contact is Spontaneously Developed

Every psychotherapy is a unique story where commitment takes different shapes. I hold that Gestalt therapy, with its hermeneutics of perception at the contact boundary, can offer a new perspective to the world of psychotherapy in general.

As mentioned above, the perception (and hence also the emotion) of the patient or the therapist is a process that occurs not "inside" the individual, but as a cocreation in the space "between". Feelings (of attraction or hate, for instance) point to the patterns that unfold in the therapeutic relationship. The neutral position assumed by analysts so many years ago, then contrasted by the (often naive and impulsive) emotional sharing offered by humanistic therapists, is now the subject of criticism. In contemporary psychotherapy, the therapist's emotional reactions derive meaning from the process of cocreation of the contact boundary. The treatment context gives the therapist a key for making sense of his/her personal reactions: it is always the patient's intentionality for contact that will guide the treatment. The patient comes to therapy with an excitement for contact that needs to be seen and supported. Whatever the therapist may feel or perceive must be understood to signal this intentionality and be "used" in its service.

For instance, the therapist who is attracted to a particular patient might discover that this patient is, so to speak, used to a parental love. Of course, we might say similar things when any other feeling occurs. In fact, in this way the patient shapes the therapeutic situation, offering the therapist — who responds sensitively — the access key to an intimate experience, so that the therapist will create the conditions to fulfill the intentionalities of contact that have not been brought to completion. The attraction felt by the aware therapist (who is present with all her/his senses at the contact boundary) is a sensitive, specific response to the situational field created by this particular patient in this specific moment.

Let me offer an example. A therapist comes for supervision because he is attracted to a young, good, intelligent patient. I ask him: "What attracts you?" "Her style of being a good girl", he says, "it really looks as if she wants to make me happy, as if she cares about me. She relaxes me." Obviously we all think that the therapist's narcissism in this case is colluding with the patient's openness towards and admiration for a real or dreamed-of father. But these two aspects may be the ground of the situation, whereas the figure is the fulfillment of this kind of contact that responds to the girl's "suspended" intentionality. It is precisely that old love that can be experienced by the patient in a new situation. The challenge for the therapist is to provide a clearer, more courageous response to the girl's love, to provide her love with a non-manipulative context that supports her to experience her spontaneity on the ground of a clear relationship. So, I ask this therapist: "If you imagine openly saying to this patient what you've just told me up to this point, what do you think would happen?" He says: "I don't know. Oddly, I think all the tension I feel would be relaxed. Perhaps she'd tell me that she's always wanted her father to say something of the sort to her. I think too that at that point my sexual attraction would calm down: I'd understand that the charge of attraction is actually determined by NOT saying these things. And maybe the patient would finally feel that she was seen in her affection for me, and her admiration would achieve its object. Maybe she could even become more independent of me." The therapist has grasped an intentionality of contact that was still incomplete and in stating explicitly what attracted him, he gives the patient the chance to conclude it in the here and now, in a new, real situation. The therapist's sexual attraction to the patient — like that of the father to the daughter — is an out-of-context emotion, but the fact that it happens is a response to the self-regulation of this situation.

The patient's attraction towards the therapist can be understood in the same way: the healing factor will not be the positive response of the therapist to this attraction (which instead would disorient her), but the fact that the patient feels seen and appreciated by him in her intentionality of contact. It is only this that can restore the spontaneity of the patient's love. For example, the patient tells the therapist that she has had a dream about making love with him. The therapist listens to what she is telling him and how, then he says: "I'm struck by the effort you've made to overcome your shyness and embarrassment. I appreciate the trust you have in me, and the courage with which you face your relationship with me." This answer, which is based on structures of commitment, gives the patient the sense of being seen in the intentionality of contact, not just in the feeling of attraction, which is thus confined by the therapist to the context of treatment: the patient has the right to express the most disturbing emotions, without this leading to a change in the setting she has personally chosen. To look at structures of experience helps us to see better the figure/ground dynamic.

From the point of view of transference, the therapeutic situation is artificial, and serves to analyze the external reality, to make conscious what is unconscious. We regard instead the therapeutic situation as real, the habitual relational patterns are fulfilled in it, in search of a new solution.

The Therapeutic Relationship as a "Real" Fact: The Sovereignty of the Experience

Hence the therapeutic relationship is seen as a real experience which arises from, and has its own story, in the space subsisting between patient and therapist, and not as a result of projections of transferential patterns from the patient's past. The relational dimension comes before the interior dimension, or at least cannot be explained from the intrapsychic experience.

Our phenomenological soul reminds us of the impossibility of stepping outside the field (or situation) of which we are a part, and gives us instruments that allow us to function while remaining within the limit imposed by the "situated" experience. The founders of Gestalt therapy proposed the "contextual" method (Perls et al., 1951), which long before Gadamer, posited a hermeneutic circularity between the reader and the text: you cannot understand the text (or the other) without a Gestalt mentality, and you cannot have a Gestalt mentality without reading the text à la Gestalt (or being with the other à la Gestalt) (Sichera, 2001).

Thus we can say that the therapeutic relationship represents a way in which the patient implicitly gives the therapist (and her/himself) the opportunity to remake a relational history, restoring certain intentionalities of contact that once bore the seeds of a complete, spontaneous development. It is in fact, in the therapeutic relationship that the possibility occurs of bringing to completion intentionalities of contact that allow the patient to perceive her/himself and situations differently, to feel more free and able to make her/his own contribution to relationships and hence to the world in which s/he lives.

Treatment is indeed based on real persons who reveal themselves not through techniques but rather through their human limitations. Isadore From, one of the founders of Gestalt therapy (who was my therapist), would share an example about a patient who had told him a dream beginning with: "I had a little dream". Now, Isadore was pretty short. Fully aware of this limitation of his, and knowing that it might trigger a spontaneous reaction in his patients (that they generally didn't say because it wasn't fair), he immediately commented: "Yes, like me!" The patient was shocked by the comment, stopped herself for a little while, and then burst into a liberating laugh. Her breathing became deeper, and she could get in touch with feelings of tenderness and trust she had previously blocked. It was just the human quality of that meeting in their limitations that gave the patient the possibility to open her deeper feelings in their relationship, with a sense of trust that was previously difficult to experience. This example shows how in Gestalt psychotherapy it is the real meeting between therapist and client that produces treatment, one where novelty occurs that is capable of restructuring the client's capacity for contact-making.

Multi-Contact Boundaries in a Field: The Triadic Perspective

Our culture, which has developed the cult of individualism, does not accustom us to seeing the plurality of relationships. The word "relationship" itself generally makes us think of an individual who encounters another individual. We think of the mother-child relationship, for instance, rather than of a field of relationships. In fact, what matters in the development of the child is the field of relationships in which s/he is inserted, in which it is sometimes the mother, sometimes the father, sometimes others that represent emerging figures: it is a field in which the various interweaving relationships of the ground influence the figure. The child experiences a field, a situation, which includes both the ground and the figure: in her/his perception of the father, for example, the perception of what the father knows about the mother is included, as is what the child her/himself knows about the mother, so that the child knows what the father does not know about the mother (which s/he knows) and what the father knows about the mother that s/he did not know.

The intersubjective perspective (cf., among others, Mitchell, 2000; Stern, 2000; Beebe and Lachman, 2001) may be a useful framework for thinking about perception at the contact boundary. If the mother feels neglected by the father, the child (even though this feeling has not been communicated explicitly to her/him) notices the mother's forced breathing, her sad face, her lowered eyes; s/he looks at the father and sees that the father is pensive and is peeking at the mother. So the child knows that the father knows what is wrong with the mother. But if the child sees the father continuing to play with her/him or making the usual business calls, s/he understands that the father does not know that the mother feels neglected by him, so s/he has to decide whether or not to take action so that the father will realize this. This will depend on her/his adjusting creatively to the situation. Hence the child's perception is oriented towards the contact boundary between mother and father, as well as, respectively, towards the contact boundary between her/himself and the mother and between her/himself and the father. This principle is also applied to the other people present in the field, constituting (in the case of the mother-father-child triangle) a phenomenological triadic field. (see figure 2)

Figure 2. Perceptions in a Triadic Field

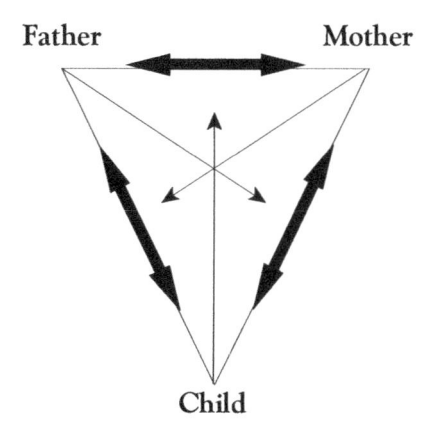

The child perceives not only the mother (or the father) but also what is happening at the contact boundary between them, so s/he knows if the father knows that the mother is sad or not, etc. In line with the phenomenological principle of the experience as happening in the here and now at the contact boundary in a field or situation, in Gestalt therapy we see intimate relationships (e.g. between family members, or between patient and therapist) as a figure that emerges from a relational field. Gestalt therapy can offer a view of the experience as a boundary event, rather than as an internalized relational pattern. This way of looking at the experience as a boundary event puts its trust in the spontaneity of being-there, in the aesthetic aspect of the relationship (being present at the contact boundary with the fullness of the senses), in the therapeutic relationship as a real event happening in the here and now.

In a word, the relationship is always multiple and complex. The child who is aware of the "fog" at the contact boundary between mother and father will develop an enduring relational pattern that fulfils her/his intentionality of contact as a child (taking care of the disturbed parents) and will adjust creatively to the situation; for instance, s/he will take steps to make the parents aware of each other, or will take on the responsibility of cheering up the mother if s/he is the only one who can do so (Stern, 2006). Summarizing, what happens at the contact boundary is a figure supported by the perceptual ground of the situational field.

Carrying this viewpoint through to the therapeutic setting, the patient never sees us in isolation, but always as part of a relational field. It would be interesting to ask the patient: "If you think of someone alongside your therapist, who do you imagine?" "What do you know about your therapist?" "What do you imagine your therapist knows about this person?" "In your opinion, what do the two of them think of you?"

As we shall see later in the clinical example, this work brings to light an interesting aspect of implicit relational knowledge, and gives the therapist a better-defined understanding of contact-making with the patient. As evolutionary theories have shown, it is impossible in life to live and grow alone, yet no one is ever only in a two-person system: we are always part of a social community, a shared situation.

Here is an example of a possible use of the triadic perspective in the clinical setting. A male patient is madly in love with his female psychotherapist. The fervor of his feelings and the desire for physical contact increase with each session. The therapist, after trying to make explicit every possible reading of the patient's feeling, is embarrassed: she cannot meet the patient in a perceptive clarity. Whatever she says or does seems to increase the patient's desire; in addition, she finds him rather attractive and is herself afraid to fall in love with him.

After some supervision from the perspective of the triadic method, she asks the patient: "Imagine there's somebody beside me. Who do you see?" The patient's expression changes at once and he says, laughing: "I see your husband (whom I don't know), or at least a man, your man. He's very different from you. I have a feeling he doesn't like me, and he's not too happy about my being with you. He doesn't think much of me. He impresses me: his presence attracts me more than yours now, though with unpleasant feelings. The experience of his glance is terrible for me. It strikes me very differently from yours. You're fond of me. You like me, don't you? It's just as well you like me!" The therapist asks: "What do I know about him? I mean, do I know that he puts you down?" "I guess so, that's exactly why you're kind to me!"

The triadic perspective brings out a new awareness in the therapeutic situation, one that casts an interesting light on the sexual feelings between patient and therapist, redressing the balance of the therapeutic relationship in the direction of the patient's intentionality of contact. It is clear, in fact, that what is moving his organism is not the "desire" to have the therapist's favors (as a dyadic view would suggest), but to understand (1) the relationship between the therapist and her partner; (2) why she appreciates him but her partner does not; (3) whether the liking the therapist shows for him derives from the fact that he is better than the other man or from the fact that he is "little", immature; (4) whether he can be independent of the therapist, i.e. be sure that she is still fond of him even if he does things she does not like; (5) whether he can reach the adult man and win his regard; and (6) whether the therapist can intercede with her partner to bring this about.

Summing up, in the triadic perspective what emerges is very different from what is seen in the dyadic context. In the triadic perspective a more complex dynamic emerges from the relationship between male and female, and between generations: the child always makes reference to one (or more than one) couple relationship in growing up, to contact boundaries between couples, more than to the dyadic relationship with one or the other parent.

The therapeutic intervention is modulated in this perspective in a way that is much more effective, and not only in the event of sexual feelings, whether on the therapist's or the patient's part. In the specific case of the example I have given, the patient's answer made it possible to move the attention for contact on to what had previously remained in the ground, and to what, remaining in shadow, lit the fire of sexual attraction. Focusing attention on the patient's relationship with men made it possible to talk about his fear of not being up to the mark (with both men and women), about the compulsions that characterized his seductive behavior towards women (sexual atttracttion to a woman in a maternal role allowed him to avoid the anxiety that comparing himself with men brought about), and to understand that, basically, starting a sexual relationship with the therapist would have frightened and confused him, burdening him with a responsibility he did not want. Going through the humiliation of comparing himself with men enabled him to offer himself spontaneously to a woman on equal terms, with desire and the sense of risk.

Psychotherapy as a Positive Look at Relations: Improvisational CoCreation as the Norm of Good Form

Gestalt therapy is a procedural approach that arose in order to overcome the dualism, with which Freud's thinking had concludeed, between the individual and society (Spagnuolo Lobb et al., 1996). It originated with psychoanalysts who had had an idea of human nature that, in comparison with the then current psychological models, was revolutionary: it was characterized by a positive anthropology (the human animal is a contact creature, one that functions by creatively adjusting to the situations in which it finds itself) and by a love for phenomenology, in which the basic concept of the intentionality inherent in every experience was seen as intentionality of contact. This means that every human behavior is to be understood as tension (excitement) for contact, insofar as it is a spontaneous occurrence of contact between organism and environment. Thus psychic suffering becomes the consequence of the failed fulfillment of an intentionality of contact (Salonia, 2001) and behaviour — even behavior which is defined as "pathological" by external norms — is always a creative adjustment to a difficult situation: it is a being-there in the here and now of an occurrence that is always relational, always physiologically and phenomenologically contact. The therapist assumes the relationship is a context for fundamental excitement to contact, rather than a defense to be disrupted in the service of an acceptable "sense of reality." This procedural, holistic "pro-tension" is constantly noted by the therapist who is focused on the now-for-next, on the support of the patient's movement "in gestation." Considering the central importance of the developing of the relationship between patient and therapist, the technique of the empty chair is conesquently revised: the client will undo his/her retroflections speaking to the therapist, instead of to the chair (Müller, 1993). This change enables us to bring into the core of the situation, into the field of the present contact, the relational block, the physiological, emotional, rational pattern of contact that covers (prevents from feeling) the anxiety linked to the unexpressed excitation.

This is the way we look at psychopathology in a psychotherapy setting: as a physiologically and psychologically creative adjustment that happens at the contact boundary between client and therapist. The concept of awareness in our approach is in line with this view. It represents a revolutionary version of the Socratic "know thyself" in which the intellectual power of knowledge and control of oneself is replaced by: 1) a human being's ability to "be awake", alive to her/his own senses, as a condition of normality; 2) the experiential direction given by intentionality of contact (the way the self is at the contact boundary and contributes to its creation); 3) the strength and the courage implicit in the holistic (at once bodily, mental and spiritual) reading of the charge of energy that accompanies this being at the boundary, no longer seen in a prevalently intellectual way (Spagnuolo Lobb, 2004).

Hence neurosis is the maintenance of isolation (in the organism-environment field) by means of the function of consciousness. Awareness performs an opposite function, or rather denotes the development of the opposite function, the function of spontaneously being at the contact boundary. In the first theorizations and examples of awareness in Gestalt therapy we find a particular movement. This passage is from the psychoanalytic culture of "making Ego all that is Id", as Freud maintained, to the culture in which it is the primacy of experience that is in use. In the existential perspective proper to early Gestalt therapy, (exploding from the 1950's to the 1970's) the value of experience (Erlebnis) was opposed to the value of knowledge; the creative strength of the organism (creative adjustment) opposed sublimation as the only possibility of adaptation to the demands of the community; and self-regulation of the organism and holism was positioned in opposition to the need of the Ego to control the Id.

This concept gives the therapist a mentality with which to be present at the contact boundary with the patient, and an ongoing dialogical tool to diagnose the situation — from the etymological root of diagnosis, that is "to know through". This is the kind of awareness that enables her/him to find a new therapeutic solution every time.

The Gestalt therapist feels therefore part of the situation, keeps her/himself "aggressive" and differentiated, casts her/him-self in the treatment role, stays at the contact boundary with her/his senses, more than with strictly mental categories. Furthermore, the therapist asks her/himself: "How do I con tribute to the patient's experience at this moment?" For example: the patient tells the therapist of dreaming about a shut door the night before the session. The therapist wonders: "In what way was I or the situation a shut door for this patient during the previous session?" This is not a reference to the transferential logic of projection, but to the figure/background dynamic. I (therapist) ask myself why it should be that of all the many possible stimuli that the patient can gather from his/her background in that moment, s/he extrapolates certain ones and not others. The hypothesis I form is that that particular stimulus is experientially attached to a relational need that the patient is motivated to resolve. The "projection" (better called perception) of the patient always has a hook in the therapist (as Miriam Polster loved to teach), whose personal characteristics are considered necessary aspects for the cocreation of the relationship.

Normality for the therapeutic situation is, according to Gestalt therapy, improvisational cocreation: the art of spontaneous good form — neither impulsive nor uneducated or unexperienced, but heavy and light, painful and joyful, experienced and fresh, in a word — harmonic.

Here is an example: A patient says, "You don't give a damn about me. I'm never going to depend on you again," to the therapist who has not answered her/his insistent calls late the night before. The therapist's experiential background is still in the pleasure of closeness experienced during the last session with this patient, who had at last managed to experience warmth in the relationship. This situation (often generated by patients diagnosed with borderline disorder) triggers anger in the therapist: a sense of being manipulated by the patient's expectation that s/he will be listened to on the telephone late in the night, and of frustration because the patient seems not to grasp or assimilate the positive experiences of the previous session. Rather than trust exclusively the anger that such provocation arouses in the therapist — following the old humanistic mentality that stressed trust in the therapist's emotion (rebeling in his/her turn against the presumed neutrality claimed for psychoanalysis) — the Gestalt therapist today asks her/himself questions referring to the field and the situation. For example: "What is the background from which the expression of these words arises?" Certainly the patient expressed during the previous session the desire for closeness, and fear that achieving such closeness would immediately be followed by coldness or withdrawal, an outcome in conflict with the spontaneously emerging need. The Gestalt therapist's faith in the intentionality of contact leads her/him to detect in the patient's words a request for contact, not just a need for separation. A good translation of the patient's words would therefore be: "Why didn't you answer the telephone last night? I thought I could count on you. Where were you last night? You're just like everyone else. I'm afraid I can't trust you." Faced with the patient's actual words, the therapist might therefore answer: "I'm touched by the dignity with which you say that." Understanding the words in terms of a challenge, and thus making the therapeutic choice to "train" the patient as to who makes the rules in the relationship (no late-night calls, no therapy outside the setting, etc.) would fail to grasp this patient's relational need, namely, to be confirmed as having the right to advance, and withdraw, to protect her/himself in the relationship.

We are a long way from a concept of spontaneity that is confused with that of impulsivity (typical of Freudian anthropology), in that, differently from impulsivity, in spontaneity there is the ability to "see" the other. We are equally far from Rousseau's idea of childlike spontaneity: it is quite different from art, which is learned over the years, to integrate all experiences, including those that are painful, in a personal harmonious style, fully present to the senses, which are the physiological means by which we enter into relationship.

The CoCreation of the Contact Boundary and the Aim of Psychotherapy as Relational Confirmation

The aim of treatment is that the patient recover spontaneity in contacting the environment. According to Gestalt therapy, what is being treated is not rational understanding and hence control of the disorder, but something that has to do with procedural and aesthetic aspects. Treatment consists in helping the patient to live fully, respecting her/his innate ability to regulate her/himself first of all in the therapeutic relationship, and this not only on a verbal level, but above all at the level of spontaneous activation of the neuro-corporeal structures governing relational life. Spontaneity is the art of integrating the ability to choose deliberately (ego-function) with two kinds of experiential background: acquired bodily certainties (id-function) and social — or relational — definitions of the self (personality-function).

What are the ethics of Gestalt psychotherapy today? We have seen that from one side researchers demonstrate how basically we are interconnected, while on the other side we can see how clients' social-relational discomforts have changed in these last decades: they seem to be characterized by a "liquidity" (according to Bauman's metaphor). The experience of post-modern wo/men is less grounded on traditions and more sensitive to relational details of the here and now. In this evolved context, psychotherapy is called to give a support that is quite different from that of "what is Id has to become Ego" (the value of rational or moral control), an outdated support that is no longer capable of giving dignity, and the rights of existence and growth to any individual (as in the humanistic movement). Today psychotherapy is called to contain the chaos of existences that live without points of reference (as in post-modern living) and give support to the possibilities of mutual recognition in relationships. In this way, potentialities of the therapeutic relationship and contact become fundamental tools for treatment. Therapeutic inter-connectedness is not a mentalized relation but a real contact experienced in the fullness of the senses and with the real limits of the situation and the people involved.

The analytic relationship — the analysis of transference, — endeavored to work in depth on the client's intimate relationships. The interpretive method required that the patient depend on the analyst's interpretations. What seems clear today is that our being interconnected doesn't imply the need of dependence from the patient on the therapist: it is merely a new way of looking at our being interconnected that now holds sway.

The healing relationship cannot be a long-term relationship any more in a fragmented world: we need to support autonomy inside an uncertain relationship. This is what this chapter has dealt with and the cocreated contact boundary is the place where we can give our clients the experience of a nourishing relational process in the present moment as well as in longstanding relationships.

References

Bauman, Z. (2000). *Liquid Modernity*. Cambridge, UK: Polity Press.
Beebe, B. & Lachmann, F. M. (2001). *Infant Research and Adult Treatment: A dyadic Systems Approach*. Hillsdale, NJ: The Analytic Press.
Blakemore, S. J. & Decety, J. (2001). From the perception of action to the understanding of intention. *Nature Reviews, Neuroscience, 2*, 561-576.
Francesetti, G. (Ed.). (2007). Panick Attacks and Postmodernity: Gestalt Therapy Between Clinical and Social Perspectives. Milan: Angeli. (or ed 2005).
Galimberti, U. (1999). *Psiche e Techne*. Milano: Feltrinelli.

Gallese, V. (1995), The 'shared manifold' hypothesis: From mirror neurons to empathy. In E. Thompson (Ed). *Between Ourselves* (pp. 33-50). Charlottesville, VA: Imprint Academic.

Lasch, C. (1978). *The Culture of Narcissism: American Life in an Age of Diminishing Expectations.* New York: Norton.

Mitchell, S. (2000). *Relationality: From Attachment to Intersubjectivity,* New York: Analytic Press.

Müller, B. (1993). Isadore From's contribution to the theory and practice of Gestalt therapy. *Studies in Gestalt Therapy, 2,* 7-21.

Philippson, P. (2001). *Self in Relation.* Highland, NY: The Gestalt Journal Press.

Port R. & van Gelder T. (Eds.). (1995). *Mind as Motion: Explorations in the Dynamics of Cognition.* Cambridge, MA: MIT Press.

Robine, J.-M. (2001). From field to situation. In J.-M. Robine (Ed.). *Contact and Relationship in a Field perspective* (pp. 95-107). Bordeaux: L'Exprimerie.

Robine, J.-M. (2003). "I am me and my circumstance" — Jean-Marie Robine interviewed by Richard Wallstein. *British Gestalt Journal 12(1),* 49-55.

Salonia, G. (2001). Disagio psichico e risorse relazionali. *Quaderni di Gestalt, 32*(33), 13-23.

Salonia, G. (2006). Il lungo viaggio di Edipo. Il trivio della verità e della relazione. In: M. Spagnuolo Lobb (a cura di). *L'implicito e l'esplicito in psicoterapia. Atti del Secondo Congresso della Psicoterapia Italiana* (pp. 281-287). Milano: Angeli. (DVD allegato).

Spagnuolo Lobb, M. (Ed.). (2001a). *Psicoterapia della Gestalt: Ermeneutica e clinica.* Milano: Franco Angeli.

Spagnuolo Lobb, M. (2001b). From the epistemology of self to clinical specificity of Gestalt therapy. In J.-M. Robine (Ed.). *Contact and Relationship in a Field Perspective* (pp. 49-65). Bordeaux: L'Exprimerie.

Spagnuolo Lobb, M. (2001c). The theory of self in Gestalt therapy: A restatement of some aspects. *Gestalt Review 5*(4), 276-288.

Spagnuolo Lobb, M. (2003). Therapeutic meeting as improvisational co-creation. In M. Spagnuolo Lobb & N. Amendt-Lyon (Eds.). *Creative license: The art of Gestalt Therapy* (pp. 37-49). Vienna & New York: Springer.

Spagnuolo Lobb, M. (2004). L'awareness dans la pratique postmoderne de la Gestalt-therapie. *Gestalt, Societé Français de Gestalt* ed., vol XV, n. 27, 2004, pp. 41-58 (translated into Spanish *Revista de Terapia Gestalt*, No. 25, pp. 24-33, and Italian in: P. L. Righetti (Ed.). with cooperation of M. Spagnuolo Lobb (2005), *Psicoterapia della Gestalt. Percorsi teorico-clinici,* Upsel Domeneghini Editore, Padova, pp. 59-71.)

Spagnuolo Lobb, M. (2005). Classical Gestalt therapy theory. In A. L. Woldt & S. M. Toman (Eds.). *Gestalt Therapy: History, Theory, and Practice* (pp. 21-39). Thousand Oaks, CA: Sage.

Spagnuolo Lobb, M. (2006), Malcolm Parlett's five abilities and their connection with contemporary scientific theories on human interconnectedness. *British Gestalt Journal, 15*(2), 36-45.

Spagnuolo Lobb, M. (Ed.). (2006a). L'implicito e l'esplicito in psicoterapia. Atti del Secondo Congresso della Psicoterapia Italiana. Milano: Angeli (DVD enclosed).

Spagnuolo Lobb, M. (2007). Why do we need a psychotherapeutic approach to panick attacks? In: G. Francesetti (Ed.). *Panick Attacks and Postmodernity: Gestalt Therapy Between Clinical and Social Perspectives* (pp. 27-45). Milan: Angeli, (or ed 2005).

Spagnuolo Lobb, M. & Salonia, G. (1986). Al di là della sedia vuota: un modello di coterapia. *Quaderni di Gestalt, 3,* 11-35 (paper presented at the 8th International Gestalt Therapy Congress, Cape Cod, Massachusetts, 1986).

Spagnuolo Lobb, M., Salonia, G. & Sichera A. (1996). From the "discomfort of civilization" to "creative adjustment": the relationship between individual and community in psychotherapy in the third millennium. *International Journal of Psychotherapy, 1*(1), 45-53.

Staemmler, F. -M. (2007). On makaque monkeys, players, and clairvoyants: Some new ideas for a Gestalt therapeutic concept of empathy. *Studies in Gestalt Therapy: Dialogical Bridges,* 1(2), 43-63.

Stern, D. N. (2000). *The Interpersonal World of the Infant: A View from Psychoanalysis and Developmental Psychology.* New York: Basic.

Stern, D. N. (2001). Lo sviluppo come metafora della relazione. *Quaderni di Gestalt* 17(30-31), 6-20.

Stern, D.N. (2004). *The Present Moment in Psychotherapy and Everyday Life.* New York: Norton.

Stern, D. N. (2006). L'implicito e l'esplicito in psicoterapia. In M. Spagnuolo Lobb (a cura di). *L'implicito e l'esplicito in psicoterapia. Atti del Secondo Congresso della Psicoterapia Italiana* (pp. 28-35). Milano: Angeli (DVD enclosed).

Stern, D., Bruschweiler-Stern, N., Harrison, A., Lyons-Ruth, K., Morgan, A., Nahum, J., Sander, L., & Tronick E. (1998a). The process of therapeutic change involving implicit knowledge: Some implications of developmental observations for adult psychotherapy. *Infant Mental Health J. 3*, 300-308.

Stern, D., Bruschweiler-Stern, N., Harrison, A., Lyons-Ruth K., Morgan, A.. Nahum, J., Sander L., & Tronick E. (1998b). Noninterpretive mechanisms in psychoanalytic therapy. The "something more" than interpretation. *Int. J. Psycho-An*al. *79*, 903-921

Stern, D., Bruschweiler-Stern, N., Harrison, A., Lyons-Ruth, K., Morgan, A., Nahum, J., Sander, L., & Tronick E. (2003) On the Other Side of the Moon. The Import of Implicit Knowledge for Gestalt Therapy. In M. Spagnuolo Lobb & N. Amendt-Lyon (Eds.). *Creative License: The Art of Gestalt Therapy* (pp. 21-35). Vienna and New York: Spinger.

Torras, C. (1985). *Temporal-Pattern Learning in Neural Models.* Amsterdam: Springer Verlag.

Trevarthen, C. (1974). Conversations with a two-month-old. *New Scientist 2*, 230-235.

Trevarthen, C. (1988). Universal cooperative motives: How infants begin to know the language and skills of the culture of their parents. In G. Jahoda & I. Lewis (Eds.). *Acquiring culture: Cross-cultural studies in child development* (pp. 37-90). London & New York: Croom Helm.

Wheeler, G. (2006). New directions in Gestalt theory and practice: Psychology and psychotherapy in the age of complexity. *International Gestalt Journal 29*(1), 9-41.

5

Embodying Field Theory in How We Work With Groups and Large Systems
Catherine Carlson & Robert Kolodny

There is a growing literature describing what a field-relational Gestalt practice looks like in the therapist's office, but little about how to embody a relational stance in non-therapeutic contexts — working with groups, organizations and larger systems. Here we will attempt to fill that gap.

Our focus is aligning our practice with our theory — how do we as consultants incorporate in our moment-to-moment experience and way of relating and intervening the core insights about human nature that makes Gestalt theory so powerful.

Introduction

A number of Gestalt theorists, all working primarily with individuals and families, are pointing to the power of more fully embodying in our practice the deeply relational, field-embedded nature of human experience that is at the radical core of Gestalt theory. These writer-practitioners in the therapeutic domain have been demonstrating how to work with their clients while embracing field theory in a more thoroughgoing way (Hycner and Jacobs, 1995; Jacobs, 2001; Jacobs, 2003; Lee, 2004; Wheeler, 2000; Wheeler, 2005; Yontef, 1993; Yontef, 2001). In the parallel universe where the authors of this article live — consulting to large systems — we have been exploring how we might embody a field-relational, dialogic way of working in more complex settings. Based on the small number of articles we could find reporting on such work, we believe that we are still at the beginning in developing experience and guidelines that point the way to a deeper realization of field-relational theory in our work (Carlson & Nabozny, 2002;. Chidiac, and Denham-Vaughn, 2007; Coffey & Cavicchia, 2005; Fairfield, 2004; Francis, 2005; Harvartis, 2006).

Clearly much creative work has been done on taking Gestalt theory and practice and applying it to complex human systems. Our own teachers at the Gestalt Institute of Cleveland were the pioneers in this work more than 30 years ago, and the adaptations and translations they made, building on the work of the first generation of Gestalt therapists, created what we consider the most integrated and effective methodology available anywhere for intervening in and supporting the growth and development of groups and organizations (Nevis, 1987). Their work has had enormous impact on the entire field of organization development, although this influence is not widely recognized or acknowledged.

So, the reader might ask, isn't this already well-mapped territory and what is new or different in what we are pointing to. What is different about a "field-relational" way of working from the stance that distinguished the Gestalt approach from the beginning, where the practitioner was never seen as a detached, objective observer, independent and separate, but a living, breathing presence in the field of engagement? Because phenomenological field theory had so much influence in the development of Gestalt practice, it is easy to overlook the ways in which it was not fully integrated into how we actually work and think about our work. It is not surprising that we could miss noticing the significant remnants of a more individualistic world-view in how we actually behave and relate to our clients. (Commentators have pointed out that Perls and Goodman didn't always notice this either — see for example, Jacobs, 2005, pp. 43-44; p. 69)[1]. These remnants can subtly position us as more independent and detached, more observing than part of the mix.

What we find compelling about the work of our therapist colleagues is their dedication to re-examining what it means to be truly "of the field" and their willingness to do the hard work to realign what they actually do with what our theory espouses — to close a gap between theory and practice that none of us noticed before. In our own training in Gestalt organizational and system development, we learned to work at the boundary, to help the client system to engage in processes that we are

---

[1] As we note Perls, Hefferline and Goodman's (1951) inconsistencies, we are reminded of our own fallibility — the difficulty of recognizing those times we slip back into familiar Cartesian ways of thinking and expressing ourselves in this very piece of writing.

separate from, to raise awareness — but mostly about them, to encourage experiments that we have concluded are at their developmental edge. We are now reflecting on how following these once persuasive and still powerful guidelines can orient us such that we find ourselves aiming our clients more than joining them.

A field-relational way of working highlights the co-emergent relationship among the client, the consultant, and the larger field within which the relationship exists. What are the themes of this field? What is the co-emergent striving? What wants to make itself known? We are looking to support our clients and ourselves to be more field-minded — to see problems not just as discreet issues attributable to someone or something, but as co-emergent functions of our inter-relation and shared context.

One challenge of doing this is to simultaneously respond to how our clients see the world, to respect their needs and their wish for concrete solutions and answers in a form that is familiar. We are not talking about getting rid of the analytic and rational and problem-solving and replacing it with the intuitive and field-sensitive. It is not a replacement model that we are trying to describe, not a rejection of one paradigm in favor of another, but a practice that incorporates both perspectives in a new synthesis. A second challenge, from our experience, is how much more vulnerable a truly relational, field-theoretic stance leaves us as practitioners. This helps us to see why, as practitioners, we might not have been so quick or so ready to notice disconnects between our practice and our theory.

The focus of our work is large complex systems. Sheer increase in size changes things, as does the greater relational complexity, and the ways people respond emotionally and cognitively to finding themselves being of a large human field. Said another way, a critical impact of complexity is that it can make contacting considerably more challenging. The translation we are exploring here is not simple or linear, not a matter of taking a relational approach to individuals in therapy and multiplying it to fit a large systems scale. Our sense is that a field-relational, dialogic approach in therapy is often equated with being "in-the-moment" (here/now), non-strategic (meeting, rather than aiming, the client), and intimate (personally or interpersonally focused). As we move to larger levels of system, this picture needs to take into account differences in context. Working at an organizational level involves more anticipation, strategic thinking and attention to whole-system context. We face the question of how to support ourselves and our clients to function creatively and effectively in an environment marked by increased scale and complexity.

In what follows, we try to identify ways of responding to this increased complexity while simultaneously embodying a relational stance, supporting emergence of that which wants to make itself known. Our exploration has given us a new way of thinking about our work and framing our role. Our part in the shaping of field conditions that support greater awareness has become a key orienting principle. Our focus has widened to include the context for contacting as well as contact and contact processes themselves.

Because the very structure of our language reflects existing paradigms, it does not bend easily in the direction we are asking it to go. Rather it tends to reinforce the split between self and field our theory considers an illusory one. It asks words firmly attached to old concepts to do new duty. Moreover, it has difficulty keeping up with the speed with which, in this way of understanding human experience, influence and impact occur simultaneously and shape rapidly changing field conditions —

difficulty in capturing the sheer multiplicity of what is emerging. In response to these dilemmas, we will turn to a piece of actual work to help us convey our understanding — an intervention with a large group that the authors were both involved in and found instructive.

Background to Our Story

Ty Francis makes a similar observation in the notes to his article on moving to a more experiential notion of field in our consulting work. "While I believe that we are profoundly a part of, rather than apart from the field, there is no holistic, non-dualistic field language that adequately communicates this in English" (Francis, 2005, p. 31, italics in the original). Addressing the limitation of language in trying to convey "the reciprocal, mutual cycle of inter-influence" that is at the core of field-relational understanding, Lynne Jacobs comments that "the linear nature of words on a page frustrates my attempts to capture the simultaneity and multi-layered quality of interactions in the therapeutic process" (Jacobs, 2005, p. 50).

This article draws on the experience of designing, facilitating, and participating in a large group experiment at a conference held at Esalen in November, 2005 titled, "The Evolution of Gestalt: Intervention for Change in a Complex Field." It is also a response to the challenge inspiring that gathering — the need for Gestalt theory and method to evolve if its unique potential to contribute to the evolution of human society is to be realized.

The conference brought something vividly home to us: while the thinking and presentations were at the cutting edge of field-relational Gestalt theory, when it came to our total community sessions, being able to embody the very relational stance we were hearing about proved to be a challenge. When we were in the mix ourselves, we and our Gestalt colleagues got stuck in some of the very tendencies and habits that we believe make truly living the theory difficult.

The Events We Will Describe

There Are Two "Chapters" To This Story

Monday Evening Session of the Whole Conference Community.

Monday was the first full day of the Conference. Monday evening we met as a total group for a "community building" session designed to explore conference "process" (in contrast to the "content" focus of the day's seminars and workshops). The authors had no role in organizing or facilitating this session. We were there as participants along with some 80 others. Our story begins with that evening because it set the stage for what followed. The themes that became visible Monday evening significantly influenced the work we were responsible for designing and leading later in the conference.

Designing and Facilitating the Experimental and Experiential Part of the Thursday Morning Session.

The authors were deeply involved in this work. This session was intended to explore conference themes at the community level of system. Cathe had primary responsibility facilitating this part of the conference. Bob worked with her on the design, and was a participant in the session along with roughly 80 conference attendees. Our insights from this experience form the core of this article.

While the authors have been equal collaborators on this article, we had different roles at the conference, and there were others who played important parts. Mark Fairfield and Robert Lee were, with Cathe, the team responsible for the plenary session on Thursday morning. Because of her large-system experience, Cathe wound up playing a major role in developing the experiment and a lead role in facilitating it. Prior to the conference Bob Kolodny had been a sounding board for Cathe for ideas about this session.

At the conference, she brought him into the final meeting with the other two session leaders to help shape the high-level design of the experiment, and thereafter consulted with him on details of design and timing. During the experiment, Bob was a participant along with some 70-80 others. Cathe wants to acknowledge Mark and Robert, her Gestalt therapist friends and colleagues, for their contributions in supporting the facilitation of the experiment that is described in this article and for their collaboration on the design.

The Conference Unfolds

The leaders of the Monday evening session asked the conference participants to reflect individually on "what supports do you need to be most fully present at the conference." The stepwise process was to discuss this with a single partner, then in groups formed with four other people, and then again with our original partner. Next, we convened as a total group. A number of people commented on how much more comfortable and at home they had felt in the small groups and how disorienting and difficult it was to be in a group of the whole. An extended discussion followed where a lot of sentiment developed to revise the format for the evening and for the remainder of the conference in favor of more small-group activity. Mixed in were comments about not liking the seating arrangements, the way they reinforced power differences, and proposals for rearranging our chairs. To our ears there was a critical, blaming edge to many of the statements — mildly attacking those leading the evening program.

Here is our interpretation of what occurred: when confronted with the complexity of an 80-person gathering, a large part of the conference community moved with some energy to try to simplify the situation and their experience. We know that this urge to simplify, to break down, was rising in us, and we imagine for others in the room. We believe this points to the strength of our reluctance to stay with complexity for very long, particularly when we get overwhelmed and need to calibrate how much emotion we can tolerate. It also suggests how much more there is for us to understand about the kinds of support we need to manage our emotional response to complexity and to build tolerance and resilience in the face of it.

As it happened, the two of us were the primary voices advocating for staying with the large group process that evening. Even as we did so, little of the understanding we think we have now about what was occurring was available to us. We were struggling, as we think others were, to orient ourselves and find some firm ground in this new experience. We were speaking from our own individual preferences, from our concern that the energy building to spend more time in smaller groups was going to dominate and that something of particular interest to us was going to get lost.

It was our understanding that exploring Gestalt theory and practice in light of complexity and working with increasingly more complex human systems was the very intention behind the conference. In this sense, the conference was pointing to the same question we are asking here — what does the embodiment of field-relational Gestalt theory look like in working in and with large systems. If we had not thought that staying with complexity was part of the conference purpose, we would have been more reluctant to speak up. It was this belief and the implicit support we felt from the conference host and organizers that enabled us to take a stand that night. Without experiencing support in the field, the impulse that says, "let's break this down so I can feel more comfortable," is hard to resist. We think it is easy to miss the degree to which anxiety accompanies the familiar questions — who am I in this large group, and how do I find support here?

Cathe and Bob take full responsibility for any limitation or deficiency in the description and interpretation of the events recounted here.

Indeed, as we have reflected on that evening, the need for support in the face of complexity has become clearer to us. Cathe's attempt to recapture some of her awareness of the unfolding complexity of the field during that session appears below:

> For me, what is uppermost is how this session might lay the ground for my role co-leading a community–wide session later in the week. I hear the instructions to pair up with someone I don't know and wonder if anyone will ask me to join them. I am relieved when someone asks me. As we move into doing the task, I pay attention to my comfort level with my partner. I imagine that many in the room are having a similar experience. I feel like I'm being carried along by some underground current but don't know where we're heading.
>
> My thoughts periodically return to how what is happening could shape the later community building session. I'm appreciating a chance to get some data about

our conference community as this will help me formulate something for later. Next we form groups of five to do a new task. The intention once again is to help us speak to what would make us feel more supported in this community. I feel less supported in this group than in my dyad. I attribute this to a new group getting started. As we shift back to the total group, I notice a shift in the mood of the room, which while subtle, is palpable. I sense an aggressive energy (not in the PHG use of the word, but in our everyday use) and feel uncomfortable with it. At the same time I wonder in what ways I am contributing to it. I don't have a feeling of being part of a community or have clarity about who we are or what we want.

I sense a lot of "push back" against the session leaders and wonder what they are experiencing in the face of the "complaints" and suggestions about what they need to change so that people are more comfortable. This is a place I identify with, having been there often in my work. I sense dimly that there is something deeper going on but that there is not enough support for it to be said out loud.

I'm getting concerned as I hear the energy building to spend more time in smaller groups. I'm not in favor of this. I think that our community edge is staying in our largest present system to see what we can learn. Part of what drew me to the conference was learning more about embodying field relational theory when working with large, complex systems. I am concerned that we will lose an opportunity to stay with our discomfort and step into an unknown. As I give voice to this, I feel some anxiety. I weigh and hesitate whether to speak up. I wonder if I am cutting across the intention of the leaders, or if a room full of therapists will have any interest in what I am proposing. I do not (nor do others) inquire more fully into opposing positions. Without directly hearing the longing beneath the desire to stay small, I attempt to influence the community to consider an alternate possibility — one that had only been spoken to directly by one other person, Bob. So it is not clear if there will be support for what we are proposing.

Here are Bob's recollections of his experience that evening:

What is uppermost for me is some uncertainty about where the evening is headed. Even though the "drill" is familiar, I am not sure I know why we are doing it. I feel some hesitation in my pair and in my group of 5 to say a lot about what is on my mind. I "discount" this as my usual tentativeness with new people and situations, and feel I should push myself to "get with the program." One of the things I do not report is my sense of how thoroughly the conference seems oriented to the therapists. I assume that others know a lot of the people present, while the circle of people I know seems to me pretty small. I am able to identify only a handful who work with organizations. Since Cathe has asked me to help her in thinking about design possibilities for the community building session that will occur later in the week, I find myself watching and listening for community themes. As the evening develops, with expressions of discontent, I feel some relief that I am in a background rather than leadership role for her session.

I find myself get energized as I sense support is building for a significant redesign of the conference. Somehow on this issue, I feel less hesitant to say what I think, even though it is in the opposite direction of what most speakers are urging. I am conscious of wanting to acknowledge in what I say the complex relational challenge of working in the total group that I sense people are responding to. I say that in my work this level of complexity is a frontier in the evolution of Gestalt theory and practice. I encourage us to stay with the design — not turning away from the complexity of size but rather using the conference as an opportunity to explore it and manage the anxiety this might create. How do we manage ourselves in the face of our own anxiety not only as individuals but also as a collective is a compelling question for me. Meanwhile, I am feeling somewhat put off by what I sense is an "angry" energy directed at the session leaders and also mystified and a bit curious about it. I am relieved when Cathe and then one or two others speak up, expressing interest in taking the opportunity to engage with the complexity. I feel supported in having taken a position and find myself feeling more engaged and part of things thereafter.

As we reflected together about this first evening session, and as we reviewed our experience over time, we had a growing sense of the richness of what had unfolded. Taking advantage of the perspective hindsight can bring, we now have this sense of what was going on:

- While the intention of the "community building session" was to help individuals identify the supports they needed, when we moved into being a total community, many people did not appear to experience the very support they required to stay comfortably with the task. Indeed, as people got more in touch with feeling inadequately supported, some got angry and focused their feelings on the session leaders.
- The task to reflect on our experience of the conference so far and talk to another about what we need to feel

more supported morphed into an evaluation of the conference design. Our creative adjustment as a system was to go with what was easier — talking about what is "out there" rather than sharing my experience (including my "neediness"), particularly when I feel vulnerable (unsure of where I stand) in relation to a new community.

- People were identifying the greater relational complexity of the larger group as "the problem" and were responding by wanting to revert to a more comfortable (more familiar) relational field — small groups. Efforts at structural intervention (i.e., changing conference design to emphasize small groups and revising the seating arrangements) were attempts to deal with this.

- As doubt arose or grew that the current field could meet our collective needs, the room became more overwhelmed by the complexity and became more individually focused than relationally oriented. We were each struggling to find our place and so less able to attune to ourselves, one another, and the larger community. While we and others put forward solutions to whatever we perceived the problem to be, there was not much inquiry into the experience that was stirring us in these ways, or the anger and frustration. Yet these proposed solutions had no shared meaning except in relation to our relevant but still largely undisclosed ground.

- We (the authors) began to interpret some of the comments made at the total community level (particularly those we described as having some aggressive energy attached to them) as a reach for support. What seemed clear is that participants were trying to influence one another about finding solutions. What was less clear was that many of us were simultaneously trying to engage others in helping us to feel more comfortable. What got missed was not just the longing beneath the proposals and complaints, but in some fundamental way, the person got missed. This contributed to a buildup of anxiety, frustration, and perhaps even a belief that this may not be a place where I belong. Had some of us been able to understand the "aggressive" comments as expressions of how vulnerable people were feeling, we think it likely that there would have been a more empathic response and more inquiry into their experience.

- Our sense is that many participants shared a growing concern that a familiar pattern from other conferences would be reenacted here. Events like these can reinforce class differences (feelings of inclusion/exclusion) within a group. The unspoken fear is that what we want to be a nourishing experience will somehow leave us feeling "less than" — not valued as a contributing member, not perceived in the way we would like to be, and not seeming to matter much to those who matter to us — all fertile conditions for triggering shame.

A Word About Complexity

One thing that we explore in this chapter is our experience when we encounter increased complexity in human systems. There are a number of contributors to the experience of complexity.

Probably the most obvious is scale. The word "complex" is routinely used to describe systems that are bigger and have more moving parts (i.e., groups and organizations are said to be more complex levels of system as compared to individuals or couples). Sometimes complexity is seen as an inexorable byproduct of modernity, encompassing escalation in the speed of events and greater organizational and technological intricacy in addition to sheer size.

Another contributor to the experience of complexity is the multiplicity of layers and kinds of relatedness. We experience greater complexity in human systems where people have long histories with each other, are important and matter to each other, and have related to each other in many different ways than in a group of strangers of the same size.

Finally there is a contributor to our experience of complexity that Gestalt theory is particularly tuned-in to — the existential complexity of being embedded in a profoundly interrelated world, our fundamental nature as being "of the field."

Some of the ways we can respond to the experience of complexity — feeling overwhelmed, confused, anxious, less safe, wanting to withdraw or simplify — we often attribute to size alone. Our sense is that complexity is more complex than that, as we think is illustrated in the story we tell. Even when we acknowledge intellectually the reality of our embeddedness in the field, we may still not see that our emotional response to the experience of complexity has more to do with our difficulty in truly embracing this reality and embodying it in our behavior. It is operating as if we can stand apart from it that helps make complexity so daunting. It is holding the image of our self as separate, acting as if we are an independent agent, in the face of being so thoroughly influenced by our context — being part of a world that is continuously co-shaped and co-defined with us by multiple others. We are so habituated to an individualistic way of looking at things, that even as we give intellectual assent to Gestalt field theory as an accurate descriptor of our world, we find it difficult to behave as if it actually is true. In our view the reality of radical relatedness, particularly in working with large systems, is our growing edge, but much of the time we are not even aware that it is our edge. Our accustomed way of looking at things keeps us from noticing the disconnect between our theory of self (not unitary or even constant but continuously being recreated at the boundary with the other) and our daily practice of trying to operate as a separate, pre-established self.

We do not mean to imply that people do not have choice or that they are not at the same time organized by phenomenological fields that are apart from and different from a particular collective or organizational field.

Intentionally Working with Complexity: A Gestalt Experiment

There were other data points in succeeding days that suggested the issues and dynamics that began to reveal themselves that evening remained alive and well in the conference community: our collective hopes and aspirations not yet shared in any full way, anxiety about working in a large group, struggling with how to support better contacting in our total community, concerns about power and access. All of this influenced our thinking about the program for Thursday morning, which was to focus on the community level of system and include an experiment involving the total participant group.

The intention of the experiment was to create an opportunity for participants to become more aware of their experience of increasing levels of relational complexity, and to stay with their experience and see what could be learned. Our rationale was that working with the complexity of our total conference system was our growing edge. Moreover, this fit with the overall intention of the conference — to explore new directions in Gestalt theory and practice in an age of complexity — as well as an instrumental goal — to build a learning community over the course of the week.

The way we chose to get into the experience of increasing relational complexity was by inviting people to talk about their longings, aspirations and hopes — what they wanted to happen for themselves, for this conference community, for the larger Gestalt community. We chose to focus on aspirations, desires, and longings based on two considerations. First, we saw this as a way to build self-support — creating space for people to talk about what really matters to them and to be listened to by others. Second, we believe that a defining aspect of community is a sense of shared aspiration, and therefore one outcome could be a deeper sense of us as a community.

In presenting the experiment, Cathe clarified that the "learning figure" was awareness of one's experience in the face of complexity — to draw attention to what happens to each of us experientially as we encounter relational complexity. She noted that the assignment or task — "talk to one another about your hopes, wants, aspirations" — was in service of fattening this figure and deepening this awareness.

The experiment started in self-selected groups of 4, where people were asked to talk to one another about hopes and aspirations. Then three groups of 4 joined, forming groups of 12 and continued this task. Next we heard from people regarding what they were noticing about their experience in going from 4 to 12. To get a broad, representative sense, people were asked to call out into the total group one word that best described their experience.

Finally we moved to a fishbowl structure where 3 people from each group of 12 formed an even larger group of 18 and continued the task. Cathe asked the rest of the room, all observers of the group in the center, to attend to what they were experiencing while we increased the level of complexity through the fishbowl format — what was their experience while attending to this new, more complex configuration.

After the inner group worked for about 20 minutes, Cathe called a stop in the action to hear from outside. Most observers commented, at least initially, on what they saw happening in the fishbowl group as different from reporting on their own responses while witnessing it. Cathe raised awareness of how little the people outside the fishbowl were focusing on their own experience. Cathe's recollection of her state of mind while facilitating the experiment conveys something about her experience in the face of complexity:

> At this point I am aware both of wanting to support our intention (hearing how the observers were themselves impacted) and also not wanting to cut people off (even as they assess how "well" the fishbowl is doing). I intervene saying that I am concerned that comments from observers could be heard as evaluative, resulting in the fishbowl group feeling judged. This is something I wanted us to guard against. As I intervene with the observers who comment on what the group was or was not doing and ask them to focus instead on their own experience, I feel some anxiety. I am aware that given my role I could be heard as saying "you are not doing it right" in front of the entire group. My intention is to help foster conditions that will facilitate learning so that people can become aware of their own experience.

Otherwise the dialogue is likely to stay "out there," about the other, similar to what happened our first night when people were evaluating the conference design rather than reporting their experience or need. I wonder about the impact of my comments on the inner group. I am struggling to balance the work of the inner group — where there is a lot of energy — with the work of the observers, who had the more explicit task of exploring their reaction to complexity.

Intermittently I shift my attention to my colleagues, Mark and Robert. I wonder, where are we as a facilitating team in relation to the rest of the room? While all of this is going on, the clock is ticking and we still need to give the total group a chance to process what we learned. Just then Mark informs me that we need to end in order to accommodate other demands of the day's schedule. I thought we had more time, and I am now confronted with the dilemma of how best to end while not being done.

What the Experiment Highlights about Groups and Large Systems

As people moved from groups of 4 to groups of 12, many commented on the increasing complexity and difficulty of knowing how to proceed. Just before we moved to the fishbowl structure, our next level of complexity, people were asked to say one word in the total community that captured their experience in their group of 12. A few spoke of being energized, but the words used by many reflected some sense of being put off or challenged by the shift to a larger system.

Bob's recollections of his experience as a participant illustrates some of the challenges he was aware of:

Even though I know more than others about what is coming next (and the thinking behind the design), I find myself struggling with how to manage when we shift to the group of 12. I feel like I am starting over and feel more isolated and less connected to others than I did in my quartet. We seem to spend as much time discussing how to organize our process and how to insure hearing from everyone as we do tackling the assigned task of speaking about our hopes and aspirations. Six or seven distinct proposals for how we should work emerge in the first few minutes, each somewhat different and not building much on the prior suggestions. I comment that we as a group have generated multiple figures, but when asked, find I can only remember a few. Even though I am not formally charged with managing the session, I feel invested in its success. I am worried about the impact of a late start and whether there will be enough time for the experiment to develop and for learning to emerge. I worry that people will get bored with answering the same question each time they move to a larger group. I wonder, given the discomfort being expressed, if enough people will volunteer for the fishbowl.

It turned out to be easy to get 18 people to swim into the fishbowl. Each group of 12 had been asked to identify 3 volunteers, and in several groups there was encouragement for those who had issues or felt marginalized in some way to join the fishbowl and speak up.

In the fishbowl conversation, with the entire community present, there was markedly more risk-taking, self-disclosure, and readiness to speak from a deep and private place than in either the small groups or the larger ones. This seemed significant in light of how uncomfortable people said they were feeling in larger groups. The very first person to speak noted his alternating desire in this community: to be seen (recognized, appreciated, given a place) and then not to be seen (to be invisible and thereby less vulnerable). He commented on the difficulty of acknowledging this so publicly. Another poignantly reported his sense of not being received and feeling alone in the community after making many approaches and getting little response from others. A third described a constriction and tightness in her chest and throat and spoke about her feelings of aloneness and how difficult it was to get her affiliation needs met in the conference community.

People were now speaking to others about what it was like for them in this community, and they were saying what had before been unspoken — the feelings of not fully belonging or being excluded. These feelings had multiple sources of course, but in the current field we had cocreated at the conference, they pointed to different levels of inclusion, access and support available to people in different roles — reflections of how central or how peripheral different ones of us felt in this social field.

Much of what the fishbowl members said pointed to disappointment and relational pain. While this was clearly there, we also experienced in their exchange a deepened intimacy and greater sense of people "being met". We believe this quality of their conversation was widely felt in the room. It appeared that as a group we had discovered what would support better contacting among us, and the field conditions conducive to this. The very act of speaking to others about our feelings of alienation (rather than just having them as a private experience) and then being responded to, appeared to have the effect of grounding us, helping us attune affectively to our environment and calibrate where we were in relation to others.

We often experience complexity as something separate from us, something out in the world, created by others, that we have to understand so we can try to reduce it. When we hold this perspective, it seems natural to turn to thinking and trying–to–figure-out as ways of orienting. This is one of the reasons we get so overwhelmed by complexity and the very thing that makes it harder for us to get in touch with what is going on "inside" of us. Paradoxically, it appears that being aware of what is going on in one's own experience is the first step in working with complexity. Sensations and feelings help orient us and can lend a level of support to the individual and the field as a whole, creating support that can be experienced at a system-wide level. So, a principle we take away from this experiment is that giving people the space to get in touch with their experience, their feelings and sensations, in the active, responsive presence of others, is one way to help people to be less thrown by — to stay present in the face of — relational complexity. (While this principle is familiar in therapy, it is not familiar in its application to large systems. Thus it stands out as an underutilized means of support, a missing part of our consulting repertoire.)

For the experiment, we mainly defined complexity in terms of group size. While complexity has many dimensions, not just scale or multiplicity of potential figures, we chose to shift group size because it was an observable difference and one that people expressed difficulty with early in the conference. We thought that increasing scale (essentially, creating progressively larger new groupings) would keep the group at a learning edge. We discovered, however, that this community's developmental edge was not dealing with size, per se. Its edge in this moment was members' willingness to speak their truth — finding the opportunity (support) to own their experience in this community, especially where it was painful. The non-visible aspects of complexity were actually more compelling than the visible ones, in this case private concerns about how I am being received by others.

Many people in this community matter to, and have a history with, each other. They have been each other's teachers and students. Some met each other as peers, and then one achieved more celebrity or "success" than the other one. They have been in therapy with each other, some in romantic and sexual relationships with each other. There are "generational reversals," where younger practitioners who now are leading theorists are "instructing" their seniors. Some are members of collegial groups that others are not part of, but might wish to be. Among the professional sub-disciplines (therapist, organization consultant, academic, and people altogether new to Gestalt), some seemed to be more highly valued, as did some orientations and training alma maters. Thus, there were a number of sub-groups within the Conference community that went un-acknowledged. There was the complexity of who is "in" and who is not, of deciding if there is room for who I am and what I want here, of how I work across cultural, language, power and status differences.

While in theory, the floor was open to everyone, we believe participants anticipated different levels of receptivity were they to give voice to their experience. People with higher "status" in the conference community (for example organizers, presenters, and others who felt included in their circle) seemed least constrained in speaking up. For us, this is an example of one of ways support (and its absence) is experienced in the relational field of a large human system.

One implication we take from this is that until we could acknowledge issues of access, privilege, inclusion and exclusion — speak our unspeakables — we could not really become a community where members felt included, supported, and enjoying some rough sense of parity — a community embodying the principles of a field-relational way of being with one another. As Gordon Wheeler (2005, p. 112) points out, in writing on the complexity of our multi-cultural world, "the working rule of thumb is always: whatever is out of bounds (gender, perceived power, other positional/membership issues), is potentially controlling the conversation. If it's not on the table (at least potentially), it's under the table."

Time pressures are another contributor to complexity in large systems, and time constraints resulted in the fishbowl ending prematurely. For us, the big loss was the lack of adequate time to process what people learned about managing relational complexity. Our impression is that many others saw the major loss as the fishbowl having insufficient time for its process, for people to speak about their conference experience and be heard. This seems to us further evidence of a sea change in the system. At the Monday evening session we described earlier, many were put off by the large group and wanted more comfortable and familiar smaller ones. As recently as the group-of-12 meetings that morning, people were still struggling with the challenges of scale. Now people were saying they want more time to stay in a total group configuration. Quite a shift, and what shifted was not simply how we were relating to scale, but discovering a different way of being in contact with ourselves and with each other that responded to and accommodated our experience of relational complexity. In a certain sense it really did not matter that we did not get to finish. If you look at the state of the community as we ended the experiment, what was needed to free up the collective capacity to speak our truths with one another seemed to have emerged.

In some ways the most remarkable shift that emerged from the fishbowl experience became visible the next day during the conference's closing session.

The fishbowl member who spoke most painfully about feeling alone stood up to report that he no longer felt marginal and indeed was feeling increasing levels of being received. Most strikingly, as he expanded on his current sense of his relationship to the conference community, he felt enough support and/or feeling of belonging to give voice to what he knew would be an unpopular view — his support for the Iraq War. For us this demonstrated a remarkable willingness to declare his "difference" from what we think were the views of the large majority of participants (opposed to it). We believe that the receptivity he experienced during the experiment the day before helped make this possible for him and for us. It points to some of the transformative power of support in a field where someone is able to shift from feeling alone and isolated to feeling a sense of belonging and connection.

What the Experiment Highlights for Gestalt Practitioners Working with Groups and Large Systems

We began this article with the realization that the conscious embodiment of Gestalt field relational theory is very new in organizational work. (It is less new in therapy, although even here its implications are not yet widely appreciated or integrated into practice.) Below is our attempt to tease out the key features of a field-relational way of practicing and how we think it differs from the consulting practice we are familiar with. While we identify three key features and take them up individually to support descriptive clarity, they are actually closely connected and can be understood as different facets of a single integrated relational way of being.

Being Strategic While Supporting Emergence

Being strategic in terms of being planful, structured and having a clear intention informing one's actions has traditionally been seen as a key factor in working with large systems. Strategic forethought and intention brought to a situation provides a container, a way of channeling energy and possibility. If everything is open and all choices are possible, then the field is too unbounded and it is difficult for energy to gather and focus.

The experiment underscores the value of structure and forethought, which when applied in a measured way, can reduce anxiety and allow systems to be more creative. It also highlights the importance of sensing into the field — of paying attention to our embodied experience and of tuning into the developmental striving that is seeking expression. By tapping into the collective wisdom of the field, shifts will occur naturally. From a field-relational way of understanding our work, the value of being strategic is that it enables conditions that facilitate the flourishing of self-regulation (more accurately, mutual co-regulation).

In retrospect, the form of the experiment Cathe facilitated looks kind of obvious to us (and not particularly revolutionary in design). It does seem well-tuned to the circumstances. But this was hardly true prospectively. In fact it only took shape after many options were considered and discarded. Much of this winnowing process was the result of repeated testing of possibilities against the multiple considerations. Does it address the "developmental strivings" of this community and so make sense to the group? Is the proposed activity clearly linked to this figure (aspiration)? Are the steps and activities clear? Is there enough self/ environmental support for what is being proposed?

Does the timing make sense — will the community have moved on to a new place that makes the intention behind this design no longer relevant? Will it provide an opportunity for learning something new (not necessarily what we as practitioners might think the client needs to learn, but possibly something that neither we or they could predict on the front end)?

In suggesting an experiment in a large group, it is not possible to get explicit assent to participate from everyone. In moving forward with the experiment she had proposed, Cathe had to rely on her own attunement to what was going on in the larger field, and then trust that self-regulation would take over with participants and design mutually adjusting.

Here are Cathe's reflections on the choices she faced and some ways the experiment unfolded differently than expected:

> Since I had a task focus for the experiment, I expect to hear more about the task I assigned — what it was like dealing with the complexity as people moved through a series of new and larger groupings. I discover that there is more energy for keeping the conversation going and hearing how people are being impacted by their experience in the conference so far. I can now see that had I supported just a task focus, the feelings of alienation, elitism, and being outside might not have been voiced. I am reminded that all data is relevant. Privileging one part of the field I see as an act of power which would increase the likelihood of me triggering shame as well as shutting down other possibilities. By consciously trying to support emergence, I and we are discovering deeper levels of relational complexity than would be possible had I/we stayed with a narrower view of the complexity to be attended to.
>
>   Even though increasing the size of each new grouping is the aspect of complexity we identified at the start,

a fuller appreciation of complexity has emerged. What I am learning from this experience is that maintaining a field perspective requires balancing and holding the creative tension between supporting emergence and being strategic. While privileging one part of the field over another is an act of power and sets up a non-relational situation, this does not mean that as an intervener I cannot have a strategic focus or a task to propose. Rather, I simultaneously need to hold in my awareness other aspects and possibilities (all elements of the field can potentially emerge) and support emergence of what most wants to become figural (that aspect of the field that is most relevant in the current time and place).

Being strategic while supporting emergence is a different positioning than those we were trained in. One powerful model we have used calls for heightening awareness of a system's strengths, then heightening awareness of its underdeveloped side, then designing an experiment that is developmental for the system. It now occurs to us that this positioning can have us, as consultants, operating at the boundary. It puts less emphasis on being in relationship with the client. For us, it has more of a sense of doing to (aiming) rather than being with. The essence of a field-relational stance is joining clients where they are as contrasted with trying to change them — true to a paradoxical understanding of change. Our story also reflects a different way of conceiving of an experiment than one that has been very familiar to us. This different way rested on listening for the developmental striving, tuning into latent aspirations, while being an embedded part of a jointly-organized field, as contrasted with standing largely outside the system and architecting an experience that could make the client system more effective (i.e., identifying a theme for them, coming up with an experiment for them, etc.)

The Practitioner's Relational Stance and Presence

We are all of us, in our relational lives, shuttling between what is going on that is visible and our experience of forces that are not visible. At the Esalen conference on Thursday morning, it was as if each of our concerns and hopes about what might happen — for us individually; for us with someone else; for us with some subgroup — were running like an underground stream, or sea current, beneath the surface, and this current was governing much of what happened. In a sense being a Gestalt practitioner in such a field is like riding a surfboard. You can choose some broad positioning and direction, but you cannot aim, you cannot manage the complexity but must respond moment-to-moment to the visible and non-visible forces at play. People came to the conference expecting to be nourished, stimulated, feel a part of something. Given what emerged in the experiment and after, we speculate that such an underground stream, while different in depth and speed for different people, was a live force of our field. We were in the current and we were all getting wet, but the flow could not be channeled or forced in a particular direction, and could only be" seen" as it emerged in the dialogue among us.

Given this understanding of the context of our work, we would characterize the practitioner's fundamental stance-in-relationship in this way: I do not know what this system ultimately needs, nor do I know in any certain way how I can best contribute, so I will step into the unknown with you. I am joining you committed to explore whatever emerges in this encounter. At the same time, I have taken responsibility to develop some picture of how I might be helpful and am willing to lead and make proposals for action.

Working from this orientation feels risky because it throws us back on being able to deal with whatever comes up in the next moment rather than holding onto what we planned; it requires increased readiness to manage ourselves in the face of our own anxiety — to avoid the tendency to push our own agenda or move towards premature closure as a way to diminish our own uncertainty and fear that we will get to a place where we won't know what to do.

It is pretty well understood that a certain strength of presence is called for in working with large complex systems — in this case, the presence needed to support mobilization among a group of 80 people. One dimension of this presence is a readiness and willingness to lead. Leadership in this sense involves clarity of intention backed by the strategic thinking that goes into knowing what you want to get across, how to orient people to what you are proposing. However this kind of leading — in our example, putting out a clear figure (proposed experiment) for the group to engage with — needs simultaneously to embrace the spirit of joining — genuine openness to being influenced at the same time I convey the conviction that comes with thinking deeply about what I am proposing. As we have tried to convey in discussing being strategic while supporting emergence, embracing both sides of this continuum is one of the ways large-system relational skills are embodied.

Cathe got feedback from participants about her presence in managing the experiment. There were comments on how readily she seemed (in the words of one) "to take charge in a way that felt supportive." When the person leading conveys she knows what she is doing, participants feel more freed up to attend to their own desires, wishes, and roles in the experiment. Presence helps answer the inevitable question we ask in the face of relational complexity — will there be enough support in the field for me to be authentically who I am?

Bob, a witness to and participant in what unfolded, noted a "transparency" to Cathe's presence. The way she used herself conveyed that she was there in the service of the community — that there was no additional agenda of self-promotion. This minimized the "multiple figures" that can arise when people find themselves asking "what is in this for the person leading," and "can I trust this," at the same time they are considering what might be in it for them. It occurs to us that one might describe effective presence as the appropriate use of relational power — neither exercising it as a means of self-gratification or self-protection on one side, nor being unduly reluctant to provide leadership from a place of positional power, on the other.

Another dimension of transparency is the "availability" of the practitioner. This is significantly influenced by the degree to which the practitioner has a preference for things going a certain way. When you are genuinely available — not pushing your own agenda — you are more open to hear from others. You are no longer captive to a particular set of voices that may seem more articulate, "well-behaved," or sensible (usually meaning, like yours). When the practitioner is not locked into their own view, they have a real interest in other perspectives represented in the field, and are naturally inclusive. We distinguish between being inclusive as an injunction or technique, and being inclusive as a way of being that springs from not privileging any one aspect of the field and having a genuine interest in the multiplicity of perspectives, needs and aspirations present. Supporting emergence requires this kind of availability.

With large systems you have much less direct information about the impact of what you do. You lack the ready access to feedback you have with a smaller number of people. In a sense this requires us to be even more field-minded, to use our senses more acutely, to keep tuned to any signal that we are missing certain members or that we have impacted them in some unintended way. In the experiment, this consideration prompted us to encourage, particularly, those people feeling less included and more marginalized to give voice to their experience.

This way of being is different from one that has been familiar to us, where we ask ourselves the question, "is there enough of a critical mass to move forward?" If the answer is yes, then we move forward and find some way to deal with the "drag factor" of those not on board. In this "theory of practice," the minority is seen as a distraction or diversion from what we or some majority are ready to do. We are pointing to a distinction between attending to the whole field, and positioning oneself to gauge if there is enough energy to go ahead anyway. The former demands that we have the capacity to hold multiple perspectives simultaneously, particularly minority or divergent positions, and to see how these might be a pathway into other aspects of the field — accessing a fuller totality of what is available and recognizing the divergent as a necessary part of the whole. Our task as field-relational practitioners is to encourage our clients' awareness that we are part of a field where we all co-influence and co-regulate what is happening. Supporting everyone is, for us, a surprisingly different way of thinking about our role.

Support

We want to underscore the central role the provision of support plays in a field-relational orientation to working with large systems. Support is a core concept in Gestalt theory and therapeutic practice. (The very first paragraph of Perls, Hefferline, and Goodman announces, "contact...is the simplest and first reality" (1994 edition, p. 3), and Laura Perls made it clear that support is a precondition for contact. She famously counseled, "as much [support] as necessary, but as little as possible" (Bloom, 2005, p. 84)). It dawned on us during our Esalen experience that as organizational consultants, we do not pay much explicit attention to the principle of support. While one might argue that it is implicit in our practice, attending to the need for support and meeting it does not seem to be viewed as a core competency in Gestalt work with large systems. (For example, it does not show up in the extensive list of competencies in Nevis's seminal Organizational Consulting, A Gestalt Approach (1987), or in the book's index.) At least, our theory for working at larger scales has not developed and elaborated what support would look like and what forms it would take. Rather, we tend to focus on raising awareness, mobilizing energy, developing experiments, etc. — a sequence of actions to be followed that now seems to us to risk under-attending-to the vulnerability and sheer humanness of our clients (for example, anxiety and disorientation in the face of complexity).

At the conference's Monday evening session, we had not yet discovered what would support better contacting among us. If we compare our experience at that early stage of the conference to our experience during and following the Thursday morning experiment, the shift was dramatic. There was a clear difference in our community's willingness and capacity to stay with the relational complexity of our total system, and it was moving to witness this. In our view the difference had to do with the level and nature of support. For example, the orienting question for Monday evening was — what would support you at this conference. Attention was being drawn to each of us as individuals. In the experiment, attention was also drawn to us as a collective — what are your hopes/aspirations for this community, and beyond to the larger gestalt community and the world, as well as for yourself. Attention to the larger level enables people to hold the possibility that they are part of something greater than themselves and serves the function of providing support to the group-as-whole, not just individual support. When people are asked to identify individual needs early on in the life of a group, this often interrupts the opportunity to think in terms of group-level needs. We believe that as members of our community began to experience themselves as "being met," the resulting feelings of inclusion and belonging dissolved an earlier sense of being there only as an individual. We think that what blocks people from being able to focus on something larger than themselves is their experience of isolation. By enabling fuller contacting, support makes for resilience in the face of complexity. In our minds, support is central to working with complexity.

In the experiment, support also came from the practitioner's presence as well as through structure and process and clarity of intention — all of which are particularly important when working with increased levels of complexity that are inherent in large systems. Being explicit and offering a clear way of going about a task provides support.

Other examples of support include the task itself — the invitation to give voice to one's aspirations supported people to be more present. Speaking about one's hopes helps to enhance the sense and the possibility that they might be realized. An example of structural or environmental support was the design, which while not particularly original, was finely calibrated in the way it unfolded. It progressed in managed increments, providing support that was adjusted step by step. The very nature of support is that receiving one form of support strengthens the basis for subsequent forms to be utilized. When a support is assimilated, it reorganizes (transforms) the system, and becomes part of its capacity to build additional supports (Jacobs, 2006). Initially in the experiment, people engaged in groups of four. The experience in the group of four was integrated in such a way that as we moved into larger groups, we were better able to engage at higher levels of complexity.

The fishbowl format provided structural support. It reduced the sheer number of people immediately involved in the conversation, while still allowing it to occur in the total community. Those in the fishbowl were not required to speak their longings and aspirations to all of the 80 or so people in the room, but rather to 17 others who had volunteered to do the same. And they had been given a chance to practice this level of sharing, first with three others and then in a group of 12. Moreover, many volunteers received encouragement from their groups to take this opportunity, since their views were felt to be important and deserving of a wider hearing. It is worth noting that, at each stage of the experiment, everyone had a task to do. This created a field of responsibility-taking and sharing where each had the possibility to contribute to the whole.

Our point in contrasting the events of Monday evening with those of Thursday morning is not to be critical of the earlier design. It is to suggest that the support on Thursday appears to have been better calibrated to the then current state of the conference community. We are not suggesting that there is a catalog to choose from — a standard list of supports that work. Support is always contextual, always in relation to the conditions in the field. What occurred on both occasions was the system's best accommodation possible given the nature and level of support available.

Support is a moment-to-moment phenomenon — it is useful in one moment but then something shifts and now it no longer is. In addition to contextual attunement, continuous calibration is needed — how much is enough to be helpful without being too much, which can evoke feelings of resentment and shame (Carlson and Kolodny, 2008). The practitioner needs to be ever mindful of the temporal and contextual nature of support, and to attend to how useable any particular form of support is — is it accessible and enabling; is it timely, not premature or too late; is it enough, neither too much or too little? The practitioner's best monitor is whether the form of support itself has become an issue — has it become figural or is it part of the background? If it is an issue, it has not been assimilated. Needless to say the phenomenological tracking this entails is that much more challenging as system size grows.

Table 1 (on the following two pages) summarizes some supporting principles for working with large systems from a field-relational orientation.

Embodying Field Relational Theory

In order to do what we describe above — work with complexity as the emerging order, sense into the field, and provide adequate levels of support — we need to be emotionally attuned to and more profoundly joined with our clients. In our view embodying field relational theory means committing to being in relationship with our clients. We no longer work at the boundary as if we are not fully part of what is happening, nor shield ourselves from the vulnerability that comes from truly working from a relational orientation. We step into uncertainty and contingency. This often means not knowing what to do next, being unsure of what is needed, doubting our effectiveness and relying, perhaps uneasily, on unfolding emergence.

Table 1. Some Supporting Principles for Working with Large Systems from a Field-Relational Orientation

• Stay connected to our own experience—particularly our feelings and sensations — and follow how it changes moment-to-moment, as well as shift attention back and forth between self and other, noticing the experiential shifts that occur as we impact others and in turn are impacted by them. Support field conditions that encourage those we work with to do the same.

• Cultivate deep attunement to others (not simply understanding, but actually experiencing in our own body and being, at the level of sensation and feeling, what we imagine to be the experience of another). Endeavor to become attuned to the larger field (not simply understanding what is going on in the larger field — as if studying it apart from it — but fully experiencing our embeddedness and embodiment...our being of the field. Our degree of attunement determines the quality of contact and our capacity to support growth and development.

• Support emergence, even when being strategic. Having a task focus or clear intention is different than aiming a client where we think they should go. Our capacity to really "meet" the client system has to do with our capacity to embrace ambiguity and uncertainty, to hold other perspectives as legitimate, as well as to refrain from privileging our reality.

Table 1. Continued

- Stay mindful of the importance of orienting, i.e., helping people understand what you are proposing, why you think it will be useful, how you propose to proceed, and giving them the chance to get in touch with what they will need in terms of support.
- Stay mindful of the temporal nature of the need for support and continually calibrate our on-going provision so that it is "just enough" without fostering conditions that could induce shame. This is beyond being broadly supportive in attitude or emphasizing support primarily at the outset of the work. Support is something that needs to be continually modulated in relation to client needs over the life of the relationship.
- Be field-minded (remain aware that everything is of a field, inextricably linked to everything else, and cannot be understood separate from the context within which it occurs), phenomenologically aware (valuing experience over our interpretation of experience), and embody a dialogic attitude (committing to engagement among different felt experiences and learning from differences, replacing answers with questions, inequality with equality, power with respect — listening to ourselves and others in a fresh way that supports emergence of new possibil-ities)...and foster field conditions supporting our clients to do the same.
- Use one's presence to contribute to something beyond oneself — consciously aim at supporting and enriching a larger whole.

In this journey we do not privilege our reality as somehow truer or more valid. We see all behavior as co-shaped and co-emergent. We begin to uproot the most fundamental and deeply conditioned way we see ourselves — as independent selves — and simultaneously know and own our own co-responsibility for what is taking shape. By acknowledging the reality of our embeddedness, we recognize that we are never not in contact. We see change occurring naturally. So as practitioners we don't need to make something happen. When we don't need to make something happen, we are freer and more resourceful in the face of complexity. The ability to work with increasing levels of complexity seems inherent in the very nature of field-relational understanding.

References

Bloom, D.J. (2005). Celebrating Laura Perls, *British Gestalt Journal*, 14(2), 81-90.

Carlson, C. & Kolodny, R. (2008). Have we been missing something fundamental to our work? In D. Ullman & G. Wheeler (Eds.). CoCreating the Field: Intention and Practice in the Age of Complexity (pp. 173-207). New York: GestaltPress/Routledge, Taylor & Francis Group.

Carlson, C. & Nabozny, S. (2002). *Field theory and its implications for organizations*. www.keypartners.ws.

Chidiac, M. A. & Denham-Vaughn, S. (2007). The process of presence: energetic availability and fluid responsiveness. *British Gestalt Journal*. 16, 9-19.

Coffey, F. & Cavicchia, S. (2005). Revitalising feedback — An organisational case study. *British Gestalt Journal*, 14, 1, 15-25.

Fairfield, Mark. (2004). Gestalt groups revisited: A phenomenological approach. *Gestalt Review*, 8(3), 336-357.

Francis, Ty (2005). Working with the field. *British Gestalt Journal*, 14(1), 26-33.

Harvartis, Adam (2006). Dialogue in groups. *British Gestalt Journal*, 15(1), 29-9.

Hycner, R. & Jacobs, L. (1995). *The Healing Relationship in Gestalt Therapy: A Dialogic/Self Psychology Approach*. Highland, NY: Gestalt Journal Press.

Jacobs, L. (2001). *Pathways to a Relational Worldview. How Therapists Change*, Wash., DC: American Psychological Association.

Jacobs, L. (2003). Ethics of context and field: Practices of care and inclusion and openness to dialogue. *British Gestalt Journal, 12*(2), 13-27.

Jacobs. L. (2005). The intersubjectivity of selfhood. *International Gestalt Journal, 28*(1), 43-70.

Jacobs, L. (2006). That which enables: Support as complex and contextually emergent. *British Gestalt Journal, 15*(2), 10-19.

Lee, R.G. (Ed.) (2004). *The Values of Connection: A Relational Approach to Ethics*. Hillsdale, NJ: GestaltPress/The Analytic Press.

Nevis, E. C. (1987). *Organizational Consulting, a Gestalt Approach*. New York ; Gestalt Institute of Cleveland Press.

Perls, F., Hefferline, R., & Goodman, P. (1994 edition). *Gestalt Therapy: Excitement and Growth in the Human Personality*. Highland, NY: Gestalt Journal Press.

Wheeler, G. (2000). *Beyond Individualism*. Hillsdale, NJ: GestaltPress/The Analytic Press.

Wheeler, G. (2005). Culture, self and field: A Gestalt guide to the age of complexity. *Gestalt Review, 9*(1), 91-128.

Yontef, G. (1993). *Awareness, Dialogue, and Process*. Highland, NY: Gestalt Journal Press.

Yontef, G. (2001). Relational Gestalt therapy: What it is, and what it is not. Why the adjective 'relational'? *Contact and Relationship in a Field Perspective, Gestalt Therapy International Network*, pp.79-94.

6

Have We Been Missing Something Fundamental To Our Work?

Catherine Carlson &
Robert Kolodny

A Consulting Story

I sign on to facilitate a high visibility meeting and discover that the client and I have different understandings of my role. I am unable to get access to the chief sponsor of the event and have to deal with his deputy, who only finds time for me at the last minute. I am unable to influence the design of the event very much and am increasingly aware that the foundation for this work is weak, but I feel compelled to proceed because of a larger relationship with this client, involving a project with much significance to my colleagues and many other stakeholders. And it is too late to back out. The audience invited to this meeting is more hostile and dissatisfied than we anticipate, and the rules that have been set, such as prohibiting answering questions from the floor, are exacerbating an already difficult situation (the plan is for the executives at the front to be there only to hear views, without responding). I have made an implicit commitment to the client to stick with this script. I fear that walking across the room to try to privately re-negotiate the format with the chief sponsor risks embarrassing him and his organization, since my purpose would easily be guessed by those present, and he might well refuse to make a change. Lacking a personal relationship with him, I have little sense of how he will respond to my increasingly more desperate thoughts about how to shift the tone and direction of the meeting. I determine to forge on. While I maintain outward composure, I feel increasingly alone and less and less able to think clearly and to be resourceful. I am running on automatic. By the time he intervenes and begins responding directly to questions, the meeting is in an uproar. He controls the one microphone for the balance of the meeting. While I am still there, my role is over. The evening ends and no one from the client system speaks to me. I leave feeling totally responsible for an awful outcome. In succeeding days I find myself replaying the event, blaming myself and trying to imagine how I could have made it come out differently.

Another Consulting Story

It is the first night of a three-day program for new senior executives — a major intervention that I have developed for a client system I have been consulting to for the past year. It is not planned that the sponsoring client will attend this session, as he has no assigned role. An hour before the session begins, he tells me he will attend just to observe and that I am to continue to take the lead. I am excited about the design — it is something that the organization has not done before and I've built excitement among the attendees and sponsors. I am looking forward to the culmination of a lot of work. We begin with a "go-around," hearing participants' hopes for the program. My client responds as if he is in charge of the meeting. His comments and instructions are contrary to the plan I shared with him earlier for the program, one that he said he really liked. When it comes time for facilitator introductions, he goes before me and identifies himself as the person who designed and developed the program. I am stunned and confused. When it is my turn to speak, not only do I not know how to introduce myself (what he just said has already claimed my role) but I feel that almost anything I say will contradict him and potentially create a tug of war as to who is running this meeting. I make a few remarks to try to bring the flow back closer to the design. (Unlike the situation in the first story, I have a solid, long-term relationship with my client.) I'm caught totally off guard by his behavior and don't know what to do about it. There is no time to talk with him about it during the session. I am feeling increasingly distracted and trapped. When I approach him at the end of the session, he tells me how well things are going. This makes it even harder for me to tell him how dismayed I am, and I don't. Inside I'm churning, but I'm maintaining enough of a façade so that neither he nor others probably know what I'm experiencing. My confidence is waning and my energy is going into hiding how awful I'm feeling. I spend a fitful night trying to figure out how to proceed when so much of what I had planned has been derailed. Moreover the first evening session was intended to build a foundation for the next two days. While I'm feeling angry, and at some level, even betrayed, I can't figure out what is happening and keep wondering what it is that I've done to create this mess. I don't recall exactly how I got through the remainder of the program, but clearly after this things were never the same between us. What made it more difficult for me was that my client kept telling me how pleased he was with the design and that he felt it took real courage to try something so "out of the box" with this level of executive group.

What's Going on in These Stories

These experiences have haunted us. While we tried many strategies — sometimes blaming the client, sometimes blaming ourselves, other times deciding the outcomes weren't really "that bad" — the stories kept nagging. They would come back to mind unbidden or be triggered when the going got rough during another consulting assignment. The memories would return with unwelcome emotional force, our feelings of chagrin and self-judgment seeming nearly as strong in recollection as in the original experiences. Whatever internal processing we tried did not banish them, and they seemed too embarrassing to discuss with anyone else. Part of the difficulty in integrating them was their nameless, formless, quality.

It was only when we came upon the concept of *shame*, as it is understood in a deep sense by field-relational Gestalt therapists, that we were able connect with these experiences in new ways (British Gestalt Journal, 1995; Gestalt Review, 1997; Hycner and Jacobs, 1995; Lee & Wheeler, 1996; Yontef, 1993). Reframing these experiences, using shame as a diagnostic lens, shed important new light on old mysteries. Suddenly, they began to make sense to us, and we became able to stay with the recollection without recoiling and to talk out loud about what had happened. We arrived at a deeper and fuller appreciation of these experiences and why their impact had been so long lasting.

We believe we are not alone, that others who work with groups and organizations have consulting experiences that have this kind of recurring grip on them. We know that we could tell other stories of consulting assignments gone "sour," though most are less dramatic than these. Sometimes it is just that things shift in a subtle but unexpected way, and the understanding we thought we had with the client no longer seems to hold. We sense that something has gone wrong, but we are not sure what it is. Sometimes, the client ends the work and no reason is given, or the explanation doesn't seem like the real one. Though we revisit the chain of events, we feel confused and can't seem to get a grip on what happened — the experience remains unsatisfying and unfinished. There seems to be some sort of breach or impasse in the consulting relationship and insufficient time, access or support to work it through.

Our growing appreciation of the potency of shame, of the ways it is related to power and how much it influences behavior in human systems, has given us a new window into these experiences. In this article, we want to talk about some of the ways shame has helped us to understand them. Three fresh ways of understanding shame have been particularly important to us:

- We experience shame in situations when we put ourselves out — reach for something we want, need, even long for — and experience ourselves as dependent on the response of others;

- Our sense that others are responding to or seeing us in ways contrary to how we would wish is a common trigger for the onset of shame feelings or the fear they are about to arise; in the scramble, often self-defeating, to protect ourselves from these painful feelings, we become even more at risk for an acute experience of shame;

- We typically interpret this flood of shame responses as negative information about ourselves rather than usable information about the degree of receptivity and support in our relational field; it is this self-referential interpretation that spirals into a vicious cycle of disempowerment, paralysis and further waves of shame.

We also want to explore a realization that surprises us — how inherent shame is in the very nature of our work. We have come to see that it is not possible to do consulting without shame being triggered in us or in our clients, or both. We think this discovery has profound implications for our practice. Because as a profession we do not generally talk about the potential for shame in the consulting relationship (to say nothing of organizational life in general), we believe we are being unconsciously controlled by it. As consultants, we see how easy it is to be chronically motivated (although we believe this motivation is largely out of our awareness) to avoid this powerfully unpleasant emotion that is rarely even named in our journal articles or professional conversations. Our sense is that this "dread of shame" greatly limits how willing we are to put ourselves forward, how much risk we are willing to take, how we relate to clients who are particularly likely to stir shame in the way they use power.

The Nature of Shame

We want to look more closely at this emotion, which we so creatively strive to avoid, to better understand it. Why are the fear and avoidance of shame so pervasive? Shame strikes at the very core sense of who we are, which is the key reason for its potency. It is the ever-present possibility that we will not be *received* by others who matter to us, and that we will take this to be a sign of our inherent *lack of worthiness.* It is not, "I *did* something wrong," but rather, "there is something wrong with *me.*"

> Shame...is the affect of indignity, of defeat, of transgression, of inferiority, and of alienation. No other affect is closer to the experienced self. None is more central for the sense of identity (Kaufman, 1992, pp. xix-xx).

Mark McConville (2001, p. 289) summarizes the Gestalt understanding of shame as follows.

> In Gestalt theory, shame is understood as the polarity of support, and both as the major regulators of the field of contact, the experiential boundary of self and other. Shame, in this view, is what occurs when an individual discovers that some aspect of interior experience, some want or interest or longing, is not sufficiently received and accepted in the social field. In its milder forms, shame is extremely useful in helping us to find and build connections with others, informing us when it would be best to pull back from expressing some piece of ourselves, or when some reshaping of expression might be better received (Lee, 1996). In its more severe forms however, shame can lead us to chronically deny and disown aspects

of our interiority, creating a silent background of worthlessness and inadequacy.

We would amplify McConville's picture in this way. One of our most basic human longings is to be seen and received, completely apart from whether we are agreed with or have the effect we want. Not being received can be a crushing experience. Thus, I put myself at risk for shame whenever I put some part of myself forward into the social world — an actual request for something, a point of view or belief, a wish to be included, or the simple desire to be acknowledged and treated as inherently valuable as a human being — and what I put out is at some felt risk of being ignored or judged negatively or punished by others who are important to me. But the shame becomes disorganizing, even paralyzing, if I also believe that the inadequacy of the *response* — the shortfall in support coming from others — is my fault. There is a critical step in meaning-making here — seeing the insufficient support as a statement about my own self-worth — as contrasted with seeing the shortfall as a function of the social field.

Thus shame's disabling impact occurs not simply in reaction to being thwarted in realizing some want, interest or longing, but more particularly in response to the feelings of inadequacy, deficiency, unworthiness that follow, coupled with the belief that we are not just deficient in our own eyes, but in the eyes of others — others who matter to us. We want to underline that shame is not just about failing to get our needs met, but more importantly a response to *the message* we give ourselves, or read into the reaction of others, about why. By the same token, overpowering shame is not just about the disappointing or insufficient support coming to me from the social field, but also about my own interpretation that the lack is due to some basic deficiency in me. Wheeler (2000) reminds us how just the mention of this sensitivity (dependency on others) is often enough to stir protests of denial, which themselves may be the sign of shame avoidance strategies at work. In the insistently individualistic ideology of our culture, we are not 'supposed' to be sensitive in this way. Thus admitting any sensitivity may itself feel shameful, inhibiting the very discussion of these powerful feelings and dynamics and leaving them difficult to be with.

We think the consulting stories that begin this article capture some of our felt sense of shame experiences in their more extreme and direct form. Typically this degree of shame is accompanied by a wish to pull back, even to escape, to be anywhere but present for this experience. (People recounting shameful moments say they want to hide, disappear, to sink through the floor.) Because shame is, initially at least, a social experience that occurs in the presence of others, the thought of fleeing can seem potentially more shaming.[1] The net result can be a sense of paralysis, with no adequate response possible, other than numbing. It can be accompanied by speechlessness, disorientation, blushing, sweating and a number of other physical reactions that can add to the feelings of disarray and exposure. One of the strongest memories evoked by both our stories is the sense of helplessness and the inability to think clearly so as to find a way to help ourselves. The experience of shame is powerfully unpleasant. Unless we remind ourselves of this, we can miss understanding how compelling the wish to avoid it can be.

---

[1] To be sure, shame is often relived privately, which simply amplifies the sense of aloneness it brings. Strong or chronic experiences, particularly those occurring in childhood, typically lead to the internalization of shame so that it can be triggered in any social interaction.

We have been describing the direct, unmediated experience of shame. While the effects are profound on the person experiencing shame, they are often partly or totally concealed from others. What are typically more visible are the secondary reactions that either follow shame — such as *fear* and *hurt* — or that arise to avoid or limit it, or to cover it up. Shame is concealed not only from others — but quite regularly from the self, so that we no longer quite know what it is that we are avoiding, or even that we are avoiding at all. Kaufman, in his seminal book, *Shame: The Power of Caring* (1992), describes strategies — such as *striving for power* and *perfectionism* — that serve to defend against experiencing shame — or *anger and contempt*, serving to transfer it (making someone else feel the shame in order to reduce our own), typically meaning from stronger to weaker, even though the weaker in one setting may be the stronger in another. Together these two modes comprise a process of defense that both protects against shame and deals with it once it becomes activated. Likewise, narcissistic processes can be understood as creative character adaptations intended to compensate for hidden feelings of inadequacy and can be seen as a strategy for keeping shame at bay.

Shame and Shame Avoidance in the Consulting Relationship

Our focus in this article is actually not on shame itself, in its full manifestation. Our sense is that the deepest and most pervasive impact of shame is the *anxiety* (ranging from beneath awareness, to vague, to acute) that shame could arise at most any time in our interpersonal encounters. The anxiety is critical because it prompts our ongoing efforts to avoid having shame happen to us in the first place. In other words, we are interested in the behind-the-scenes, subtler impact of shame — its barely visible, chronic effects. And we are interested in the impact of the avoidance and fear of shame in our everyday professional activities — the way we consultants, trainers, and practitioners in organizational settings show up in the workplace and routinely orchestrate our behavior to stay out of the line of potential shaming fire, or alternately behave in ways that threaten to shame others with no awareness of this potential (partly because shame is not something we are trained to recognize or taught how to work with in ourselves or in organizations).[2]

If shame is the emotion stirred by not being adequately received (and faulting ourselves for the inadequacy), then all human interactions are opportunities for shame. And, the consulting relationship is a particularly fertile field. Yet we consultants hardly notice or talk with each other about the ever-present potential for shame — about the client's vulnerability or ours, or about the various ways we each organize the consulting relationship to keep shame at bay. Since we see the primary vehicle for our work as being *the relational experiment between us and our clients,* what unfolds in this relationship is analogous to and a window into what goes on in the larger system. Similarly what happens in the consulting relationship

---

[2] One reason shame is not in our awareness is noted by Wheeler (2000). A fundamental difference in understanding anxiety is a hallmark distinction between a gestalt field-relational model, and the more familiar psychodynamically-derived models of personality that underlie many consulting approaches. Freud saw anxiety as the keystone of his model for understanding behavior — but the anxiety was essentially libidinal drive energy itself, with shame as an immature manifestation of this anxiety. In a relational model, the anxiety is about shame itself — where shame is understood as the indispensable regulator of the social field, or "contact," as noted by McConville (above).

will effect what's possible in the larger system. If we cannot attend to and work with our own dynamics around shame, and support our clients to do the same, we cannot expect that this core issue will be addressed anywhere else in the organization.

We are also interested in the way shame anxiety and avoidance diminishes human functioning and creativity, again with an eye on us as consultants. Shame can be understood as an expression of relational vulnerability and an attempt to protect oneself. A natural response to even the perceived threat of shame is to close down and withdraw from social contact, focusing energy inward. A consequence is that we are less able to take in and utilize new information — less able to stay complex in our thinking. In Gestalt terms, shame interrupts awareness and contacting. We are also less able to deal with subtleties, ambiguities and multiple layers of meaning. As we move into a protective mode, we become primarily reactive and thereby limit our capacity to adjust and change — to respond choicefully, with clarity of intention and agency. We lose degrees of flexibility and freedom.

In particular we are interested in looking at how the dread of shame and the behind the scenes impacts take shape in the consulting relationship — how shame emerges as a function of the moment to moment flow of reciprocal mutual influence occurring between client and consultant and how each can be influenced by the anticipation of shame.

The Beginning of a Consulting Relationship

> I have been working with several senior executives of a large financial services organization and their departments. The HR person who brought me into the company asks if I will meet with a third senior manager. She describes him as "old-school command and

control," harsh with his people and resistant to changing his ways. Indeed, I am already aware of his reputation as their "most difficult" manager because of my prior work in the system. After asking the HR person why in the world she thinks I would want to take on this apparently thankless assignment, I agree to meet with him. As our first meeting approaches, I ask myself a related question: why would he want to meet with me, since he doesn't sound like someone who sees any need to change his manage-ment style or worries how people feel about working for him? I guess that because another manager who reports to the same vice president has done some team building with my help, my prospective client needs to at least make a show of doing something similar himself. I almost always feel some anxiety before a first meeting with a client, but I anticipate this one with more trepidation than usual. He sounds like someone who, carelessly or deliberately, has a way of hurting other people with his caustic judgments. Simultaneously I am aware that this meeting may be hard for him too. Apparently he does not have much experience requesting help or having other people look over his management shoulder (on the other hand his financial performance is constantly reviewed and he gets very high marks here). The fact that we are meeting in itself puts him potentially in a dependent or one-down position, open to being seen as "needing" outside help and lacking the ability to deal with issues in his shop. Despite his self-confident manner, he cannot be unaware that others in the system see him as requiring "fixing". Now he needs to talk to a stranger about this. In this sense he is potentially more vulnerable than I in this encounter. However, we are meeting on his turf, and while I can decline to do the work (he doesn't know that I am very actively considering this), he presumably feels in the stronger position to determine whether I get hired. There is no mistaking that this is a kind of employment audition. He strikes me as wary when I sit down in his office, but not heavily defended. I find I like his gruffness and directness, which is not what I expected, but feel myself still waiting for "the other shoe to drop" — for him to say or do something designed to put me in my place, question my competence, or the like. While he blames others for many of the problems in the unit, he also seems able to entertain that he may contribute as well. I find myself silently struggling with the mismatch between his "reputation" and my more positive actual experience of him. I am still unsure about trusting these initial impressions. My going-in resolve — to say no to the assignment if there is anything I don't like — has faded, but my instinct still is to slow down the process of engaging around the work and to find a way to spend time getting to know him to be more sure I can trust him. When I propose we not rush into planning a retreat for his staff (what I had done with his colleague), he seems surprised, and I am afraid that the "honey-moon" part of this meeting is over. Instead I suggest we meet every couple of weeks during the several remaining months of the year, so I can get a better sense of what he is up against in his leadership role and so he gets a chance to know me better. (I already sense how action-oriented he is, and realize that this slow process could be a challenge for him.) He seems agreeable, but adds the suggestion that I start meeting individually with his most senior people. I agree to the importance of this, but observe that he and I will be able to be clearer about the purpose of these meetings after we have taken some

> time just talking together. This seems to be OK with him, and we schedule a follow-up meeting. (In retrospect, it occurs to me that the slowing down may be a relief to him, something he might have been embarrassed to suggest himself because it would signal indecision or doubt, and that it may actually have increased his comfort level in working with me by giving him more time to test how far he can trust me.)
>
> I leave feeling lighter, having shed a fair amount of apprehension, even looking forward to our next meeting. I am still not fully ready to trust my first impressions, but I can't deny some growing confidence that I can work with this person.

This initial client meeting has features we think most consultants can identify with. It took place some years ago, before we had the conceptual framework we are outlining here regarding shame anxiety and avoidance. We are revisiting the story because the shame lens that is now available allows us to see the underlying dynamics at play here in a fresh way — to better appreciate the subtle, cocreated dance consultant and client were engaged in.

Since shame is a phenomenon of the field and gets cocreated in relationship, looking at this meeting through a shame lens requires that we understand what was going on from a field-relational perspective. The dynamic emerged from our shared experience, which each of us was trying to influence and regulate. In the absence of a field perspective, I (the consultant) could choose to see the story as mainly about me — for example, that I have a problem with nervousness when meeting new clients.[3] I could then get caught up in what to do with "my

---

[3] Since only one of the authors was involved in this experience, we use the first person in revisiting it.

anxiety." How do I build myself up to be more confident, or how do hide it before I show up. Alternately I could focus on the client's "defensiveness" or "narcissism" and see him as the problem, rather than seeing our reactions and responses as based on our co-emergent experience, as opposed to being the product of some personality deficiency on one or both sides. (Similarly, we can speculate that the negative judgments of others in the organization were expressions of their own ways of avoiding shame. They were blaming the executive for what happened in their encounters and not seeing the ways that they were cocreating the experience they were having with him. They were disowning their contribution and making him the problem.)

From a field perspective, we can see my (the consultant's) tentativeness as my own out-of-awareness desire to avoid getting embarrassed or to embarrass myself, and we can guess at the likelihood that the same concern was organizing and motivating the client's behavior as well. Furthermore, we can see that together we were creating and then trying to manage a relational field which was primed for the activation of shame. Shame is an ever-present potentiality of the relational field, even when things are going "well." For example, as consultants in such a meeting we can feel that we are being auditioned — asked to demonstrate how we can address a problem we only barely understand. The client's vulnerability to embarrassment about needing help can prompt a wish to put us in our place, perhaps by pressing us for a plan, noting how little experience we have with organizations like theirs, making an off-handed comment about how little help they got from the last consultant, and the like. We may respond defensively, meanwhile making some internal negative judgment about the perspicacity of the client, which then colors our response. The near certainty that we will be different in perspective, values and attitude means our views are likely to be misunderstood, greeted skeptically, or even dismissed. We each stand a good chance of being asked questions that will make us feel incompetent, even when the intention is just to get more information so as to understand better. The vulnerability both our clients and we feel in the first meeting can continue to arise, albeit in new and subtler forms, throughout the relationship. We are each unsure how the other will receive us.

Viewing this story through a shame lens helps us see the subtle and often nuanced way shame relates to power, namely, that shame is more likely to be activated where there is a power differential, such as when a client puts us in our place or makes the off-handed comment that is intended as a put down, or when we make a judgment about the client, try to change them, or in some way make them "wrong." In each of these examples, one party positions themselves over and above, making the other in some way "less than" — not treating the other as a co-equal in the sense of valuing their perspective as equally legitimate as our own.

As we have seen in this story, the power balance in the consulting relationship is a shifting and unpredictable thing. One minute it feels like the client has more power, and at other times I imagine the client could experience me as having more power. Unlike the power dynamic in most encounters that senior managers have (with either subordinates or superiors, or in established relationships with peers), the relative balance existing between power and vulnerability in this interpersonal encounter can change momentarily. The power-vulnerability continuum is like a teeterboard and is constantly subject to a little push in either direction. There is a more equal distribution of the opportunity both for shaming and for being shamed.

While the vulnerability is shared, there is a particular impact the positional power attributed to the client can have on us as consultants. The natural tendency is to try to protect our self. While this can well take the form of distancing and differentiating from the client, we believe the more common and harder to recognize reaction is aligning with the person we experience as having more power and focusing on or deferring to the needs and expectations they have rather than our own. This is a natural and understandable creative adjustment to avoid shame, since the person with the most perceived power has the most latitude to shame others. Our attention to shame and power brings to light what we consider a *fundamental consulting dilemma*, harder to see clearly without this lens and without understanding how shame and power interlink. Where we have not developed awareness of shame's role and the resilience required to stay present in the face of it, we are in danger of colluding.

In traditional Gestalt understanding, this is to become "*confluent*." We are likely to be afraid to differentiate ourselves because we fear not being liked, not fitting in, or in some way being rejected — all triggers for shame. While we see the "confluence" as a function of the field, we want to highlight the impact on us as consultants. Professionally we are caught in a double bind. On one hand we are there to make a difference, and on the other we aren't freed up to do so because we fear being dismissed, both literally and figuratively — losing our ability to influence and have impact. Similarly, if a client just goes along with us, we lose the value of their independent perspective. They comply but there is no real conviction on their part. The net effect is that we and our clients can end up perpetuating the cycles of shame-avoidance and shame-begetting-shame, not just for ourselves but for others in these organizations.

Looking back, we sense that one reason this meeting went as it did was that I wasn't trying to get the client to be somewhere other than where he was. I was not trying to correct his contact process, not deciding that he is at "action" and I need to get him back to "awareness," not judging him as inadequate. In short, I was not working with the client from a power stance. Mostly I was just being with him, taking him in, letting him know when I had a view that was different from his, but not pulling expert rank.

It is clear that I didn't experience him as others reported they did. And it appears that he experienced me differently than he did others who thought their job was to get him to be different. Our guess is that this was a big part of why I settled down as the meeting progressed and why he seemed to also. The paradox is that I was so alert to my own vulnerability, that this had the result of my being also attuned to his potential vulnerability. So I was paying attention to myself but also to him and our co-emergent relational field, even though at that time I didn't have the language or conceptual clarity to explain to myself why things unfolded as they did. Had I positioned myself differently, as having somehow to fix this person, my options would have narrowed considerably. I can see him as the problem, which almost guarantees that I will shame him. Or I can get intimidated by him and find myself colluding in order to minimize the chance of getting shamed myself.

One other thing about this meeting — I didn't spend much time trying to convince him that I could help him. This itself can be a kind of shame-avoidance strategy for us as consultants, while also being potentially shaming for the other party, who is positioned as 'needing help.' Many shame-avoidance strategies turn out to be potentially shame-*inducing* in this way. Paradoxically we can also evoke shame when we orient around the very thing the client explicitly wants help with — their problem. Moving too quickly to address their issue can miss the vulnerability in how they are feeling — that this is something they have been struggling with, a dilemma they would like to be seen as competent to deal with and instead feel helpless to fix. Our jumping to the problem, and thereby missing the *person*, can be taken as a confirming message that they *are* 'deficient,' just as they feared.

We have been looking at the way shame operates and how ever-present it is, even in a situation where shame was more potential than active. Nevertheless we believe it played a big role in organizing and regulating what emerged between the two of us. It is important to note that the meeting could have gone in a more problematic direction had I not been sensitive to my own and the client's affective state and paid attention to the impact I was having on the client moment-to-moment, so that if my words had a different impact than I intended, I could address the miss.

This observation leads us to propose that not only is shame ubiquitous, but the ability to work with shame (i.e., working inter-subjectively, not us working on theirs) is a critical variable to consultant success. This proposition is supported by two prominent commentators on the significance of shame in therapeutic work. Lynne Jacobs (1996, p. 298) observes, "*much* of the success of any in-depth therapy is contingent upon the therapist's capacity to tolerate the ever-present risk of shameful exposure and on her resilience in the face of shame itself (*emphasis added).*" Reflecting on therapy with families, Gordon Wheeler (2002, pg. 267) concludes "that shame plays a crucial, often hidden role in *nearly every* difficult interaction or breakdown of parent-child relations...(*emphasis added).*"

We see parallels in consulting, particularly when the consultant is working from a field-relational perspective. In line with Jacobs' assertion, we believe that much of the success of any sustained organizational work is contingent on the consultant's ability to stay present to the risk of shameful exposure and to work with shame as it surfaces. We suspect that most difficult client-consultant interactions ultimately trace back to shame. When things aren't going well, when there is an impasse, we believe that shame dynamics are likely to be at play. And we think awareness of our own shame responses as consultants, and the ability to hang in when they are stirred, are indispensable skills in our kind of work.

Working with Shame

Our awareness of shame has changed more than how we under stand organizational dynamics; it has shifted how we work as consultants, *calling for a different way of* **being** *with our clients.* A core dimension of this difference is recognizing both our own vulnerability and our power — how subject we are to being shamed in our consulting role and how readily and unintentionally we can trigger shame in those we work with.

Accepting Our Own Vulnerability

A starting place for us is to become more familiar with our own shame reactions — to recognize shame or, more often, shame anxiety as it shows up, and to develop skill to notice it even when it is just a faint premonition. Familiarity with the felt (phenomenological) experience of shame has helped us become more sensitized to the early signals, as has being more accepting and more forgiving of our own vulnerability.

Having learned to recognize shame more readily, the challenge is then to develop resilience to stay with our experience. Shame anxiety, along with the various strategies we employ to keep shame at bay, narrows awareness, interrupts contact and blocks us from remaining complex in our thinking. Resilience helps us stay present and have access to a fuller range of capabilities to address whatever is emerging. Without this sturdiness relative to the triggers that evoke our feelings of shame, we risk losing much of our agency and effectiveness. The challenge we face is to be able to use our experience of shame as a signal or navigational device — a guide to what may be going on in the client-consultant field. If we do not develop some resilience, we are likely to act without awareness to protect ourselves from shame. In one direction, we can defend by blaming the client —judging them as dysfunctional, difficult, resistant — typically in an indirect and disguised way. In another direction, one we particularly want to draw attention to as a core consulting dilemma, we can find ourselves colluding with our client as a way of buffering ourselves from painful feelings. Our experience is that it requires a significant shift in habitual response and real courage to acknowledge to ourselves the dynamic of collusion and call it to the attention of others. If we do not, we contribute to the perpetuation of shame and block ourselves from doing the very thing that attracted us to organizational consulting in the first place, namely, to help make a difference in the lives of the people we work with.

2. Creating Support

Supporting ourselves in the face of our own vulnerability is key to working with shame. Equally important is supporting our clients. You will recall our earlier observation that in Gestalt theory, support (being received in the relevant social field) is the antidote to shame. At a fundamental level, support involves the process of transforming the experience of shame from one of isolation and disconnection to one of belonging and contact. There are various ways of being with the client that increase presence, contact and agency in the system (meaning, in us as well).

- Letting go of the belief that our perspective is the "right" one and instead seeing our view as one possibility;
- Being equally interested in others' perspectives — allowing ourselves to take in what our clients are saying as meaningful and relevant, rather than dismissing their picture, particularly when it differs from ours;
- Staying as close as we can to phenomenological experience — ours and our clients'. Asking our clients what they are experiencing and sharing our experience as it is occurring moment-to-moment;
- Listening for what the client may be most trying to tell us, often the "subtext" that lies below the surface of their words;
- Being willing to be vulnerable by reporting how we are being impacted and by sharing with our clients what is getting evoked in us as we work with them (in this way the consultant teaches how to manage and transform potentially shaming interactions);
- Acknowledging our contribution — appreciating that our words and our behavior, indeed our very presence, have the potential to evoke shame;

- Having a preference for understanding clients' behavior not in terms of "what they are doing to me," but rather "what they are attempting to do to establish more of a sense of balance for themselves" (Jacobs, personal communication; see also Jacobs, 2004, pp. 37-38.);
- Providing support in a form that can be assimilated and used by the client system, as well as attending to the support we need in order to remain present and available.

In its consideration of support, Gestalt has often focused on guarding against offering too much or too little. This can have us paying a lot of attention to calibration and technique, which is not a particularly relational way of being (in the dialogical or horizontal sense) with a client. In our mind the issue is less about how much and more about the *quality* of support. Lynne Jacobs (2006) describes support as "that which enables" — enabling our clients and ourselves to do or experience something that we might otherwise not be able to — either because it's not in our current repertoire or because our access to it is being blocked by fear or some other avoidance. Focusing on the quality rather than the quantity of support gives the way we think about it new meaning. Support becomes more contextual and emergent, requiring a field sensitivity to what is required moment-to-moment in the client-consultant relationship. The question becomes what would support the next step for both of us. This is different from the sense that it is mainly the client system that needs our support in their confusion, distress, etc., which can have the effect of objectiying them without our realizing it. This, in turn can leave the client feeling dependent and needy, a set-up for shame.

We can often trace the times when we are less attentive to support to our own reluctance to reach out fully to the client, to risk being seen as weak (i.e., too soft or sensitive) or to risk touching their vulnerability out of fear that it will stir our own. If we choose safety — not to be vulnerable (i.e., being unwilling to speak to our own experience) — we collude (together with our clients) to keep the range of permissible contact limited such that we cannot address what is also going on in the relationship. This in turn limits the larger client system's capacity to address what is going on in its process.

De-Shaming the Field

One way to look at the notion of supporting both ourselves and the client system is to have as an operating principle the objective of "de-shaming the field."[4] We have found this phrase a very useful conceptual handle. *De-shaming* involves noticing vulnerabilities and continuously scanning for possible sensitivities in ourselves and in the people with whom we work. This process then requires finding *appropriate* ways to acknowledge our own vulnerability and to respond to our clients when we sense that potential for shame is arising for them. The challenge in applying this principle is being aware of the ongoing possibility that drawing attention to the presence of shame can itself be shaming.

Here are some examples from our experience of working with clients, seen through the lens of de-shaming the field. In a workshop we were leading, one group member started to tell another member what he "needed to do." This advice-giving was prompting the recipient to withdraw. In fact he told the advice-

---

[4] Thanks to Mark McConville for introducing us to this concept. He describes its application in psychotherapy in McConville, 2001.

giver he could feel himself shutting down. The speaker kept going (most likely an attempt to re-establish his own sense of balance in a situation that had gone differently than he expected), and the tension seemed to mount. Certainly it was mounting in us. One of us intervened by acknowledging to the advice-giver that we could see how much he cared and how much he wanted to reach the other person and offer him something he thought would help. Following this observation, there was a noticeable change in the speaker–he seemed to relax, and then to proceed in a way that more fully owned his own desire rather than putting it on the other. The other person reported feeling less defensive and more engaged once the person offering advice owned his want rather than making it something the recipient 'should' be doing.

While this intervention was mainly intuitive and in the moment, at some level we were sensing the potential for shame, not only in what was being cocreated between the speaker and the person he was addressing, but also in the feelings that could arise for the speaker following my intervention. As a consultant, we might not have ventured into this difficult situation without a conscious sense of the importance of de-shaming the field that was developing in the context of this new group. One way to look at this exchange is that the speaker felt *met and seen* in terms of his good intentions, which were uppermost for him, rather than in terms of his impact. The intervention required being able to see his striving to be helpful beneath what, on the surface, could be judged as a clumsy and even paternalistic attempt to give guidance.

Only after the fact were we more fully aware of the risks, both in intervening and in not intervening, in this situation. The observation we made risked shaming the speaker by explicitly and publicly drawing attention to an effort he must have sensed was "not going well." Had one of us or someone else not intervened, the speaker was likely to continue "missing" the member he was trying to reach, in all likelihood leading to growing embarrassment for both of them. It is more speculative to forecast the impact on the group. Our guess is that many members were already sensing the potential for shame and, had the pattern not shifted in response to the intervention, would have become even more wary of actively engaging with others in the public setting of the group.

Here is another example of de-shaming the client-consultant relational field. We were meeting with a relatively new Executive Director. The purpose was to flesh out plans for a series of interviews with his staff that he had promised to sponsor, as a way of addressing their belief that their grievances weren't being taken seriously. Much of his concern focused on how and how widely the interview data would be communicated — in what form and forums. The limitations he proposed were so tight that we feared they would undermine the credibility of the results.

As our meeting progressed, he began reporting a litany of new staff complaints and accusations that had come his way, adding to a list of staff discontents that he had previously described to us. His dismay was palpable. Our initial response was to describe the impact this new list of indictments had on us and to comment on how crummy and discouraging it was to hear them. It made sense that he would be wary of inviting even more criticism by having us conduct these interviews. We sensed that his experience of shame at how some staff were judging him was uppermost, and that trying to resolve the interview issues would risk missing this and what was most immediately real to him. At the same time, we had growing anxiety about the interview process, since it had already been committed to. We were having our own parallel shame preview as we contemplated widespread criticism of us for conducting a 'controlled' and therefore what could be perceived as selective sharing of staff views.

We also had a different take on the staff complaints, seeing them as flowing from a historic set of organizational dynamics, and greatly exaggerating his mistakes and shortcomings as a leader. The dilemma was that presenting this different perspective would be like trying to talk him out of his own reality and risked shaming him as 'once again being wrong.' Only after awhile, when he seemed to believe that we had truly gotten how difficult his situation was, did we put out our picture. We asserted that there was no way that his presence alone could be responsible for all the commotion arising in the organization. We then reminded him of how much hope his arrival had engendered, and how widely he had been seen as a person with the right temperament and skills to take the organization to the next level. Following this, he seemed more flexible and open about how the survey should proceed and ready to let the process unfold rather than needing to predetermine outcomes.

One way to see his shift is in reaction to the de-shaming effect of our responses. Simply being there with him in his distressed state without trying to move him anywhere—staying with his reality — had the effect of de-shaming our smaller system. We speculate this freed him up to be less fearful and anxious about the larger system he was dealing with as well as enabling him to now be interested in our sense of things. We then confronted him (in a supportive way) with our different picture of his situation — waiting until we sensed he was better able to hear it. We asserted that there was no way that his presence alone could be responsible for all the commotion arising in the organization. We then reminded him of how much hope his arrival had engendered, and how widely he had been seen as a person with the right temperament and skills for the job. Letting him know that we saw how hard he had been working in spite of being the lightning rod for complaints, we were, in effect, responding to him in a way closer to the way he was hoping to be received by the organization in his new role.

Seeing Our Relationship in New Ways

One thing these examples tell us about de-shaming is that it requires us to *be with* our clients in a particular way — *meeting them as they are, rather than aiming them towards where we think they should be.* Often, when we think we are being helpful by working to raise client awareness, or sharing our perception of what is going on *with them,* it is actually less helpful than *being in the relationship* with the client and telling them what is going on *for us. Being in relationship* means that we authentically care about, and have an active, sustained interest in the client's experience. This goes beyond caring about their issue. It requires us to be empathically attuned to our client's experience as it unfolds with us — to get as close as we can to the way they are experiencing what is happening. When we orient and relate to our client this way there is an immediacy — we are interested in what's happening *now* — in our relationship — from the client's perspective.

This is different than positioning ourselves at the boundary, observing the client system to better figure out what's going on with them. We are invested in knowing their experience, and at the same time we stay connected to our own experience. From our frequent struggles to enact our new appreciation of the centrality and power of shame, we find that we need to pay close attention to the effect we have on our clients, to notice subtleties and nuance in how they respond to what we just said or did, and not to assume that the impact we have is the one we intended to have. Above all, we must be willing to put ourselves out, to be vulnerable and risk being not received or met as we would like to be by the client.

Let us look at another example. The context was a training situation. One of us was coaching a consultant while he worked with a client system. A number of our peers, his peers and other participants were present and looking on. Even though we were aware of the potential impact of onlookers, we did not recognize how vulnerable the consultant was feeling being observed while being coached in his work. Meanwhile, the consultant was unaware of how vulnerable we were feeling being observed doing this coaching and teaching. What was most helpful occurred in a debrief after the actual work. There, instead of talking about how he was working with the client, we shared with the consultant how vulnerable we were feeling in the coaching role. His response was to say that he found this sharing of what was going on with us in our role more useful than all the other interventions. The reason we believe this was so is that he experienced himself as no longer alone and singularly at risk.

So while de-shaming can be thought of as a strategy, "being in relationship" can be thought of as the core philosophy or practice ethic that guides this strategy. In order to work with shame we have to be willing to join client systems where they are, without an attempt to get them to be somewhere else. This asks us to go beyond working at the boundary, or raising awareness intended to guide the client in a direction, or making observations intended to move them along some process cycle. It is even something other than trying to understand them or to help them. It is about being with the client wherever they are and exploring our and their experience as it unfolds moment-to-moment as a way of supporting emergence of what wants to happen naturally. It involves a commitment to remain engaged in dialogue and to stay in relationship whatever comes up. We recognize that the shift we are trying to describe is subtle, and in fact can seem to be no shift at all since many of the words we use may be familiar. We do experience this as a fundamentally different way of conceiving our role.

Working at the Edge of Our Competence

Even as we have tried to distill what we understand about working with shame, we feel we are just beginning to appreciate what is needed to support work of this kind. This is new territory for us, and we imagine for most others who work with organizations. Even as we become more familiar with it, the challenge of working with shame is formidable. There are times when we feel too vulnerable or unsupported to take it on. When we are caught in our own shame response as consultants, we can lose access to our own agency and ability to hold complexity, which we need to work with shame skillfully. There are other times when the organization itself and the people in it are just not available for work at this level. Members may have limited access to their own interiority, which limits self-awareness, or they may be highly defended or affectively closed down, interrupting contact. In addition there are many organizational cultures where the field conditions reinforce leaders in not acknowledging shame. Sometimes clients use the power of their position to keep shame at bay. This can take a number of forms, most common being pulling rank to limit our access or avoid contact with us. So a client's shame response can result in our being cut off even before we can try to address it.

We need to respect the challenges shame presents, and we need to respect the limits set by our own sense of competence and skill. There is no one way to work with shame — no checklist or formula. Much depends on the context, the relationship and ground we have with the client. Initially we may work with it simply in terms of ourselves — developing more resilience in the face of our own vulnerability. We believe that greater understanding of shame and its dynamics, along with our own awareness of how shame gets activated in us, can offer a lot even if we are not ready or able to engage a client around these dynamics in an explicit way. One major contribution is a deeper appreciation of the dance of power in a consulting relationship and a heightened awareness of how readily our sense of vulnerability can prompt us to either collude with those in power or to turn against them and in some way take them on.

Conclusion

"Have we been missing something fundamental to our work?" Our answer to the question that launched this article is, yes, we have been missing something, and it is fundamental. Not only is the potential for shame unavoidable in our work, but the experience of shame is core to who we are as humans. It is an expression of our fundamental nature as relational beings, of our ultimate dependence on each other for our sense of having integrated and worthwhile selves. And yet, as organizational consultants, we don't take much note of it, we don't talk to each other or our clients about it, and we haven't been trained to work with it. We have been unaware of and therefore have missed how shame operates to limit us — how it prompts us and our clients to orchestrate our behavior to avoid being shamed, and how it can cause us all to align ourselves with power, or to get into power struggles with those in authority thereby

compromising our ability to support development and change in human systems.

Our exploration has taught us that our more familiar positioning does not support us to do what we now see as central, namely, working with shame anticipation and shame defenses as they arise, thereby contributing to de-shaming our relationship with our clients as well as the wider relational field in their organizations. We see that we cannot do this work effecttively from a stance that is outside the relationship or at the margin looking in. In fact, this positioning increases the likelyhood that we will trigger shame. In contrast, the orientation to "being in relationship" implies a field-relational world-view, where we accept that we cannot understand behavior independent of the context in which it occurs. We are each impacting and being impacted by others, and we mutually co-create and co-regulate the field. In this view, we are able to see shame as a function of the field. We each have a role, and when shame is evoked, it does not reside in just one person. It is in the larger field, and we each, to varying degrees, are impacted by it. In this picture, we consultants are active players, like everyone else. This understanding frees us up to speak to our experience rather than having to figure out exactly what to do or how to "help" our clients. We can speak from our own awareness — how we are being impacted by what we understand to be going on — which can be the support others need to do the same.

As we complete this article, we have a residual concern that because our subject is an emotion that seems so personal, what we describe will continue to look like work for therapists and not for consultants. We want to be clear that we are not asking consultants to turn into therapists. At the same time, we do believe that working with shame requires a new measure of courage and skill. It requires us to join our client's world—not just their issue or figure — such that we "*get*" them and their experience in a deeper way. This demands of us a new level of vulnerability — our willingness to be "*gotten*" too at this deeper level. In moving beyond our comfort zone, we foster conditions that facilitate new levels of human experience. Developing resilience in the face of shame and exploring these new places together would be transforming, both for our clients and for ourselves.

References

British Gestalt Journal (issue w/ multiple articles on shame). (1995). *4*(2).
Gestalt Review (issue with multiple articles on shame). (1997). *1*(3).
Hycner, R. & Jacobs, L. (1995). *The Healing Relationship in Gestalt Therapy*. New York: Gestalt Journal Press.
Jacobs, L. (1996). Shame in the therapeutic dialogue. In R. G. Lee & G. Wheeler (Eds.). *The Voice of Shame* (pp. 297-314). San Francisco: Jossey Bass.
Jacobs, L. (2004). The ethics of context and field. In R. G. Lee (Ed.). *The Values of Connection: A Relational Approach to Ethics* (pp. 35-55). Hillsdale, NJ: GestaltPress/Analytic Press.
Jacobs, L. (2006). That which enables—support. *British Gestalt Journal*, *15*(2), 10-19.
Kaufman, G. (1980). *Shame: The Power of Caring*. Camb. MA: Shenkman.
Lee, R. G. & Wheeler, G. (Eds.). (1996). *The Voice of Shame: Silence and Connection in Psychotherapy*. San Francisco: Jossey-Bass.
McConville, M. (2001). Shame, interiority, and the heart-space of skateboarding: A clinical tale. In M. McConville & G. Wheeler (Eds.). *Heart of Development: Gestalt Approaches to Working with Children and Adolescents. Vol II - Adolescents* (pp. 286-298). Hillsdale, NJ: GestaltPress/Analytic Press.
Wheeler, G. (2000). *Beyond Individualism*. Hillsdale, NJ: GestaltPress/Analytic Press.
Wheeler, G. (2002). Between parent and child: The power of shame. In M. McConville & G. Wheeler (Eds.). *Heart of Development: Gestalt Approaches to Working with Children and Adolescents. Vol I - Children* (pp. 265-284). Hillsdale, NJ: GestaltPress/Analytic Press.
Yontef, G.M. (1993). *Awareness, Dialogue and Process: Essays on Gestalt Therapy*. Highland, NY: Gestalt Journal Press.

7

Digital Storytelling with Tibetan Adolescents in Dharamsala, India

Iris Fodor

Introduction

Drawing on my experience in working on digital storytelling projects with various youthful populations around the world, I will demonstrate the power of constructing visual narratives for working with children in crisis to foster resiliency within one particular community: Tibetan refugees in Dharamsala, India. The photographic work in a digital story workshop is a collaborative, group communication process, which begins with brainstorming a story, and ends with making a short digital movie. Moving beyond individual therapy, digital storytelling engenders creativity and resiliency in marginalized communities or those in crisis. The work helps individuals create narrative art projects within the supportive context of their community. Digital stories also serve to foster awareness of social and cultural concerns and often generate social activism that leads to social change.

A Picture Is Worth a Thousand Words

I am a psychologist and a photographer. As a Gestalt trained psychotherapist I am interested in how my more recent passion for these photographic learning projects with young people in different cultures can translate into a new way of working that goes beyond individual therapy. Central tenets of an evolving Gestalt perspective focus on field theory (which emphasizes our interconnectedness), a dialogic approach to therapeutic interaction and, most recently, constructivism which posits that we are creators of our own experience and stories (Fodor, 1998). Yet, in all of our discussion of Gestalt therapy — which mostly focuses on working therapeutically with individuals or in organizations — the emphasis is on verbal communication and/or the written word. While there is a Gestalt approach to working nonverbally with clients, highlighting body language, the me-dium of discourse in that realm is still the verbal interaction about what the therapist notices and the client experiences.

One area that moves beyond verbal interaction is work on dreams and the creative process. In dream work the individual describes a dream (with language) and moves into enactment of the parts. The work in the visual arts, drawing, painting, as well as various creative work with children moves closer to tapping into the visual experience.(Zinker, 2001, Oaklander, 1971).

The major narrative art form of the 20th century, moving beyond words is the development of photography and film. The moving picture, whether still or film, captures, more than words, a person's visual take on the world and a viewer, with images, could be moved to understanding the person's experience. Early in this 21st century we are discovering new ways of interconnecting via the Internet. Visual communication is one of the modalities that has been supported through this still growing/ evolving global technology. Furthermore, while a great novelist such as Herman Melville in his graphic writing could create a world of the sea and the white whale, for us all to grasp, nowadays, with the advent of inexpensive digital cameras for everyone to use, we, who do not have a novelist's or poet's gift of visual description, are all capable of using our own pictures and images to describe our experience and show what we have seen to others.

In Gestalt therapy we are mostly still operating in a verbal/ narrative descriptive model. What I am proposing in this chapter is the use of photography as a window into the inner world. Visual experience expressed through digital storytelling is a constructivist, interactive medium that transcends our usual modes of communication. In addition, moving beyond fostering awareness and intercultural communication, digital storytelling provides a cultural visual framework for the storyteller and can be a tool for empowering marginalized groups and thereby promote social change.

In writing this chapter, which was originally a slide show and movie presentation at the Esalen conference, I am again left with the limitations of language and the written word to describe visual experiences and photography projects. What I will do is focus in this chapter on the process of creating two digital stories: "The Spirit of Music" and "Yeshi's Story" with Tibetan refugee children living in exile. These adolescents want to tell others about their lives and situations, and importantly they view themselves as responsible for holding and continuing their Tibetan cultural stories at a time when their cultural traditions are under sustained attack. To view these two short movies and the many movies made by the children at the Tibetan children's village, as well as the stories of children from cultures in other parts of the world, go to the Bridges to Understanding web site: www.bridgesweb.org.

Digital Story Projects

.."it is assumed that photography, a form of iconic communication, is a universal language". Ziller (p.10, 1990).

Photojournalist Phil Borges founded Bridges to Understanding as a non-governmental organization (NGO) in order to explore possibilities with teaching indigenous children throughout the world to give expression to their experience and their culture. Over the four years I've participated I have been a mentor in five digital story telling projects sponsored by Bridges to Understanding. These have included working with Andean children in Peru, and with young people in a settlement school outside Capetown, South Africa, as well as the work with youth in the community of Dharamsala, India. I will focus in this chapter on the work with Tibetan refugee adolescents at the Tibetan Children's village. While I will not present the work from other cultures here, other projects I have worked on go beyond highlighting cultural awareness of issues to work toward social activism and social change (see the Bridges web site for Women's Empowerment (2007) and Ubomi Bam, Impilo Yam, My Life, My Health (2008) .

Bridges, by using the internet, encourages communication among the children from these various cultures about their projects. Bridges is now expanding to focus on educational exchange programs between schools in the Seattle area and the international Bridges schools.

While, I have been working with Bridges as a photographer/ teacher, I did not relinquish my understanding of these children's lives as a psychologist. These adolescents are from cultures that were still in or are recovering from crisis. The Tibetan refugees, as I will describe later, have been and are still dealing with the impact of the Chinese occupation of Tibet and the assault on their cultural traditions, and are living in exile, often parentless. Resiliency researchers report that, "One of the most important and consistent findings in resilience research is the power of schools, ...to turn a child's life from risk to resilience...especially in the absence of positive family relationships" (Bernard, 2004).

Central to resiliency research is the emphasis on helping marginalized groups give voice to their experience, development of communication skills, use of creativity and art projects with social and community support. I believe that digital story telling is an effective technique, moving beyond individual therapy for working with children and communities dealing with crisis and trauma.

Dharamsala, India,
The Tibetan Children's Village Project

In May, 2004, a dozen Americans boarded a bus for the 14-hour bus ride from New Delhi to Dharamsala. We were teachers, photographers, filmmakers who had signed up to be mentors in the Bridges program to work with the children in the Tibetan Children's Village. The group's leader was Phil Borges, photographer and teacher, who specialized in photographing indigenous people from many cultures. On the bus we examined each other's cameras and traded digital know-how. Phil wandered the aisles of the bus, talking with each of us about our own interests and the overall project.

As a psychologist and graduate professor I train graduate students to work in schools-in-crisis in New York city. My interest in coming to Dharamsala was to integrate my two disciplines, psychology and photography. As a therapist, I focus on storytelling — people's experience of their lives. I am also strongly interested in Buddhist beliefs and practice and I was excited about living in and participating in the community of the Dalai Lama.

The Tibetan Community in Exile

In 1950, China invaded the independent country of Tibet and the Dalai Lama, the leader of the Tibetan people, fled to India and established a government-in-exile. For over 50 years now, over 80,000 Tibetans have been living in India as stateless people. The Dalai Lama is not only the spiritual leader of the Tibetan people, but also the head of state in exile. The Tibetans report that over this period of time the Chinese have occupied Tibet, destroyed monasteries and religious communities, moved Chinese into Tibetan communities and have persecuted hundreds of thousands of Tibetans, including Buddhist monks and nuns. About forty percent of the Tibetan culture is said to have been destroyed and hundreds of thousands of artifacts and religious treasures have found their way to Dharamsala and the West.

What is most evident in visiting Dharamsala is the continued preoccupation with the repression, trauma and flight — it's as if the holocaust has been going on for 50 years and in spite of the Dalai Lamas' prominence on the world stage. With the exception of a handful of human rights organizations, until recently, the world has stood aside. The Tibetan community in Dharamsala is infused with images of this repression. As we go to press with this book, the 50th anniversary of the Dalai Lama's escape following the failed Tibetan uprising, a current clampdown on expression and human rights in Tibet is being covered in the New York Times among other media outlets ("Fifty Years After," 2009).

While, this situation has been going on all these years, each year about 7,000 refugees still come, take the long walk out to Nepal over the Himalayas in the cold, children on horses. They report that the arrests and persecution continues. One can feel the pressing need of the Tibetans to let the tourists and Westerners visiting Dharamsala know about what is happening. The 80,000 Tibetan exiles in India are scattered throughout India which is a vast country. Of these, 35,000 live in Dharamsala.

Since Tibetans have been fleeing China to Nepal and Dharamsala for over half a century, there is a well-established community ready to help with the aid of the international community. What I also discovered is that each year hundreds of parents still in Tibet will give their children to someone fleeing to be raised in Dharamsala. I visited the refugee center, which is the arrival point. On the third floor there is a room with walls that are covered with vivid pictures drawn by children after they arrive.

The Tibetan Children's Village in Dharamsala

The Tibetan Children's Village (TCV) was founded in 1960 to provide an education for the Tibetan refugee children. The Dalai Lama's oldest sister, Tsering Dolma Takla directed the School and when she died, the younger sister, Jetsun Pema succeeded her. She has written a moving biography describing her exile and her efforts and international fund raising to care for the thousands of refugee children in the TCV(Pema, 1997).

There are 2,400 children in the TCV in Dharamsala, and there are now seven other schools in different parts of India serving the Tibetan refuge community with 14,000 children. The TCV is a model for the other schools. From a Western perspective, it is an unusual boarding school. The buildings are traditional Tibetan houses. The children live in such houses in groups. There are forty children with two foster parents in each house. One out of three children in the school is a refugee without parents here or is an orphan. Many of the children are being raised communally with the other children seen as brothers and sisters. There are infants, toddlers, all the way up to high school age children. Older children take care of younger ones. The children do the work of the house (cooking, cleaning, washing etc).

There is a rigorous curriculum based on Montessori ideas which features instruction in the Tibetan language and learning traditional culture and crafts. The curriculum includes prayer and a Buddhist religious core, but also a heavy academic education: the children learn at least three other languages and most are prepared to enter Indian Universities when they graduate from the high school. Athletics are also featured. What is most special about the school is the grounding of Tibetan Buddhism into the every day life of the school. The Dalai Lama is both the spiritual leader who embodies Tibetan Buddhism and he is revered and loved by the children and community in Dharamsala as their cultural/political leader (e.g. when he leaves and returns, people line streets for hours to greet him and there are numerous *puma* (ceremonies) ongoing.

Central to the Dalai Lama's Tibetan Buddhist philosophy is a need to cultivate a "universal responsibility for one another and for the planet we are in" which serves as an educational grounding for the Tibetan Children's Village. All over the school and the extensive grounds are signs and posters, which foster these beliefs (e.g. "Others before self").

I am strongly interested in Buddhist beliefs and practice and I was excited about living in and participating in the community of the Dalai Lama. As I worked in this community that had experienced so much trauma, I was impressed with the resiliency of this refugee community, its spiritual grounding, concern about children and education. I saw this story telling project further promoting the development of resiliency in so many of these parentless children.

The Photography Club

For a few years there has been a photography club in the high school. The students have taken pictures in the school and the community and when we were there they had a show of their photos in the gallery in the community. Our group worked with high school students from the photography club.

Digital Storytelling

The photographic work with the children is a group collaborative process and is typically done in a week to ten days. It involves:

- brainstorming a story idea
- writing a script
- instruction in taking photos with a digital camera
- reviewing and deciding what stories/pictures they like and want to show and which photos fit the narrative (the photos are edited on Photoshop)

- entering the selected photos into a computer movie program such as Adobe premiere or I move
- recording music often to be added

Finally, the movie is put onto the web on the Bridges web site.

Making "The Spirit of Music"

The first digital storytelling project I worked on was "The Spirit of Music." I worked with another mentor photographer, Judy Hoffman. We were assigned three adolescents: Tselha, Tenzin and Tenzin to work with. We were guided in our work by Susan Natayama, the then director of Bridges who was an expert in the application of digital storytelling and a wonderful teacher to us all. First, we met with the three teens and asked what movie they would like to make. They decided they wanted to form a band and make a movie about Tibetan music. They were not yet clear about the script. (In later projects we worked on the narratives first which supported stories becoming more personal). We spent the first few days focusing on photography and enjoyed watching the students increased mastery of their digital cameras. I felt I was getting to know them and their cultural world through their pictures.

By the third day, they were able to come up with a rough narrative script about their love of Tibetan music. It was decided that Tselha would provide the narration. They worked on putting their band together and taking pictures of each other playing in various sites on the grounds of the school. We next worked on putting the images onto the computer and sizing and editing the photos. They recruited another student to help with the sound. Phil Borges recorded the final narrative and music. After much discussion, the students decided on the title. Tselha began "The Spirit of Music" by saying: "Tibetan music is part of our culture and we all appreciate Tibetan music." This was followed by the photographs of their band playing the Tibetan flutes and guitar. The digital film ended with a hermit monk playing Tibetan music in his hut.

"Yeshi's Story: the Babyroom"

I returned to the Tibetan Children's Village the following year. This time the teenagers wished to work on their ongoing projects for the photography club. They wanted to make a movie about the Babyroom, the home for the infants and toddlers. We worked with the director of Bridges, Susan Natayama, and four high school students. When we went to formulate a narrative we learned that Yeshi had been raised in the baby room and we decided to focus on her story. The other teens, Dolker, Drukam and Jangchup were separated from their families and were very interested in making this movie.

We followed a similar process to that of the year before when we made "The Spirit of Music." However this time, the story had a more focused script. Yeshi spoke about her life in the baby room and her appreciation of the *Amala's,* the women who were like mothers who raised her. The photos were mostly taken in the baby room showing the toddlers in their daily activities such as brushing their teeth, washing, eating, playing, and singing and the loving care they received from the caretakers. The teens were wonderfully affectionate and playful with the children as they were photographing.

The students seemed to have had quite similar experiences, and as we worked on this project they spoke openly about missing their parents, being appreciative of growing up in the school, their bonding with the housemothers and other students. Most of all, they emphasized the importance to them of being Tibetan. Almost all the students had a strong political consciousness. Yet, they were also in many ways like students everywhere. They had read the Harry Potter books and were very identified with Harry Potter.

Resiliency

As we look at these children who are separated from their families we see that they do very well. They are good students, engage life, care about each other, and yet are able to talk about their personal situation and the plight of the Tibetans. They are also ambitious, want to go to University and become doctors and scientists. Yeshi asked me many questions about being a psychologist. These children are raised in a communal environment. They do not have therapy or mental health consultation. There is only one counselor at the school. In other words they are resilient. Bonnano (2004) in discussing resilence talks of finding meaningful purpose in life, growing from all of life's experience, positive and negative, the development of self-confidence, and the ability to use social support.

The community of Dharamsala holds a strong commitment to these children, to fostering the resilience of these adolescents. Everyone in the community is in the same boat. Everyone is a Tibetan. There are loving caretakers, there is close bonding and affection among the students and they care about and take care of each other. The Dalai Lama is looked on as a father figure. He has an active spiritual and physical presence in the school. Buddhist teachings on compassion, forgiveness, mindfulness, interconnectedness are the mainstreams of the education community. These teens work hard, do well in school, want to learn, many want to grow up to serve the community. I believe that we are fostering resiliency with the digital storytelling projects we have engaged in so far. By utilizing artistic/creative means to support children to tell their stories, putting them out for others to hear/listen develop skills for articulation of cultural experience/communicate with children from other cultures, these Tibetan children feel pride in themselves and their culture.

Intercultural communication is our hope for the future. These children by putting their stories on the internet are inviting dialogues that can lead to greater cross-cultural understanding.

References

Bernard, B. (2004). *Resiliency: What We Have Learned*. San Francisco, CA: WestEd.

Banaszewski, T, & Hastings, M. (January/February 2002). Digital storytelling finds its place in the classroom. Multimedia Schools.

Bonnano, G. (2004). Loss, trauma and human resilience. *American Psychologist*. 59(1), 20-28.

His Holiness the Dalai Lama (1975). *The Buddhism of Tibet*. Snow Lions Publications.

Lambert,J. (2002). Digital storytelling Capturing lives, Creating Community. Berkeley, CA: Digital Diner Press.

Oaklander, V. (1991). *Windows to Our Children*. Highland, New York: The Gestalt Journal Press.

Ohler, J. (2008).*Digital Storytelling in the Classroom: New Media Pathways to Literacy, Learning and Creativity*. Thousands Oaks, CA: Corwin Press, A Sage Publications Company.

Pema, Jetsun (1997). *Tibet My Story*. Great Britain: Element

Wong, E. (2009, March). Fifty years after failed revolt and Dalai Lama's flight, Tibetans face clampdown. *The New York Times International*, A1-A10.

Ziller, R. (1990). *Photographing the Self: Methods for Observing Personal Orientations*. Newbury Park: Sage.

Zinker, J. (2001). *Sketches: an Anthology of Essays, Art, and Poetry*. Hillsdale, NJ: GestaltPress/Analytic Press.

Web sites:
Center for Digital Story Telling: www.storycenter.org
Bridges to Understanding: www.bridgesweb.org

8

Mindfulness, Magic and Metaphysics

Deborah Ullman

I *see my light come shining from the West down to the East*
Any day now, any day now, I shall be released.
Bob Dylan[1]

There is a secret that jumps off the pages of my favorite books, sacred texts, poetry, novels and other favorites, something achieved by my favorite authors... and musicians, for that matter — it is this: we are alive. Life is a remarkable experience. Life is transformational. It is rich with mystery that unfolds over time, or in a moment, and in relationship to World. We can wake up and take notice. This attitude, or this weaving of attitudes, keeps me enchanted. "To breathe and to know you are alive is wonderful" raves Vietnamese meditation teacher, Thich Nhat Hanh (1995, p. 58). But must a loved one die for me to remember my awe and gratitude at the experience of being alive? Or must we each face our own mortality due to illness? Or face nature in crisis, as during devastating weather events like

---

[1] The Band, *Music from Big Pink*, 1969.

hurricanes, floods and wildfires, to feel really alive? Maybe just as we say in Gestalt about the self, it only comes into relief at the contact boundary with other, so life only becomes deeply precious at the encounter with death. Many of my practices help me to remember that my own death is possibly just over my left shoulder, perhaps a single breath away. And yet, I forget.

For Gestalt-oriented people, how we experience life at the edge of what is familiar is the mystery that draws us to its bosom. How do we make contact with, and make sense from, what is just beyond our known world? Because I am a seeker and Gestalt is about organizing experience, these reflections address how my Gestalt tools help me organize my life in a search for truth. Now truth is a loaded word but the truth I seek is a process, not a stasis (Keller, 2007, p. 15). It is a growing green thing, if a thing at all, more like a way to wonder. What does it mean, then, to be organized as a life-long seeker? Theoretical physicist Henry Stapp reminds us (2007, pp 4-5) that "no influence upon human conduct, even the instinct for bodily self-preservation, is stronger than beliefs about one's relationship to the rest of the universe and to the power that shapes it." So here is a discussion about beliefs, how some of mine have developed, how beliefs interface with values. Stapp, again, "for what we value depends on what we believe, and what we believe is strongly influenced by science" (ibid). William James adds that religion is "belief that there is an unseen order, and that our supreme good lies in harmoniously adjusting ourselves thereto" (in Smith, 1992, p.viii). Here I will explore how science and spiritual inquiry all add up, informing my life choices, in the context of the world's urgent crises of imbalance and distress.

This essay is also about wanting to share words regarding my life of seeking with my Gestalt community, a sense that as sense-makers some of us collectively share the good sense to stop making sense and awaken to our senses and perceptions in subtler, less rational domains. And I feel a call for this yearning to be expressed in a collected volume that is about the evolution of Gestalt in this age of complexity, about intentionally co-creating the field we want to share. I am also unable to divide my sensually informed life of spirit from my political soul. Meanwhile, issues about beliefs in these shared stories and reflections may suggest ways to integrate this longing into intentional practices among colleagues and friends because, like that second generation Gestalt psychologist, Kurt Lewin, I always find it easier to think in dialogue with others. Issues about beliefs, practices, and whom to share them with, already arise with clients every day.

Provenance

Even in the quietest moments, I wish I knew
What I should do ...
Supertramp[2]

The year is 1987. It is still grey, about an hour before dawn. Mother has agreed to have me wake her up and join me on Fort Hill to watch the sunrise. The place overlooking Nauset Marsh and the Town Cove has long been a stop on my dad's "50 cent tour" for new guests to Cape Cod. Today it is to be our sacred site, our chapel, Mother's and mine. There was a Mayan prophecy that has been receiving a lot of attention. As the story goes, if a certain number of people gather at sacred sites around the world at this time in the name of peace, we might bring in a new era of expanded consciousness and avert global catas-

---

[2] *Even in the Quietest Moments ...*, 1977

trophes in 2012, a year conveniently over the horizon from daily considerations, but established as pivotal in prophetic Mayan calendars dating from before the 9th century.

The minister at the Provincetown Unitarian Universalist Meeting House has been working with eight or ten of us all summer to organize beach meditations and other gatherings over the designated weekend. Her point is — it might be incredible to think our actions will have such an effect, but if enough people want to engage with these intentions to build a more equitable and peaceful world, why on Earth not? After all, other prophets and prophecies have been ridiculed in their day.

My dad has written an editorial in the weekly paper where he presides. He proposes that if tens of thousands of young people decide to commit themselves to affirming the need for world peace based on our shared concerns, why wouldn't every sane elder support them in any way possible?!

Mother and I are surprised to find half a dozen other cars in the small parking area on the hill facing the ocean inlets on this overcast morning at 5AM. This is a significant moment, but not one of the events that has been organized. We park and get out of the car. The air is fresh. There is a cool breeze off the Atlantic. People are quiet and reverent. I feel excited. The sky is brightening in the East. Mother is quiet with her own thoughts or prayers.

I grew up in a decidedly secular family environment. God was not disrespected. He just didn't come up much. Daddy worked at a distance for seven of my early years. His visits included walks in the woods, my hand in his large, soft palm, watching for box turtles, salamanders (under rotting limbs), owls (among the tall pines), lady slippers, deer. No chattering. Stillness was the way to discover the natural world going about its business.

These early life influences, no doubt, contribute to my attraction to the metaphysics of panpsychism (see Mathews, 2005). This radically sacred world view re-enchants my life by suggesting that the world of animals, plants, and minerals is communicating all the time. We need only take the beans out of our ears to hear what is being said. This sort of listening is found by some in practicing meditation. Others find it in fasting or in artistic practices. Still others reference psychotropic drugs or relationships with pets as how they heighten awareness and connect with the world around. One effect is universal. When you experience, or imagine deeply, a consciousness throughout the material world, your priorities become instinctively those of a vigilant steward of the environment. When the "vital principle that animates all living creatures ... is minded", as in the shamanic perspective examined and advanced by anthropologist Jeremy Narby (1998, p. 104), your every action is informed in a different way.

Scientific exploration of the natural world, of course, generates an ability to listen intelligently to patterned behavior and to note anomalies. Those anomalies are in one sense, able to help us hear what is being expressed by other life and energy forms. In Freya Matthews' *Reinhabiting Reality: Towards a Recovery of Culture* (2005), Xenophon Barbor distinguishes a tension between scientific method's aim to uncover law like patterns in the behavior of things and evidence of intelligence in nature. Intelligence, as his argument goes, is often manifested in deviation from expected lawful behavior. It is when an animal is confronted with novel situations for which instinct is not useful, that it is necessary for the animal to *think*. This behavior is more likely to arise in communication than in laboratory research (ibid, p. 207*)*).

These experiences, these encounters, our meditations and reflective practices or sacred[3] rituals, can nourish openness to other than human-to-human dialogues. I find it grounding to remember to communicate with the natural world simply in conversations with nature, not in the abstract but in its particularity.

Story is the language of panpsychism. Sacred storying is the practice of panpsychism. Story is the language of World, as every being and every energy force has a beginning, a middle and an ending. All stories are nested inside other stories. A story is also a *gestalt*, a configuration of meaning. Gestalt theory offers a friendly framework for managing our lives as we learn to hold our experiences in self-forgiving and life-enhancing stories. My stories need space for the magical streams and even sacred attitude that has spirited my life experiences. Too much of my life since returning to college in my forties, has been spent in secular/rational surroundings with my more sacred and creative inclinations hidden away.

Experience

If you can just get your mind together
And come across to me
We'll hold hands and then we'll watch the sun rise
From the bottom of the sea.
Are you experienced?
Have you ever been experienced?
Well, I am.
Jimi Hendrix[4]

---

[3] This word is used to mean: "regarded with intentional respect, awe, reverence, as something holy."
[4] *Are You Experienced?*, 1967

Experience. This is an anchor for managing the strong and shifting currents of my life. Living on the East coast of the USA, where the sun rises from the sea, and playing rock 'n roll on the radio when Jimi Hendrix lived and died, his words resonate for me. In 1968, experience was code for altered states of consciousness and youthful sexual experimenting. Forty years later, in the American political discourse, the word is used to imply what every woman over 45 knows, that her skills and resilience, her wisdom, cannot be reduced to her professional resume alone. Certainly many men of my generation (and those of other generations) experience this as well. But the point holds special significance for women who have sacrificed to support family and loved ones, then found themselves limited as bread winners, their skills undervalued in the market place, in a civilization still unearthing deeply embedded assumptions about women's limitations.

The stories and experiences I share here are stops along a life journey spent as a spiritually curious person. The points where I touch down include Buddhist meditations, a sampling of metaphysical studies, a word about my yoga practice, and the mystical, magical visions I've been touched by along the way. In the words of William James, these are "a true record of the inner experiences of (this person) ... wrestling with the crises of (her) fate (2002, p. 7)."

In Gestalt when we speak of experience we mean more than what happens. We mean the sense we make of what happens. How we process events, has everything to do with who we are, the context of our situation, the culture we are now living in and the one we grew up in, the values we have assimilated, our relationships, our gender, our race, and the stories we've developed about who we are from all of this. It was German neurologist Kurt Goldstein, with whom Fritz Perls worked over a few years' time, who identified the universal human drive to make the largest sense possible out of our experience under the given circumstances. With this definition of our ongoing constructivist, gestalt-making nature how can the quest to understand our place in the universe, our origins, our relationship to our situation, what many call their spiritual quest, be anything but germane to our Gestalt discourse? In the words of Tibetan meditation master and teacher, Chogyam Trungpa:

Spirituality is simply a means of arousing one's spirit, of developing a kind of spiritedness. Through that we begin to have greater contact with reality."

Ah, contact – grist for our Gestalt mill! He goes on:

"If we open our eyes, if we open our minds, if we open our hearts, we will find that this world is a magical place."

Chogyam Trungpa[5]

One of Kurt Lewin's great gifts to Gestalt theory is explaining that from moment to moment our experience in the field of a complex life and world is organized by our most urgent concerns, our most critical needs — now, to grasp this theoretical point, now to decide if it matters enough to me to keep reading. I make these decisions based on the fluctuating urgencies around and within me. These urgencies go way beyond what Fritz Perls sometimes spoke of as the glass of water we reach for when we are thirsty. They include ways to contribute to alleviating hunger and thirst in the world when we see images of refugees, their faces "smeared by deprivation" (Rohrer, 2005). And the sail that catches the wind of my intentions is –

---

[5] Dedication page, John Wellwood's *Ordinary Magic*, 1992.

what I most need. And yet, we are emphasizing here how what I need is in relationship to the needs of those around me. Ecologically it's a truism, and as we live with an ever more advancing global communications technology we see the world on our laps or in our hands. Also important are the discoveries from research on the brain which confirm the role of relationship and community in our own brain development, sustained health and happiness, and in human evolution (see Wheeler, Staemmler, and Spagnuolo Lobb, this volume).

Interpersonal neurobiologist, clinician and brain researcher Dan Siegel, playfully reduces ancient Buddhist *Vipassana* meditation instructions to some simple mnemonics in his book *The Mindful Brain: Reflection and Attunement in the Cultivation of Well-Being* (2007). Research shows that the outcome of this practice parallels brain activity stimulated by empathic relationships, implying that this approach to meditation cultivates an empathic relationship with ourself. YODA's SOCK or "You Observe to Decouple Automaticity" describes the moment to moment process of attending to breath, sensations, and thoughts in order to interrupt habitual mental activity. The practice, therefore, involves "Sensation, Observation and Conceptualization to achieve a different way of Knowing" (2007, p. 69). He promotes teaching reflection to school children as the fourth "R" based on what brain research shows us about the healthful, life-enhancing benefits of mindful and reflective practices.

Dog Dung to Stars

So what...
 Miles Davis[6]

When Alexandra David-Neel encountered a vagabond ascetic in Bhutan around 1920, he spoke dismissively to her of the pilgrims who had traveled to receive blessings from His Holiness the Dalai Lama, saying that they were puffed up by their own importance, "insects fluttering in the dung." If the Dalai Lama really had power would he need soldiers to fight the Chinese and other enemies? — a provocative question. He then spoke of the founding father of Tibetan Buddhism, *Padmasmbhava*, "the Guru who is born in a lotus," the 8th century's first in a long line of spiritual/political leaders. *Padmasambhava* did, indeed, possess such power, he claimed. When asked by David-Neel if he, the wandering mystic himself was free of defilement, he said indeed he was not. He rolled in it like a pig. "He who tries to get out only sinks deeper." And "to fashion stars out of dog dung, that is the great work!"

Such was the spirit I caught from Jack Kerouac when I first read *Dharma Bums* and *Big Sur* in 1962-63. Contemporary Buddhist author Noah Levine engages a new generation, and me, with stories from his own path to liberation through journeys with hard drugs and jail. He speaks affectionately of "spiritual revolutionaries" in his gritty and piercing memoir, *Dharma Punx* (2003). David-Neel's scruffy, rude, magically endowed wanderer conjures these alternate paths and experiences: "defilements" I have "rolled in" through experiments in

---

[6] *So what. Kinda Blue*, 1959.

living and through periods of therapy since my earliest introduction to the dharma.

The Bhutan mystic's skepticism regarding His Holiness the Dalai Lama, however, is something I must challenge, even though the Dalai Lama he addressed in 1920 was a different incarnation from the current Dalai Lama. I personally experienced a transmission from *Tenzin Gyatso*, the XIVth Dalai Lama. The year was 1992. The site was New York city. The event was a *Kalachakra* rite of initiation: 3000 people receiving ancient and elaborate teachings regarding the symbols and meanings of a tantric mandala[7]. These esoteric advanced teachings on empowerment are also known as the wheel of time. Furthermore His Holiness calls the ritual a vehicle for transmitting world peace. On the last day of 5 days of reverent and patient practice together a mandala made of colored sand was completed by the monks. At that time His Holiness channeled the total image he had been describing all week of deities, not gods, but personified states of mind. It was very complex. Suddenly, I did see it all, in my mind's eye, from a back row in Madison Square Garden, and quite unexpectedly! The sacred image came alive inside me. I did not hold it for long but I have known since that time that this sovereign monk-in-exile and the teachings he offers have the seemingly magical power to instruct and lead millions.

Useful to remember, as we explore the force of beliefs, that in Tibetan Buddhism *birth and death are considered part of the practice.* In each lineage, the next head of the line is determined by certain actions taken by the dying lama himself,

---

[7] Tantra is regarded within particular traditions as the highest of the Buddhist teachings, based on outward ethical practices and internal altruism to attain enlightenment by employing *deity yoga*. A mandala is a sacred image used in certain Buddhist practices (Bryant, 1992).

by his highest level *tulkus* (teachers), and finally, later, by the identified youthful incarnation. In the Kagyu lineage maps are left in a sacred site before the leader or his attendant teachers die indicating where they will return, so the new *Karmapa*, head of the lineage, and his aids may be found after the proper interval (H. Macleish and W. Zimmie, personal communication, 1995).

For this discussion, I am noting a belief, a set of practices that support ways one can become prepared to die with awareness, with the purpose of returning as you intend, and as part of a multiple lifetime's intention to alleviate the suffering of all beings.

Pema Chodron, an American Buddhist teacher and student of Chogyam Trungpa teaches also from the writing of 9th century Indian *bodhisattva* or saint, *Shantideva*. She speaks of ways to transform our behavior worthy of a lifetime of practice. When something someone says or does entangles us in a reactive response: 1) we can notice that we have been "hooked"; 2) we can engage in a non-habitual way, employing any behavior that moves us out of our original aggressive response or self-righteous indignation; and 3) we can do this practice for the rest of our days, over time noticing sooner the familiar experience of getting hooked. This three step practice she calls by the Tibetan term *shenpa* (2006, pp 55-64). It is supported by some familiar Gestalt approaches to therapy and working with conflict. These include facilitated heightening of awareness, the slowing down of responding, attending to embodied experience, and fostering curiosity about our own experiences and those of others. Another Gestalt tool that supports this teaching is our understanding of shame and how this universal experience can cause us to be overly reactive. Feelings of shame and reactivity can shift when feelings of belonging are cultivated or when the individual's and the field's capacity to expect support and ask for help is developed. These experiences are able move people from isolation to intimacy.

Credo

Imagine there's no country, and no religion too.
Nothing to live or die for, above us only blue.
Imagine all the people, living for today, oh ...
You may say I'm a dreamer. But I'm not the only one.
Someday, I hope you will join us.
And the world will live as one."

John Lennon[8]

I have a credo — no ism's no ist's, having long shrunk from being committed to an ideology that carries these suffixes. Yet, I am a Gestaltist. I can more conventionally say — I practice Gestalt, and get off the ist-hook. And I am a Buddhist. This, in spite of over 2000 years of teachings that implore me not to be a Buddhist, but to be a Buddha, an Awakened One. The teachings of the Buddha, not entirely unlike those of Gestalt, offer ways to train oneself to be more aware, more intentionally involved in one's life and work [9]. There's a lot more to my "taking refuge" in the Buddha than that, including affirmations to do what I can to alleviate suffering in my own life and in the lives of "all sentient beings"; some tips on how to do that in particular ways; and some teachings to help integrate all this into daily practice. I

---

[8] *Imagine*, 1971

[9] It is important to note that Gestalt therapy is a healing art, a set of beliefs that support practices to alleviate suffering and enhance well-being. It is also used to connote a philosophy of human process. Buddhism is alternately described as a religion, a metaphysical viewpoint, a philosophy of life.

have been drawn to this wisdom tradition since I was fourteen years old. I was thirty-four before I found Gestalt.

My life in North America is distant from the mythical Himalayan nation of Tibet known as *Shangrila*, or from India's massive 9th century Buddhist university, *Nalanda*, or from the old China where *Bodhidharma* arrived in the 5th/6th century from India carrying direct transmissions and the Buddhist *sutras* or scriptures. My life in the vast USA is also far from the 14th century's Zen gardens of Japan. And yet all of these cultural traditions have inspired my studies and practices.

We are, of course, always acting out of our world view, out of assumptions we hold about the nature of the cosmos and our place in it, what we believe to be true. But speaking the truth is not the same as telling everything I know. Certainly we are entitled to our privacy if we want it concerning our relationship with divinity, or Spirit, or World or higher consciousness. My concern arises when the public discourse is a simplistic one between rigid religious beliefs and rigid secular ones, or scientific views posited as oppositional to religious insights. These positions seem to trivialize matters of utmost concern and can undermine people's access to the ground of wonder and what's universal in our human experiences and our capacity for empathic connecting across our differences. Einstein reminded us that wonder is the source of all seeking, both religious and scientific (in Lash, 1990). Enhancing this capacity for curiosity about others, about the world beyond our known terrain, underpins every hope for turning this oil tanker of a world around. It is helpful to be aware of what beliefs each of us holds and what ones we tend to hide, and around whom we hide them.

Within You and Without You

We were talking about the space between us all,
And the people who hide themselves behind a wall of illusion.
Never lose the truth, then it's far too late when they Pass away.
We were talking about the love we all could share
When we find it to try our best to hold it there.
With a love, with our love we could save the world
If they only knew.

George Harrison[10]

When Daddy died it seemed like a small step. He was 99 and had been moving in smaller circles for some time. He had retired only six years before. After a meal of kielbasa and scotch with my brother-in-law, he went to bed and a day later he stopped breathing. He had been a beloved force in my life and in the community we both shared, as a much respected country newspaper man who defended democratic principles as common sense values learned as a child and even dealt with lofty topics carrying his tongue in his cheek much of the time.

From the book, *The Tibetan Way of Living and Dying* by Sogyal Rimpoche (1997) I had learned some practices I felt might be beneficial to my dad even after the cord was cut (and surely they helped me). They included particular visualizations and affirmations. One recitation I had shared with him before he died was on a Grateful Dead t-shirt I had:

We now return our soul to the creator.

---

[10] Within you and without you. *Sgt Pepper's Lonely Hearts Club Band*, 1967

240 ... COCREATING THE FIELD

And as we stand on the edge of eternal darkness,
let our chant fill the void that others may know,
in the land of the night the ship of the sun is
drawn by the grateful dead.

But what is the soul? And who is the creator? And out of what is all this created? Feminist constructivist theologian Catherine Keller, suggests in *Face of the Deep: a Theology of Becoming* (2003) that perhaps the initial surge into materialization is ongoing, not behind us at all. From *Tehom*, a primal oceanic chaos, comes creation out of watery depths based on ancient scripture. The first two verses of Genesis give us creation from chaos and then the chaos disappears into nothingness. With its compatibility with chaos theory, Keller offers up this theology of becoming, with the key principle of "extreme sensitivity to (being organized by) initial conditions (p, 5) " We know this to reflect our understanding of human process from developmental psychology. We know this, too, as brain research has identified the neural pathways that develop in our brains under empathic conditions and the ones less developed in the face of constant early trauma. Initial conditions matter. And the call for "strong sociospiritual practice" justifies a reconnoitering with myths of creation. Where a Christian and secular dogma has grown up around God or a big bang creating the universe from nothing, the notion of Western independent originality is paralleled. A *tehomaphobic* or "fear of ocean/chaos-hating/darkness-dreading" stance can be observed in any systematic resistance to the unknown, depiction of female as evil or inferior, condescension toward indigenous cultural beliefs, denial of death (2003, pp xv-xvi, 26, 64). Much as Gestalt has found that shame is shameful in a culture where something as universal as yearning to connect implies weakness, so an originating chaos is simply denied due to its, well, chaotic, out-of-control message. Awareness of these stories of beginnings affords us a chance to encounter each present moment anew, each containing an urgency for attention, a new creation. This process theology can give birth to a greater call for intentional practices.

Emily

What a dream I had, pressed in organdy, clothed in crinoline of smokey burgundy, softer than the rain...
And when you ran to me your cheeks flushed with the night, we walked on frosted fields of juniper and lamplight
...oh, I love you Girl! Oh how I love you!
Simon and Garfunkle[11]

I first re-met my daughter when she was 26 years old, my grand-daughter was 7. There were junipers and lamplight at the Holiday Inn where we met. It was Mother's Day weekend. I drove thirty miles up the coast from a Gestalt beach retreat with Margaret "Pat" Korb, south of St. Augustine, Florida, to meet them. When I was expelled from college, my life had taken some rocky twists and turns: trouble with the police, with rough boy friends. Then I married an orphaned man, younger than my 19 years. We set up housekeeping in a hotel off Times Square in New York city the summer of 1967. I became pregnant. His violent rages soon became intolerable. After I ran home to my folks, we separated. He vowed to return for his child. I cared well for her while she was in my womb, then delivered my

---

[11] For Emily whenever I may find her. *Parsley, Sage, Rosemary and Thyme*, 1967

baby and had her placed for adoption at birth. The adoption forms asked what religion I wanted her raised in. I chose Protestant, my root religion, that of my four grandparents ... but I wished Buddhism had been an option. Later I would learn she was raised by a Buddhist mom from Japan. Theirs was a difficult relationship.

I sent her off with a hand-stitched bunting, the name Emily, and the wish she would know her own truth. The clothing item came from Gene Stratton Porter's *Freckles* (1906), where the orphaned boy knew his birth mother had loved him because of the hand-stitched baby clothes he wore when he was found in a basket on someone's doorstep.

The name Emily came from Simon and Garfunkle's "For Emily Whenever I may Find Her" (see above lyrics). And my wish for her to know her own truth – well, I learned in our first hours long phone conversation after detectives helped me track her down, that Emily, too, was radically honest, a seeker of truth. A very verbal, very sensitive Southern woman with a great sense of humor, I quickly saw she had a deep, though often complicated, sense of her own truth. Growing up in a biracial family, where she felt isolated and often unappreciated, she had developed a deep concern for the world. She brought to our first meeting my very sharp and outgoing granddaughter, and a difficult marriage. I fell in love with her.

It turned out she started looking for me around the time I got serious about finding her.

I never have married again or birthed another child. I do have one godson. And children matter a lot to me. The counseling work I do with teens is work I love.

Looking back at the truly difficult life she has lived, the startling continuities and discontinuities between our life paths, the hard work she has undertaken to integrate her lost family roots back into her story, family of a very different cultural back-ground from her southern family — I am amazed that she is as resilient and healthy a person as she is. In a new marriage now she has found Christ and remains sensitive to signs of hypocrisy around her. Our religious differences challenge us to remain loving and close while we hold, for example, different and strongly held positions on what counsel to offer young women facing unintended pregnancies[12].

I believe I have carried the ripped open wounding of having lost a child throughout my adult years. And I now carry the powerful healing from our reconnection, the enormous blessing of our finding one another and caring deeply. As body awareness training shows us a wound such as this will be deeply embodied.

Physical evidence of that injury, that loss, I experience entering the yoga asana, or posture, *setu bandha* or "the bridge pose." Being aware of the world of sensations when I work on this floor-lying back-bend, allows me to witness myself at my edge, where my heart feels exposed, I feel vulnerable, occasionally anxious, my attention wanders off, I quiver and breath and sometimes with patience I discover myself opening just a little, becoming stronger. Sri Aurobindo, the 19th to 20th century Bangalese philosopher, poet, and visionary spoke of yoga as "the art of conscious self-finding" (in Satpem, 1964, p. 13). This is

---

[12] Work I've done with Judith Hemming's NoWhere Foundation has helped me to acknowledge some deeper unattended grieving that stems from the loss of unborn children ... and lead me to reflect more deeply on this topic. These reflections have not however changed my commitment to support a woman's legal right to choose the outcome of unintended pregnancies. But they have moved me to deplore the cruel and contentious political playground that idealogues engage for exploring such a deeply difficult and personal issue as this. I long for dialogues across this deep divide facilitated by those trained in conflict resolution, a mainstay of our Gestalt toolbox.

also how my yoga teacher teaches hatha yoga. Moment to moment he reminds us that our efforts and our resistances are all "us". Yoga allows us to pay attention to how we manage ourselves as we approach difficult tasks. He speaks of the value when we move into these funny positions of learning to be good to ourselves as we approach the mystery of who we are (D. Peccerill, personal communication). I have suggested to him that he is actually a Gestaltist. From a different perspective, the vantage point of history, perhaps, Gestalt is a relational yoga.

The beneficial effects of extended yoga practice were made clear to me in 1972 when I did a one week silent yoga retreat with *Swami Satchidananda*. I had to race directly from the ashram, Yogaville East in Connecticut, to MC a Bruce Springsteen and Herbie Mann concert at the Hartford Opera House. Without a toke of pot, without a slug of beer, I was able to address a large rock n' roll audience without nervousness or distress.

Do You Believe in Magic?

We use unicorn hair, phoenix tail feathers, and the heartstrings of dragons.
No two Ollivander wands are the same ...
I wonder now ... an unusual combination, holly and phoenix feather, eleven inches, nice and supple.
Harry took the wand.
He felt a sudden warmth in his fingers.
                                  A.J. Rowlings[13]

As a morning drive radio personality during the 1970's in Boston, Hartford, Cleveland, Boulder, other cities, I believed in

---

[13] *Harry Potter and the Sorcerer's Stone*, 1997

magic. I believed in miracles. Later, returning to college in my 40's, I learned, this means I am a post-modern woman — ascribing to diverse world views, some not readily compatible with others and holding rational, linear thought as only one of many reliable gauges of validity. Fortunately, my ongoing drive to make sense from experiences, to build a coherent story and contribute to a world that supports others to live with coherence, is still underway.

Madame Blavatsky came to the US from Russia in the late 1800's to study Native American religions. She later founded the Theosophical Society out of her belief in universal brotherhood[14]. She was a student of Indian yoga and was an influential writer of the 19th century. She defined a miracle as "... not a violation of the laws of nature, as is believed by ignorant people. Magic is but a science, a profound knowledge of the occult forces in nature and of the laws governing the visible or the invisible worlds" (in Murphet, 1971, p. 12). It is taught by Patanjali in his ancient *Yoga Sutras* that with true yogic training miraculous powers begin to manifest. This is a result of the spiritual training contained in yoga and involves character development, psychic unfoldment, and spiritual evolution (ibid, p. 15). Sai Baba was one contemporary Indian yogi whose miraculous feats or *siddhis* are much discussed in certain circles. Best known is the *vibhuti* or holy ash he conjured from thin air and with many an audience. This is used for healing. Many feats of healing by Sai Baba were witnessed and recorded, including by medical doctors. Every person is a spark of

---

[14] The site of Blavatsky's Philadelphia home is now a restaurant, The White Dog, founded and run by Judith Wicks who claims she uses "good food to lure innocent people into social activism" (Wicks and Van Klause, 1998).

divinity, so say the ancient *Vedic* teachings of India. Sai Baba offered clear teachings on faith:

> ...*When faith dawns, fence it around with discipline*
>   *and self-control*
> *so that the tender shoots are guarded against the*
>   *goats and cattle —*
> *the motley crowd of cynics and unbelievers.*
> *When your faith grows into a big tree,*
> *those very same goats and cattle can lie down in the*
>   *shade that it will spread.*
>
>   Sai Baba[15]

Notice that he did not speak of lassoing or corralling those goats or cattle, only sharing the shade.

Wandering through these stories and reflections I feel a bit exposed. As my friend Catherine Keller says, I am finding "a rhythm of gratitude and hesitation." The hesitation is around so publicly exposing my many non-rational assumptions about reality, and also around claiming spiritual insights with any confidence. The gratitude comes when I suspend my disbelief, allowing myself to imagine I am surrounded by sacred story, myth of place, rooted in the natural world of where I now am, populated by conscious beings of different sorts than myself. When I do this I feel a shift. My focus moves from the familiar and endless reruns in my mind, a purgatory in which the writers of new, enchanting tales are forever on strike. I move from that place to one where I plant gardens and harvest healing herbs, talk with turtles and spiders, consult archetypal astrologers, psychics, and shamans, and listen and watch with great rev-

---

[15] Sai Baba: *Man of Miracles*, Murphet, 1971.

erence and play. Sometimes I sing to birds and get bumped into by forces with powerful life energy. I transform my life space with conscious rituals or alters, sometimes with *feng shui*. I become able to imagine a world radically changed by collective intentions and actions. My choices become more easily sustainable ones, my decisions arise in relationship to World. I feel responsible for my thoughts, and for how tightly I hold my belly, for my impact on other people and on the world around me. I climb into a life enriched by simple treasures like meaningful connections, and mindful breath, joyful feasting or fasting, ecstatic intimacy and ease in the arms of familiar comforts.

   The praxis of panpsychism includes the organizing principle of letting-be. This contradicts the high value of progress and productivity in modern capital-based society. Letting-be serves as a mantra for healthy recovery from the chronic stress of individuals making a life in a competitive society. Letting-be is also a resistance cry, a movement's motto against the gluttony of the beast of materialism and profit, an environmental and transformational thought for a ravaged and struggling planet. And it is one version of the most often quoted Gestaltism, the paradoxical theory of change of Arnold Beisser: we change by becoming more fully who we are, not by trying to become who we are not. Letting-be must also resonate for the 60's generation as a philosophical support as we learn to slow down (not stop!) as we approach our retiring stages of life. Letting-be as a value can also support millions of troubled people during economically hard times, as we all work on weaning ourselves of our addiction to the act of consuming. Chogyam Trungpa Rimpoche reminds meditators that the practice of meditation involves letting-be. Australian philosopher and panpsychic, Freya Matthews, again, speaks of "letting the world grow old."

> "Slow down, take a hike
> *catch a bus, ride a bike,*
> *and turn toward peace"*
> Harriet Korem[16]

Of course the danger is of laying aside responsibility at a time when human civilization is up against so many challenges. Nothing could be further from my own intentions as I learn to inhabit the mantra of acceptance and admiration for nature's story. Letting the world grow old means to me: less to fight over but much to hear and say, making love not war with time, fewer material embellishments to be achieved or acquired at whatever cost, defending the rights of people or places to continue living as they have or choose to, admonishing only "and harm none, do what ye will"[17].

Gordon Wheeler describes a world culture rife with the multiplicity of splits we all know about and a world view that can carry us across those divides. This world uniting perspective is a view based on relational field theory. Building on earlier Gestalt psychologists he speaks of our drive to make integrated wholes of meaning, how we are "wired" for relationships, values, intersubjectivity, and no less we are "wired" to be spiritual seekers, always moving on to make the next larger meaningful whole picture out of our experiences (2000, p. 383). He also describes a dynamic alteration between our individualized identity and our interdependent sense of who we are.

Competition exists in counterpoint to deep levels of co-operation and mutuality in most of our lives. David Korten reminds us of this in his visionary work that posits empire against Earth communities (2006, p. 309):

---

[16] Jerusha, ©2006, Turn toward peace. *Free Sky Show.*
[17] Axiom of the Wiccan religion.

The species that survive and thrive are those that learn to sustain themselves in ways that simultaneously serve the needs of the whole.
　　　　　　　　　　　　　　　David Korten[18]

Getting There

*... Sometimes my burden is more than I can bear
It's not dark yet but it's getting there.*
　　　　　　　　　　　　　　　Bob Dylan[19]

As I'm finishing these reflections it is a sparkling and beautiful autumn equinox. In the northeastern United States I am touched by the sight of birds only just growing their feathers back after molting ... and the sound of crickets. Yellowing birch leaves and bright red poison ivy dot the roadways. I am reminded of a tale told me by my longtime and beloved friend, father to my godson, George Murray, before he recently died. Along with colleague Charles Moyer, Murray stumbled upon clues to the puzzle of human literacy: indications that ancient alphabets from across Eurasia were derived from ancient lunar calendars. Our human relationship to the calendar is full of mythic significance — much of what we know from ancient cultures we've learned from the sacred myths that delineated time, the seasons, the tides of a communities life. Murray long held court and spun tales concerning what connected ancient people, earth's communities, to the larger world, and how they attuned themselves to their own health and life cycles, and those sacred rites of passage within community. He also suggested ways we disregard these cycles and forces of time at our own peril.

---

[18] *The Great Turning*: from *Empire to Earth Community*, (2006).
[19] *Time Out of Mind*, 1987.

In this story Murray ponders how oral traditions carry knowledge forward now and in the ages before the written word. He begins with conversations with folk singer Andy Cohen who over 25 years on the folk and blues circuit recounted that he knows easily 3000 songs ready for parlor picking with 150 of those in his performing repertoire. This, Cohen said, is not untypical for troubadors who by the way have always set calendarics and religious lore to tune. The old timers he knows have even grander repertoires. Contemporary attitudes of secular literacy lead us to think we have traded off the ancient ways of knowing of oral cultures for the more advanced knowledge of today, and in the process lost the memory capacities of Homer.

When Murray's friend Moyer and his wife spotted the afternoon sun shining through the bell tower of the Church of St Francis at Ranchos de Taos, in New Mexico. Moyer, a student and scholar of ancient languages was struck by the pun of the sun god Bel shining through the bell tower. He took a snapshot which revealed a 6-rayed star blazing from the arch. He recognized the 6-rayed star is a *Haglrun*, the holiest rune of the Futhark alphabet and in the photo it blazes from within a *Dolmen Arch*. *The Dolmen Arch* was said to be the home of the central deity of the Celts and central to their Ogam alphabet. In poetic extrapolations on studies involving the overlapping Ogam, Runic, and Futhark alphabets, Murray and Moyer suggest that literacy did not spread because of commerce, as has been commonly believed, but due to "sacred communings with a common diety" across great distances and among divergent regions and cultures (1989). This moment of alphabet was the transitional moment studied also by poet-scholar Robert Graves, when these ancient traveling people we call Celts moved from oral history and traditions to written narratives, a shift with enormous implications for the evolution of human consciousness and society.

> *These signs belong to rural life, where rules are rules-of-rhyme,*
> *and close is close enough to keep apace of heaven's Time.*
>
> George Murray[20]

Mixed Mercy

> *... the prophet told us we should tolerate*
> *the people and the things that make me want to hate*
> *Allah have a little mixed mercy on me*
> *to see some beauty in this human pageantry ...*
>
> Chrissie Hynde/ the Pretenders[21]

Reflecting on the current day world and our religious and cultural divisions I'm reminded of two close encounters I've had with the Islamic mystical tradition of Sufism. In 1969 I was living in Sausalito, California, and dropped in several times to the Community Center where Murshid (spiritual teacher) Samuel Lewis, known as Sufi Sam, held court and led a weekly night of Sufi dancing, whirling to flutes, drums, and stringed instruments played live by his students. The whirling and chanting felt personally liberating and collectively ecstatic! Sufism, a non-doctrinal approach to Islam that is experiential and non-excluding, is the dominant mode of Islam practiced in the two most populous states of Pakistan, Punjab and Sindh, according to a piece in Smithsonian Magazine (December,

---

[20] *Moon Calendar of the Celts*, 1989.
[21] *Break up the Concrete*, 2008.

2008). A few hundred thousand Sufi practitioners danced enthusiastically at festivals to one Sufi saint in the summer of 2008. This saint was patron to the assassinated People's Party leader Benazir Bhutto's family. Bhutto's husband is now president of Pakistan. Far from the repressive fundamentalism espoused by Islamic extremists, these practices celebrate inclusiveness with embodied ecstatic experiences in praise of Allah!

My other Sufi encounter was a weekend meditation workshop in 1974 with the head of the Order of Sufi in the West, Pir Vilayat Khan. It was he who instructing a young Pema Chodron, before she became a Buddhist nun, predicted to her that she would become a leading Buddhist teacher in the West!

The news of the world reminds me also of Vietnamese Sister Chan Khong's memoir, *Learning True Love: Practicing Buddhism in a Time of War* (1993). This compelling story tells many heart wrenching episodes from her experiences in what Americans call the Vietnam War, there known as the American war. She worked tirelessly for years both organizing student protests against the corrupt South Vietnamese government of Ngo Dinh Diem and founding a youth service agency. These college-age youths went deep into rural areas to feed and nurse the wounded and devastated villagers and rebuild the bombed villages. Sometimes they would spend weeks to months rebuilding a village only to see it bombed again just as they were finishing. Shortly after she left Vietnam the first time, Sister Chan Kong traveled to France then America with her teacher Thich Nhat Hanh and talked with people about what was happening inside South Vietnam to children and civilian families in the countryside. She has now spent many decades imploring people to help today's children of Vietnam in the wake of those devastating years of war[22]. Sister Chan Kong reminds us, "all of us, indeed, inter-are" (ibid, p. 295).

Susan Collins Marks and John Marks work and teach from a vision of "infusing spiritual values into the political, economic, and social life of our planet ...." Their international non-profit Search for Common Ground supports social entrepreneurship in pursuit of conflict transformation throughout the US and around the world[23] because as Susan told a group we shared in at Esalen, in October 2008, it is always easier to find common ground before violence has broken out into war.

"Say Yes Quickly"

... If you are here unfaithfully with us,
you're causing terrible damage.
If you've opened your loving to God's love,
you're helping people you don't know
and have never seen....

Rumi[24]

The Greeks give us the word, *kairos,* and Carl Jung applied it to our times, referencing our epoch as a time of "a metamorphosis of the Gods." For a sweeping exploration of this living universe and the dynamic rhythms of human history, I am turning briefly here, to philosopher and cultural historian Richard Tarnas. As in Copernican times Tarnas finds we are at a cosmic moment for revisioning our metaphysical understanding of our world. Tarnas invites in a perspective I have found to be most helpful

---

[22] To learn more go to www.plumvillage.org and check out "how can I help?"

[23] For more information on Search for Common Ground check their website: www.sfcg.org.

[24] *Open Secret*, 1984.

for attending to the tides, storms, and dynamic interrelations of my own life: archetypal or mythic astrology. Perhaps, he suggests, the public disenchantment which I and others grieve springs out of a culturally dominant "simplistic epistemology and moral posture spectacularly inadequate to the depths, complexity, and grandeur of the cosmos" (2006, p. 40). Where the disenchanted world view may have historically strengthened our human differentiation and autonomy in ways that greatly advanced the agenda of the Modern era, this has outlived its usefulness for these times and an urgently evolving numinous and collective world view (ibid, p. 41). He maps the archetypal and creative intelligence of the universe as expressed through correspondences between astronomical patterns and human experience, historical trends and cultural shifts. This perspective ties in with an evolutionary panentheism. [25]

Concepts like interdependence, transformative practice, the web of life, and relational process now pepper the Leisure sections of the newspapers and many of our popular magazines. Back in the early 1990's Michael Murphy reminded us that "... our practices must promote perceptual, kinesthetic, communication and movement abilities; vitality; cognition; volition; command of pain and pleasure; love ...." And, he adds, these practices must involve "social creativity, as none of us can develop without considerable help from our fellows" (1992, p. 562).

---

[25] An evolutionary panentheism is a metaphysical proposition allowing for the interrelatedness of all creatures and a creator/creative force such that God resides in all and everything resides in the Divine (Keller, 2007). The evolutionary assumption is that there is an overarching purpose that includes embodied consciousness becoming capable of greater complexity as history unfolds. This unfolding process includes the possibility of subtle worlds and beings (Poletti, 2007).

These reflections remind me that the Gestalt of Laura and Fritz Perls, Isadore From, even Paul Goodman and others could not articulate these contemporary strivings. They plowed the field. They planted the seeds in the shell-shocked 1950's, in the 60's, and the 70's that awakened a generation to how our emotions address the sense we're making from our experiences, often based on suppressed passions, unfinished business and unexamined assumptions. The world was a very different place then. Their ideas pointed the way so we might now extend our wondering minds and trembling hearts to the urgent concerns of a world in which the very endurance of our human family and many other species of the natural world are in question. Caring for ourselves and others now demands new skills for living better. For many of us, leaders in our families, communities or workplaces, this has turned us toward Asian disciplines or more deeply into ourselves while we find ways to wonder about what is real. How do we keep our balance with so many unleashed forces for good and ill. Also what can we do to support better ways of sharing the finite resources including our own energy in service to strengthening relationships with underprivileged populations at home and in the developing world, particularly critical as the international economic crisis unfolds. These are questions we must concern ourselves with while we learn to listen to one another across our differences. And they rightfully involve, what Malcolm Parlett describes as "the search for a spiritual home" which "is a form of reaching for a better quality of life in a non-material sense." (see Chapter 10).

I have lately been rereading *Black Elk Speaks*. Black Elk, the Oglala Sioux holy man whose words to John Niehardt recorded in 1931 tell some unbearable stories from the decades of the Custer battle, the ghost dance, and the massacre at Wounded

Knee, when the *Wasichus* (white men) entered into treaties with the Indians, then broke them, resulting in great slaughters and suffering for the Plains Indians of the Black Hills and beyond.

Black Elk's stories remind me we are all responsible for one another. Some intention to find truth and reconciliation and maybe learn a sacred attitude, an attitude of humility and of reverence for all the directions of this earth and all that live here could help us make our way — intentional practices that lift us up to honor our own sweet seed of divinity, as well as our common humanity and what I'm calling the sacred cycles of time, including whatever archetype or image we hold of the ineffable around us? While I wonder what is lost in my own eclecticism and am concerned about violating the Buddhist edict to "take the one cushion," follow one path at a time, I am grateful to have the patchwork of rich mystical and indigenous traditions to draw from, words and images of enspirited power and compassion that move me and support my ongoing quest to alleviate suffering in the world, my own and that of many others.

This brings me full circle, to Gestalt, our meaning-making tool. In Gestalt, in the contemporary field theoretically focused understanding of Gestalt, we are fundamentally and integrally part of the field, before we are separate beings. Not *in* the field only, but *of* the field. This understanding carries with it compelling ethical implications (see also Lee, 2004). And my mystical/spiritual beliefs or panentheistic assumptions about the world provide a larger context for making sense of what I see as our contemporary responsibilities. These include embracing practices that nourish me with an expanded consciousness.

For me to stay strong and open, the poems and prayers, the songs, our stories all matter greatly. They help me to cry, to keep caring, they inspire and hold me, as I seek *sangha*, community, and kindred spirits to practice with, to help enrich our world as we move along with intention.

References

Arguelles, Jose. (1987). *The Mayan Factor: Path Beyond Technology.* Santa Fe, NM: Bear & Co.
Bryant, Barry. (1992). *The Wheel of the Sand Mandala.* San Fransisco: Harper.
David-Neel, Alexandra. (1971). *Magic and Mystery in Tibet.* New York: Dover.
Davis, M. (1959). So what. *Kinda Blue.* New York: Columbia.
Dylan, B. (1967). I Shall Be Released (Recorded by The Band). On *The Music from Big Pink* [CD]. New York: Columbia Records. (1968).
Dylan, B. (1987). Not dark yet. On *Time Out of Mind* [CD]. New York: Columbia Records.
Goldstein, Kurt. (1995). *The Organism.* New York: Zone Books.
Harrison, G. (1967). Within you and without you. *Sgt Pepper's Lonely Hearts Club Band* (LP).New York: Columbia.
Hendrix, J. (1967). Are you experienced? On *Are You Experienced?* (LP). New York: MCA Records.
James, William. (1992). *The Varieties of Religious Experience.* New York: Modern Library.
Jerusha (Harriet Korem) (2006). Turn toward peace. *Free Sky Show* [CD]. Wellfleet: Permanent Wave (2009).
Keller, Catherine. (2007). *On the Mystery: Discerning God in Process.* Minneapolis: Fortress Press.
Keller, Catherine. (2003). *Face of the Deep: a Theology of Becoming.* London: Routledge, Taylor and Francis.
Korten, David. (2006). *The Great Turning: from Empire to Earth Community.* San Fransisco: Berrett-Koehler.
Lash, John. (1990). *The Seeker's Handbook: the Complete Guide to Spiritual Pathfinding.* New York: Harmony.
Lennon, J. (1971). Imagine. *Imagine.* New York: Columbia.
Levine, Noah. (2003). *Dharma Punx: a Memoir.* San Frasisco: Harper.

Lee, R. (2004). *The Values of Connection: a Relational Approach to Ethics.* Hillsdale, NJ: The Analytic Press/GestaltPress.

Matthews, Freya (2005258258). *Reinhabiting Reality: Toward a Recovery of Culture.* Albany, NY: SUNY Press.

Murphet, Howard. (1971). *Sai Baba: Man of Miracles.* York Beach, ME: Samuel Weiser.

Murphy, Michael. (1992). *The Future of the Body: Explorations into the Further Evolution of Human Nature.* New York: Jeremy P. Tarcher/Putnam.

Murray, George (1989). *Moon Calendar of the Celts.* Midwestern Epigraphic Journal. Vol 6. p. 12.

Narby, Jeremy. (1999). *The Cosmic Serpent: DNA and the Origins of Knowledge.* New York: Jeremy P. Tarcher/Putnam.

Niehardt, John G. (1979). *Black Elk Speaks.* Linciln, NE: University of Nebraska Press.

Pema Chodron. (2006). *Practicing Peace in Times of War.* Boston: Shambhala.

Poletti, F. (2007). Conference materials for CTR Study Group on Panentheism Esalen Institute.

Porter, Gene Stratton. (1906). *Freckles.* New York: Grossett & Dunlap.

Pretenders (2008). Boots of Chinese plastic. *Break Up the Concrete* [CD]. Hollywood: Shangri-La.

Rohrer, Jane. (2002). *Life After Death.* Riverdale-on-Hudson: The Sheep Meadow Press.

Rowlings, A. J. (1997). *Harry Potter and the Sorcerer's Stone.* New York: Scholastic.

Rumi. Moyne, J. and Barks, C., Trans. (1984). *Open Secret: Versions of Rumi.* Putney, VT.: Threshold Books.

Satprem. (1964). *Sri Aurobindo or the Adventure of Consciousness.* New York: India Library Society.

Schmidle, N. (2008, December). Faith & Ecstasy. *Smithsonian,* 37-47.

Seigel, D. J. (2007). *The Mindful Brain: Reflections and Attunement in the Cultivation of Well-Being.* New York: W.W. Norton and Co.

Shantideva. Padmarka Transation Group, Trans. (1997). *The Way of the Bodhisattva.* Boston: Shambala.

Sister Chan Khong. (2007). *Learning True Love: Practicing Buddhism in a Time of War.* Berkeley: Parallax Press.

Smith, Houston. (1991). *The World's Religions.* San Fransisco: Harper.

Sogyal Rimpoche. (1992). *The Tibetan Book of Livin and Dying.* San Fransisco: Harper.

Stapp, Henry P. (2007). *Mindful Universe: Quantum Mechanics and the Participating Observer.* Berlin: Springer.
Simon and Garfunkel (1966). For Emily whenever I may find her. *Parsley Sage Rosemary andThyme* (LP). New York: Columbia.
Supertramp (1977). Even in the quietest moments ... *Even in the Quietest Moments* ... [CD] London: A&M.
Thich Nhat Hanh. (1995). *Living Buddha, Living Christ.* New York: Riverhead Books.
Tarnas, Richard. (2007). *Cosmos and Psyche: Intimations of a New World View.* New York: A Plume Book/Penguin.
Welwood, John. Ed. (1992). *Ordinary Magic: Everyday Life as Spiritual Path.* Boston: Shambala.
Wheeler, Gordon. (2000). *Beyond Individualism: Toward a New Understanding of Self, Relationship and Experience.* Hillsdale, NJ: TAP/GestaltPress.
Wicks, J. & von Klause, K. (1998). *White Dog Cafe Cookbook.* Philadelphia: Running Press.

9

A Larger Field
Judith Hemming

This is a (slightly edited) version of a talk I was asked to give in 2005 as one of the series of annual lectures honoring Marianne Fry, a much respected and loved Gestalt therapist and trainer who died in 1998. It was a personal talk, given to an audience who mostly knew her. Marianne and her Jewish family escaped from Germany to Britain in 1938 when she was fifteen. She originally trained as a family therapist in the National Health Service, only encountering Gestalt in the seventies and, with Malcolm Parlett, created a Gestalt training organization — Gestalt South West — which ran successfully for many years. Outspoken, creative and warm, though not a writer, Marianne inspired many therapists in the UK. (The British Gestalt Journal carried a lengthy interview with her and also an obituary, both of which can be viewed on their website.) The talk was originally called Dialogue in the Dark, since the lecture day was created as a series of dialogues between different practitioners and theorists.

The teachings of Bert Hellinger have moved on considerably since I gave this talk, as has the development of my understanding of both the Diamond Approach and systemic work. So what follows needs to be seen as a snapshot of changing perspectives in progress.

This chapter is going to be quite personal. I'm going to be honouring Marianne Fry, whom I knew well, though only for the last dozen years of her life. She left behind many friends, grateful colleagues, students and clients. Since she died, she has remained surprisingly alive to me. I often, unbidden, hear her voice and imagine I am talking with her. I hear her laugh, and the jokes are always good. The theme of Gestalt and Spirituality was dear to her heart, and I think she would be glad I am going to be discussing something that is important to us both, and perhaps to all of us. Marianne was interested in spirituality and explored it in many different settings, whilst remaining clearly a Gestalt practitioner. Because of the broad nature of our theoretical framework, Gestalt continues to be enriched by the range of other perspectives it can integrate and include. The British Gestalt Journal has published a great range of papers doing just that — including wisdoms from attachment theory and intersubjectivity, for example. Along with others like Marianne, I have been on a journey to gather new perspectives, and until recently, I was actively devoted to that integrating process, partly through my work in the Journal and partly through having opportunities to teach. I want to say that the fact that I no longer work with the Journal or teach Gestalt students was a personal decision, not related to the capacity of the Gestalt community to welcome new developments. I have now shifted so definitively into systemic work that my community has changed. But still, I remain a Gestaltist through and through — I wouldn't know how to relinquish those ways of understanding and being in the world, and nothing I have learned more recently contradicts that inner map. I'm glad to be able to share some of my additional maps. I believe this integrating process has a healthy future. The additions I want to talk about relate to Bert Hellinger's systemic approach and to the Ridhwan teaching of the Diamond Heart School. This also connects me to Marianne, as she knew Bert Hellinger's work, and she was thinking she might join the Ridhwan School in the year before she died, so our journeys continue to connect. In her fifties Marianne decided to return to the Germany she escaped from as a refugee when she was fifteen years old, though obviously it was not the same Germany. That was a courageous action, and important for both her and those she met and worked with in Germany. Living with the aftermath of the Nazi era was one of the defining issues for those growing up in post war Europe. What kind of relationship could exist between those who had been in the war and those who came later? What part could psychotherapy play in healing the relationship between the generations? In Germany, because of who Marianne was, a Jewish German from the generation that had been gassed and killed, she found herself attending to the bigger field within the context of the individuals she met. And as I said, she got to know Bert Hellinger's work quite early on. I remember talking with her about how it impacted her work, moving her into a therapeutic environment where blaming could give way to respect, and where individuals might find peace with their past as well as shining a light on peace in a bigger context.

I must say that writing and lecturing are not my strengths. I have concentrated on being a practitioner and teacher, and when I have written, I have mainly done what I'm doing now, mediating the creativity of other people. In fact I looked recently at the collection of pieces of mine published in the British Gestalt Journal and every single piece has been about someone else — book reviews, obituaries and interviews. So, in the tradition of being the grateful magpie that I am, I shall continue to show you the bright colours in my nest and tell you about where the feathers came from.

Germany, is one answer, since that is where the Perlses came from as well as many other key contributors to Gestalt, like Lewin, and other seminal influences, like Buber. It is Bert Hellinger's home, and it is also where the original European Ridhwan retreats are held, the ones I attend. As a British Jew, I am glad that I have this connection with Germany. It hasn't all been easy but it has been a huge gift. It reminds me of those Sufi stories where you don't know whether something that has happened is good or bad in an absolute sense until you know the time frame. Germany's history, like ours and America's, has been both terrible and extraordinarily creative and wide reaching in what it has brought to the world.

I absorbed the outlooks created by these three giant approaches, in that order – first Gestalt, then the systemic and the spiritual. They overlap, cover the same territory, with each enriching the other. I hope today we can have a good conversation about their integration, their differences, and how this might contribute to a 'dialogue in the dark' that our world needs.

And I believe Marianne would be glad we are doing this. Just before she died, she resigned from GPTI, that institution she helped to found. The 'conscience' of GPTI, the Gestalt Psychotherapy Training Institute, (those rules of belonging and allegiance that push us to conform if we are to remain secure) required something of her that her own personal conscience did not allow and so she withdrew from it. It wasn't that she relinquished her Gestalt beliefs and practices. But had she wanted to continue to belong to GPTI she would have had to pay too high a price. It can take as much courage to leave a flock as to stay.

Marianne's life was rich in themes. I have taken on a bit of her mantle, and even some of her work, and I continue to explore some of those passions that were important to her — the relationship between a conscious psychological and a spiritual path, growing old gracefully (or disgracefully), the Jewish legacy, how to teach in a lively way, how to stay open and curious. And as I said, I also share with her the fact of having largely withdrawn from having an official position in the Gestalt community, with a similar feeling of affection, regret and respect.

Since this is a personal account I want to be more explicit about the ways I feel connected to Marianne. It comforted me that someone older than I knew some of my world, and I hers. Like her I have an assimilated Jewish background. Assimilated Jews, until the last war, hoped they would not stand out. My family succeeded in being safe and camouflaged in Britain, but all Jews stood out in Germany, whatever their beliefs or culture.

We have other German connections too. Lutz and Cleo, part of the same Ridhwan group I am in, learned their Gestalt with her back in the seventies in Germany. Hunter Beaumont (who lives in Munich) was friend and colleague to us, and someone who has done more than anyone to integrate many other forms of knowledge into a Gestalt-compatible framework.

The impact of the holocaust continues, especially between the descendents of the Germans and Jews from that time. Marianne grew up in Dresden, where she had to remain silent about her Jewishness. But the question of what you are allowed to say was one that was also alive for me, growing up in a family that was successful and had a public face but where there was a lot that was not to be spoken of. Marianne wrote, 'the theme of silence, fearfully kept, and the urge to break it, have accompanied me ever since'. I knew that theme too. Silence and secrets deeply distort family life. The process of unearthing a bigger truth and speaking out is also a great gift and one that can support growth. Even though Marianne left GPTI just before she died, she memorably wrote the following to her colleagues, 'I want to part from you with love, appreciation and gratitude for our past connection and the transforming work that has flowed between us.' Having been persecuted in her youth had cast a long shadow of victimhood, but wrestling with the complaint at the end of her life somehow cleared away its remaining impact. It seems that when a parting is done well, all that need remain is appreciation.

Marianne explored many wisdom traditions, and was drawn to many teachers and teachings — Mother Meera, Findhorn, Emmanuel's channelling. She had a special connection to the spaciousness and non-attachment of Buddhism and was the first Gestalt therapist to have been invited to work with the monks and nuns in one of the Thai monasteries here, work I took over when she died and which I love. They feel especially at home with Gestalt, but now they also love constellation work and several have joined the Ridhwan School.

Marianne began her career within the Jungian tradition, though she found that psychodynamic approach too cramping - she couldn't include enough of herself. In the interview I did with her she spoke about her delight in being authentic and creative once she encountered and experienced Gestalt. For her, it was Ischa Bloomberg who inspired her and her friends Ursula Fausset and Dolores Bate — they all trained together. They had met in the early 1970s at Quaesitor– one of the London growth Centres — which helped to bring over the new humanistic approaches from America including Gestalt. Those who missed out on that really did miss something! Despite the poor sexual boundaries and bashing of cushions, there was a lot of passion and vitality — different from the necessarily careful and responsible form that Gestalt now takes. I think of my teachers: Ursula, Dolores and Marianne as both part of the old way and the new.

Old and new don't find getting together always easy. For example, in the early days of my engaging with Hellinger's work I ran several workshops with Malcolm Parlett on the connection between Gestalt and the systemic approach because we both saw so much compatibility in how each understood the field, the power of dialogue and the phenomenological basis of the work. I think there has been a good relationship between the two approaches that has developed over time, but there certainly were some challenging periods where it didn't seem easy to belong to both those thought worlds, let alone two communities. I remember engaging, about ten years ago, in a GPTI debate with some who felt strongly antagonistic, and who saw the differences more than the similarities. They found it difficult to accept the process of a constellation, to work with the idea of orders that lie beyond the conscious mind. They were not happy about all this talk of the soul. Here were two big approaches, two ways of living even, and they inspired conflicts of loyalty and belonging.

Schools of therapy are a bit like religions — there are creators, followers, lineages, and specific disciplines. We have to narrow our field of vision if we are to belong, to deny or reject ideas that don't conform. Each school tends to be critical of others. There is orthodoxy, creed and practice, with institutes set up to safeguard the doctrines and expel those who deviate. As with religions there is a long apprenticeship, tests of dedication, rites of initiation and opportunities for advancement into places of influence and power. If we question things we risk censure, or maybe even expulsion. This seems to be an inevitable way of maintaining loyalty and boundaries. I understand and respect the process more now, armed with what I learned about loyalty and conscience from Bert Hellinger. I am also impressed by how welcoming of diversity is the Gestalt world I know. Most of my colleagues in the Hellinger Institute of Britain have a Gestalt background, and many Gestalt colleagues and friends have joined Ridhwan's path of study.

As far as I can see, therapy and spiritual practice do search for the same thing — the healing of the soul, the whole person, though the forms they take will change. I see them as complementing each other — therapy helps us get our egos working well enough for living and the spiritual path helps us see it for what it is, just a fixed set of ideas, not the real thing. I'm still feeling into their similarities and differences. Perhaps with my therapist hat I am committed to self-improvement, catching up on deficits, having an impact on everyday life for the better. I deal with matters of inner security, solutions to life problems, self-manipulations, shoring up a sense of self that threatens to dissolve under pressure. But most spiritual practices take suffering as the human condition — they are not concerned with the impossible task of eradicating its cause in the world. Their focus is on the inevitable suffering that comes from all attachment to desires, and on the natural instability of the ego. Their promise is that there could be somewhere else to live — somewhere far more spacious.

I remember interviewing Hunter Beaumont seven or eight years ago, for the *British Gestalt Journal*. Hunter described an interesting dilemma, back from his own early studies, of how his Gestalt training encouraged him to identify with his body or his feelings, whereas other approaches asked the opposite of him, to dis-identify, and how both felt true and valuable. I think this nicely expresses a tension I also feel, between the spiritual and the therapeutic path.

Despite, or maybe because I am a therapist, I remain addicted to poking about in myself, trying to be a better person, although what I do never works for long. And yet when I stop I often feel frighteningly empty and disorientated. So I vacillate between the familiar ways and the lightness. However, I am beginning to be able to stay in the empty spaciousness for longer. I believe in my case that is largely to do with my being a student of the Diamond Heart School of Ridhwan, a spiritual teaching created by Hameed Ali, known as A.H.Almaas, one that is now becoming quite well known in Britain. (Perhaps some of you are students in this group.) It's hard to summarise or explain a deep and complex teaching that, even though I have been a student for nearly ten years, feels only fractionally revealed to me. In great depth it illuminates the path from individual consciousness to the ultimate nature of existence. It helps its students make contact with essential states that create a different basis for living: compassion, peacefulness, impeccability and acceptance. It outlines, step by step, what Almaas calls the '"inner journey home."

The teaching of Ridhwan works with psychological processes, and exists within a western framework of thought. It's a spiritual path of being 'in the world' rather than withdrawing from it, seeing psychological and spiritual work as necessary for each other. This approach to spiritual work deconstructs the personality so we don't take it as real. And the deconstruction process is awesomely detailed and thorough, deep and relentless, lasting many years. I believe that Ridhwan's thoroughness sets it apart from most other traditions, and takes its students to an appreciation of the intrinsic narcissism of the personality, to the emptiness it hides, and eventually into an appreciation of qualities that do not depend on the personality. Matter turns out to be mostly space or emptiness, according to modern particle physics; its solidity, like the solidity of the personality, is an illusion. In my explorations I have exactly and endlessly explored what it feels like to be imprisoned in the labyrinth of my own ego structure, feeling the staleness of my stories, my fixed convictions, and the way that my past seems to recreate itself and recreate me, and how I can't escape from this by devising a better version. I have been taking a magnifying lens to this now over many years, to what in Gestalt we think of as fixed patterns of alienation and identification. It's a sobering process, discovering the small suitcases I thought we lived in don't actually exist!

Actually I didn't join the Ridhwan School with a preformed passion for this kind of investigation. Like many therapists who have been working for a long time, my need was not so much about how to develop my work but how to continue to develop myself. However valuable what we offer others, we would eventually wither without being on a similar journey. I guess that is one of the reasons we may wish to search outside our community — so we can find people further ahead to guide us, people not connected to our institutional life. Even if we can guide our clients well, we too need guidance. I didn't realise the size and power of the journey I was starting on, one that was going to change my whole inner and outer landscape. After a decade I still feel I am at the start, and that another ten years wouldn't complete it either. But I love it. I am supported by the teachers, who really do embody what they teach, and by the teaching, which is open and personal and compatible with my western mind and life style, and I am supported by doing the work in a stable ongoing community. The journey is extremely personal. I travel at my own pace, focus on what arises for me, and find my own way, or non-way.

And I appreciate how familiar a lot of the processes are — Ridhwan's style of enquiry is not so different from a Gestalt practice. Very simply, it consists of learning to be fully present and embodied, enquiring into what turns up, and not stopping in the belief that there is an ultimate resting place. That's hardly rocket science, to get interested in your own experience. You learn to unwrap in layers, going deeper through the structures of the ego. It can be very painful, so the environment of possibility and compassion created by the teachers is critically important. Everyone needs a teacher who is further ahead on the path, so that the process isn't injurious.

The biggest obstacles to an ongoing exploration of reality are introjects, the voices of our inner critics — that whole complex of the superego with its attendant imagery and its inherent 'keep-us-in-line' cruelty. Overriding introjects always brings up anxiety. There is fearfulness associated with the possibility of losing our hopes of belonging, our inner security, if we deviate from those old ways of seeing the world. It doesn't matter whether you call them introjects, in the Gestalt terminology, or superego, in the tradition of Object Relations, or Conscience, in the Hellinger frame. By any name I appreciate their power and am still learning more about how they run my life, and what strength I need to live without them.

From following the Ridhwan path I have discovered the power of going into what I haven't got rather than focusing on what I have, which might perhaps be a more familiar route for a Gestalt practitioner. Facing deficiency, if honestly done, opens up spaces, whereas strengthening the ego seems to have the opposite effect. It is through getting to know the falsity of my usual versions of will, love, happiness, kindness or power, seeing them largely as ideas and images, that I have begun to meet their beautiful and truer versions, the more essential qualities. The framework is both very personal — relating to each person's specific history — and also not personal at all. After all, everyone falls from grace as they come into the world. We all grow a compensating ego, a narcissistic shell, and it turns out to be in one of only a certain number of patterned ways, despite our personal histories. I have found it helpful to study these ways via the use of the enneagram, an ancient personality inventory that helps us see our particular ways of getting lost and the relevant healing journey for each kind of patterned 'sleepiness of the soul'.

Obviously, you have to be present to enquire since enquiry only happens in the present. You have to show up, be there. Most of us are only sometimes at home. In the Diamond Approach, as I also did in Gestalt, I have had a lot of support to witness with real curiosity, to feel all my exquisite nuances of experience at a somatic level, to persevere, to be interested in everything. In the Ridhwan tradition we mainly work in ever changing groups of two or three, taking turns to investigate an aspect of experience without interruption, or ask repeating questions. That's a very different process from being in long term dialogue with a therapist. I think it has helped me to be more independent from the response of the other. Over time, along with the practice of meditating and listening to the teaching, it has had a powerful impact. Instead of believing that my resources were mine alone, I am beginning to know, at least in flashes, the immense and benign resources of the universe. I am learning to taste the qualities of basic trust, of nourishment, love, attunement (my own) and the exquisite guidance I can experience if I settle into what is real. We also explore what the implications of this knowledge are for how we live every aspect of our daily lives. It's a delicate and subtle exploration — and difficult to talk about.

As far as I can see, the big question in all traditions has always been about the connection between the individual soul, the world of others, and Being (or God). Most traditions respond with a doctrine. Ridhwan's teaching resonates with those traditional spiritual outlooks but it does not depend on any of them. It's more a way of investigating than any kind of creed. Buddhists, for example, teach the non-existence of the separate self, but in Ridhwan we are invited to explore and experience directly. Like Gestalt it is based on open-ended enquiry, and the practice of suspending identification with the content of thoughts, as pure experiment. You could call it a scientific enquiry into consciousness, with reference to your actual lived experience. You develop a psychological understanding of the mental structures and veils of identifications without any attempt to change or improve anything but simply to understand them and thereby be less identified with them. This perseverance seems to grow a love of the truth of reality itself. We only make use of personal experience. There is no state or level of awareness postulated as the goal of the practice — in fact it challenges the whole process of goal seeking, as Gestalt does too, but which therapy clients often badly want. I have found it valuable simply to learn the precise ways I prevent awareness through my identifications, and the patterns of and on the soul. It's good to be exactly where I am and to know that is where I am meant to be. If I know that deeply I can share that belief with clients too.

So you can see there are many connections between Gestalt and Ridhwan. Much of what we practice in Gestalt forms the building blocks of a spiritual practice. The challenge for me has been to know those practices deeply enough to live them in my life beyond the clinical context, and that is what I gain from Ridhwan, since with them I am on a well organised path of study, not dependent only on what happens to be figural for me. But nevertheless it was those Gestalt practices that set me off on this journey. In Gestalt, for example, we have a wonderful understanding of the value of middle mode functioning and creative indifference. We encourage curiosity and fearlessness in the face of reality. We work with paradoxical theory of change, the understanding that self-manipulation merely ties our inner knots tighter. All of that supports mindfulness – developing a capacity to be present without judgment. It is the route into what Perls called the fertile void, the place where everything gets disorganised and from where the new arrives, where we are ever dying and being reborn.

Gestaltists also address projections and introjects, and understand the stuff of which the personality is made, that 'verbal replica' of the self, which, unlike the personality, is more process than thing, more fluid and field dependent. We enquire phenomenolgically, aim to really 'meet' people, stay in the present, value authenticity, and the novel over the patterned. So Gestalt practice is naturally expansive for the practitioner. It wants to move and travel, it is guided by the same energies as life itself. It is based on awareness and curiosity about what life is like for us, ever changing, always in relation to another, whether real or imagined.

It is a wonderful basis for the spiritual journey. However, Gestalt does not claim to be a spiritual community. We have been, quite properly I think, focusing on establishing our place in the world. And we have been plugging away to the world with a field-based understanding of the self and its relationship to others, self as a boundary phenomenon. I have always found this perspective both rich and radical, compared to the only partially relational theoretical basis for a lot of psychotherapy. So even though we may work mostly with individuals, since one on one therapy is our culture's dominant mode, we are well suited to work with field energies, to support the health of groups. Gestalt in organisations has been well developed, drawing on pioneers like Ed Nevis and Carolyn Lukensmeyer as well as by people represented in this volume.

However, through my immersion in systemic work, my lenses have shifted further even than Gestalt's radical understanding of the self, where the features of the field — its structures, memories and somatic impact, can be raised to awareness through the rather remarkable amplification process of the constellation. I have found that working with just what a client and therapist can be aware of is limiting. It seems that we sometimes operate in ways that we simply don't have any way of making sense of. It has excited me to understand better the ways we are called into service by the systems we belong to, often playing a part that damages both others and ourselves, but always because of our deep system participation, our loyalties on behalf of the group we depend on. Gordon Wheeler touched on this with his phrase, 'the structures of ground'. Through constellations, these structures can be investigated — both the universal aspects that Bert Hellinger calls 'orders', and the particular way balance is achieved for specific individuals and their systems. I'll return to this in more detail.

But I want to reiterate that, both in the understanding of the field, and in the process of healing, what both the Diamond approach and systemic work offers is not so different from what we work with in Gestalt — it comes from finding the support to make clear, respectful contact with reality. Systemic work just illuminates aspects of reality we usually can't see. You can't remain identified with someone in your system when you see how much it does not help. And you can't remain victimised by someone if you see the hapless entanglements that have encircled everyone. And if you can see the essential love in yourself and others, even when the essence has been distorted, you can begin to stretch out into a larger space.

I notice I keep using the word 'see', which is not just an idle metaphor. There is a powerful effect arising from being able to take something in of huge complexity but all in one fell swoop, the way you can when you see a picture, take in a visual representation in a constellation, compared to our usual, linear ways of organising experience. I guess there are special reorganising properties of right brain activity. They reorganise and enlarge the hearts of all who are doing the seeing: client, group and therapist. So the work is also a training in clarity and compassion for the practitioner.

Gordon Wheeler did a fine job in alerting us to how biased our Gestalt understanding of contact could be, with one end of each polarity tending to be valued more highly than the other – differentiation over confluence, expression over retroflection and so on. He took us back to seeing that all is contact and that all styles have their valued place in the field. He reminded us not to import distorting values into the theory. I don't know if I would call them values, but since I started practicing as a constellator, I am looking again at some of these drives, not as importations but as facts of human life, needs that always come first, that really do shape what is possible in communal and individual life, and not just for humans. Hellinger summarises these key needs as bonding and attachment, exchange, and social organisation, and he shows what supports us in meeting these key needs, either in a blind and destructive way, or in a way that supports love and growth. Perhaps eventually we lose our earlier needs to belong, and especially if we follow a path where belonging is so thoroughly deconstructed. But we all need to understand the power of these needs, the ones that emerge from our biology and evolution. These orders that Hellinger has found stress the way that our membership of the group comes before our more fragile sense of ourselves as an individual. Perhaps they tell of 'before individualism', just as Wheeler emphasises 'beyond individualism'. But in any case they make interconnectedness absolutely central to our process.

Everyone talks about interconnectedness now, because we can all see how things spread — AIDS, terrorism, climate changes, coca cola — evidence everywhere of our participation in a unified field, and the dangers of not seeing it clearly enough, or knowing how to respond. Our survival depends on our participation in bigger systems, but on what basis?

The process of getting to know systems through constellations has revealed to me the power of something I hadn't seen as so central, that of conscience — our inner organ that takes care of belonging. I understand more clearly why it is so difficult to expand our sense of belonging. Expansion always triggers conscience, and if we carry on, we are bound to feel some guilt or loneliness. If we halt, we may continue to feel innocent. These ideas: of conscience, guilt and innocence, are now central to how I see the world.

One little parable I once heard Bert Hellinger tell relates to mountains and little villages at their base. Imagine being born into a village tucked into the valley of a mountain range. You are close to everyone in that somewhat isolated spot. You belong to a small but complete world. It is safe and also limited, despite the sweet innocence of belonging. At some point perhaps you decide to climb the mountain. As you ascend the slopes you get your first view of the village you grew up in. It is suddenly smaller than you had realised. With each step it also looks different, set against more of the surrounding terrain. You keep climbing, seeing other villages perhaps, with the scope of your vision ever widening. Once you have seen the size of the landscape and experienced the thin and bracing air up there, the village of home may now be too small to return to. You feel lonely, but grateful to be able to see.

I've always connected Bert's parable with the story of the expulsion from Eden. It's as if First Man and Woman also feel that loneliness and loss of innocence, as well as the immense gains. There is no turning back to Eden or the village, not to the easy confidence that it once offered. The Fall is painful, and we sometimes search for readmittance.

There is a natural loss of innocence in growing up and leaving home, both literally and metaphorically. Over and over, it costs us loneliness and guilt. It was something Bert Hellinger knew a lot about, since he left many 'villages' behind in his life — that of National Socialism, of the Catholic Church, of psychoanalysis too. They each demanded allegiance he could once give but as he grew, what he saw up there meant he couldn't go back. I was touched when I heard him speaking about thought worlds he was no longer part of, because he was always respectful. He wasn't fighting or wanting to change anyone else. He just grew out of where he was. I understand he has done this again - moved on from his own teachings — beyond the orders of love, beyond the movements of the soul, into something very simple and philosophical, about the spirit and living well. Growth doesn't have to mean devaluing what you leave behind. The past remains somehow present.

What I have valued in Hellinger's philosophy is this central concern with belonging, as children and adults, both personally and on behalf of our systems. It challenges me to see all moral points of view as the price of belonging to our various villages.

There just isn't a place of independence to speak about good and bad. Suicide bombers feel innocent doing things that would make us feel guilty, and who is to say which religious or cultural outlook has value over another? We can look at this question in terms of the impact of an outlook, but not of its intrinsic rightness. It also helps me understand why so many attitudes are state specific. At a personal level we have as many consciences operating as we have groups or systems to which we belong, and we are always moving like chameleons between one conscience group and the next, even from moment to moment. Because of this multiple system participation, guilt is just inevitable. It's a sign of growth, a risky but strengthening experience. You can't climb the mountain without feeling guilty, you can't join with another in love without leaving behind your old ways of doing things, and you can't leave a person or organisation or belief without guilt. Only fundamentalists are completely innocent and in their name many terrible acts are committed.

Hellinger, now eighty years old, has already had a profound impact worldwide. Probably most of you know something about him, but here is a short summary of the ingredients he brought to this still evolving approach. He prefers to describe himself as a philosopher rather than a psychotherapist, influenced more by Heidegger and Rilke and St John of the Cross than by his forbears in psychotherapy. The impact of his years with the Zulus in South Africa and his life as a priest are also evident. But constellations grew out of psychotherapeutic concerns and approaches that already existed. The theme of hidden loyalties and dynamics, intergenerational scripts, sculpting, balancing, giving and receiving, reaching out, phenomenology, respect and order — these all predate him. Just as Fritz Perls and Goodman created a new gestalt from many sources in Europe and America, Hellinger too has made an extraordinary synthesis. As

Rupert Sheldrake once noted, his work brings together biology, consciousness, social reality, personal development, religion, purpose, creativity and healing. It is having an extraordinary impact. The conferences inspired by his work have sometimes had two or three thousand participants, aided by new forms of communication and travel, not to mention new levels of world distress. It has already, within not much more than a decade, created a whole industry — of translators, teachers, videos, websites, journals and institutes. Hellinger travels and demonstrates worldwide. He continues to expose himself to public scrutiny. His work has travelled into a host of related fields, organisational, educational, prison, law and social.

My immersion in the work has taken me from doing therapy with individuals about issues of intimacy, to working at an organisational level, working with collective issues: in education, social action, government and business. That has been enriching for me after my quieter years of individual work when I needed to be at home for my children. It's enabled me to discover how differently things work when there are large numbers, and when multiple system participation is an issue.

I knew something about personal growth, but much less about larger systems and what helped them heal or develop. There is an understandable tendency to believe that what works for the individual within the small tribe of the family may also work for bigger issues. In fact those actions turn out not to help at all. This is particularly true with regard to some key experiences that fuel conflict, notably revenge, accusation, confession and even forgiveness. I'll say more about that in a minute. If we take on the power of systems, it seems they have a way of looking after their completeness, even in ways that are full of suffering. But completeness can be achieved in more than one way. A more enlightened kind of healing requires us to include in our hearts all those who belong in our systems so that they really are complete, to see everyone in their context, including all those who have perpetrated against others. We have to take history into account in a precise kind of way as part of our karma. History lives in the present, as we glimpse it in relation to the climate, the rise of terrorism and our colonial past, those events we hope are over but which clearly live on.

But to find this unity, we have to move way beyond ideas of good and evil, towards surrender to the greater forces at work. That's why, if you care about peace or growth you have to transcend conscience. Perhaps this sounds rather ordinary, but I think of it as a demanding spiritual path. It is certainly a humbling process.

At the end of his first workshop in Israel, Hellinger spoke, 'I have a vision in which we all return...and look deeply in each others eyes, weep together over what we have suffered at one another's hands, salute one another with dignity, and reconciled, leave the past behind.' Only a German who doesn't *only* belong to his German past can have that vision, and only with a people who can find a way of being more than their particular past.

Systemic work has also developed a very striking way of understanding the place of the dead in the lives of the living. Hellinger, at the same workshop, also said 'peace only comes when the dead lie together as equals.' I thought about this when we were asked to have two minutes of silence for the people who died in the London bombings. I happened to be running a group that day and we used the silence to grieve for the dead on all sides. It gave a completely different feel to the silence.

This vision isn't just a new age personal construct. It is supported by repeated empirical experiences of what happens in constellations when the bigger cast, including the dead, emerge and are given freedom to move. We glimpse into the many different parts that the dead play in the lives of the living, despite cultural variations.

As a therapist or consultant, not to mention as a human being, it is challenging to feel respect for war as well as peace. Hellinger has often said that war is the father of peace, of everything. I spent a while last year researching whether there had ever been a peaceful society on earth, even when the community was safe from outside pressures and economically stable. I discovered not one single group, not one system that hasn't needed to create an antagonism between 'them' and 'us'. Our current level of world weaponry makes this fact awesome, but not new. It is part of being human, part of the thrust for growth. And to the extent that we can agree to it, say 'yes' at a deep level, we can also find where peace and reconciliation is possible. I remember someone quoting the Dalai Lama after September 11, when he said, 'if you want peace, be peaceful.' It is because we are connected at such a profound level that this sentence makes sense, connecting us all back to a path of soul.

At a collective level revenge fuels some terrible atrocities, and it never does what is hoped for; it does not appease the dead. Of course revenge is understandable, because the alternative is so costly — to feel grief and express it un-reactively. Grief often needs more support than a therapist can provide alone. The best support comes from contact with the whole field, being able to see everyone more clearly, and from redirecting love and loyalty in ways that have a better effect. In a constellation, as in a person's heart, when the dead or the rejected are properly seen by the living they move into the background. They seem comforted most of all if they see we who come later making good use of our lives.

Revenge and retaliation do serve connection at a personal level because they help people share their guilt. They are part of a natural impulse to give and receive, even in the negative. But at the wider societal level when numbers are big, retaliating is endless and can't create what it seeks. As I understand it, it is grief that brings things to an end, or at least moves things on. (As I was writing about this the news covered the Japanese commemoration of the bomb dropped on Hiroshima sixty years ago. I was tremendously touched by their collective emphasis on the honouring of the dead. It reminded me of when Willy Brandt fell to his knees some years ago at the Jewish holocaust memorial in Poland. They are profound gestures, with small but good effect.)

But to take on this view would create a huge shift in our basic ways of understanding the world. It is not just politicians and freedom fighters that think differently. Along with most religions, Christianity stresses the goodness of taking on the burdens of another. It is seen as a high calling of atonement and sacrifice. Jesus spoke much about forgiveness. Yet by focusing on the *consequences* of these noble qualities, things don't look so hopeful. As Hellinger says 'what I forgive I pack in my rucksack.'

And then there is outrage, another energy fuelling political action in the world. Hellinger wrote, 'A third party who is outraged takes away something from those who have actually suffered. They feel they have the right to do evil things in response without feeling guilty.' Outrage is a feeling I used to admire in others, a noble energy, highly committed, morally clear. People I knew who had lots of it were deeply tied to their causes, even as they, paradoxically, got to seem rather similar to the people who outraged them. (Another of Bert's condensed teachings lies in the sentence, 'those whom you condemn, you imitate.') Accusation burdens the accuser. It is hard to find a position that doesn't keep people entangled. Hellinger had the courage to tell the group in Israel with whom he spent some days doing constellations, that he saw perpetrators continuing to be represented in their systems, but now by the Jews themselves, because they had so deeply excluded the Nazis. The most aggressive members of the family systems were the ones most identified with their aggressors, and who carried the aggression on, shifting the target but continuing the process. It helps make sense of how many Israelis view the Palestinians, uprooted people like themselves. Hellinger wrote, 'A perpetrator can only change if he is loved'. What a big idea. Perhaps more than that is also needed, but love is central. This is because, when someone kills, even in war, they join the system of their victims. Excluding them means they are represented by those who come later. That's not how we usually view perpetrators. If we genuinely want peace there is no avoiding this narrow and sometimes excruciating path of inclusion.

I have spent years getting used to this perspective as it is so demanding on my biases. In learning to constellate, I discovered that the only position that carried the respect of all the representatives was one where I was far enough back from the situation, whatever it was, to be on everyone's side. On the side of abusers, adulterers, murderers even — of all perpetrators. I have probably been given more than I have delivered by making this demand on myself, to see all as equal, all taken into service of some kind, all acting from some kind of loyalty and need to belong, to make sense of how people have been cast out, rejected or despised. Naturally, it's not a stance that I manage in all of my life, but the more I have it the more peace I feel. Peace with the Nazi culture's history and imperatives, even with al Quaida. Everyone still has to carry the consequences of what they have done, no matter how entangled or innocent they feel. But as a stance it changes the moral climate for exploring possibilities.

And when I engage in systemic work I am given strength to hold this peaceful position. Constellations naturally generate a special atmosphere of archetypal and collective experience. We get to look at real essentials: life, death, loss, sex, war, guilt, innocence, love, and bonding. That naturally invites an expanded outlook, where past, present and future co-exist, where love shines out of people's stories, and gratitude flows. The energy generated often makes it possible for people to take courageous and difficult steps, so that they can come into an easier relationship to what they have done or failed to do with their lives. A bigger outlook, one that doesn't feed off blame and resentment and criticism, can then replace the stale old stories. Often there is depth and lightness in the new pictures. Participants celebrate ordinary, everyday actions that give people weight, like having children or staying put, not only heroic and special moments. The work keeps us focused on strengths rather than injuries.

There are additional gifts for me as a therapist, to do with getting disciplined practice in not doing, in standing aside and letting the field of the constellation reveal itself and move in ways I could never think of on my own. That, repeatedly, teaches me trust. It gives me a friendly yet separate place to stand, and endless practice in agreeing to the world as it is, with good and bad completely tied together.

Everyone here has had a long journey in therapy or they wouldn't be here. I shan't go into any detail about my own, but I do want to say that Hellinger's systemic approach really did feel as if it was taking me somewhere new, touching issues that up until then I had barely been able to give a name to. I first went into therapy at the age of seventeen, trying whatever was available back in the sixties. It was haphazard. You can imagine my first experience in a Gestalt group was a revelation — of experiencing vibrant contact, taking risks, coming alive. But there wasn't much emphasis on my family history. Somehow the individual and group therapy experiences I had didn't touch much of the *me-in-my-bigger-context*. I had no way of seeing how entangled I was in quite serious family issues. I suffered from feelings that no amount of individual therapy had addressed. My actions often continued to be confused and my intimate relationships unsettled.

It was a revelation to look at these issues through a systemic lens. The lives and actions of all those who had gone before me in my family turned out to be critically influential. Through the constellations I did, I learned how to 'separate our fates with love'. That's not just a phrase: I am blessed these days, as never before, by being in loving contact with everyone in my family, both alive and dead. I have only been given a few constellations but each one has slowly filtered into my soul, impacting and settling me. I marvel at the power of those few interventions, each of less than an hour, compared to my long years of regular therapy. (It seems important at a political and economic level, to engage in making provision for something brief and relatively cheap.) Obviously, such challenging work benefits from preparation and follow up, but it does go straight to the point and it attends to what the individual focus can't — those hidden identifications, disorders of love, lack of facing the consequences of actions — those sorry sentences that as children we are called to utter by how we live — let me carry or share that, follow you, have this burden instead of you, put this right that you could not — even if I don't know who you are. Even if it will never bring relief, and even if it damages love.

As you know, Hellinger and his colleagues have demonstrated constellations in many war-affected countries, from working with the legacy of the last war in Germany, to Israel and Rwanda. I too have had some opportunities to work with these themes. I see both personal and organisational problems that have arisen out of a systemic entanglement with past events — carried by them even when they may have had little or no knowledge of it. And I am sometimes able to work with organisations that have been attempting to do good but have been inadvertently making matters worse.

I would like to describe an incident from my work last year. By chance perhaps, it relates to finding a good relationship with the Muslim community in America. Resolution arrived through becoming humbler and accepting the fate of others.

I was invited to consult to an American political activist in Maine who ran a support agency for refugees from the Sudan. He wanted help because the take-up was low for what his agency was offering, and lowest of all was the use made of it by the Muslim woman refugees whom he deemed the most in need. He wanted to know what he could do to increase their take up. I offered to set up a constellation.

Like many political activists he felt righteously angry about certain features of the landscape he focused on. He was incandescent that the US government was financially supporting the Sudanese civil war by its arms sales. He himself took sides in the war. He was indignant that the Sudanese men seemed to be stopping the women from coming to his centre and receiving help.

I asked him to set up representatives for himself, for the men and woman refugees, several people to represent the situation back in the Sudan, and someone to be the spirit of the American government. What unfolded shocked him. There was no one in the constellation that appeared to want to have anything to do with him, and the women least of all.

I won't go into describing all the stages of the constellation. It unfolded very slowly, and often I had no idea where the next impetus for movement might come. I just had to wait, and then something would open up somewhere in the constellation. I could not initiate without support from the representatives. However, eventually the representative of my client was able to start aligning himself differently. He bowed to the spirit of America that had given a home to fleeing people from all over the world, respecting its power and its outlook. He faced the war and all its victims in the Sudan, without taking a partisan position. And, hardest of all for him, his representative bowed to the particular cultural way of being in America that these refugees felt right about, with all its gender discrimination. As his representative enacted each humbling movement my client watched the constellation relax and unfold, melting tight positions on all sides. Spontaneously, the women stepped out from behind the men and smiled at him, as did the representative of the dead in the Sudan. The representative for the American foreign policy also reported feeling more generous and flexible.

This was not the outcome he expected at all, and it winded him for a while. There was a long silence, as there often is after a constellation. His friends and colleagues who were present felt equally affected — they began wondering if their ideological positions were part of the problem rather than the solution. But how could they possibly give them up? It was precisely those beliefs that defined their community.

Fortunately this brave man continued to explore these questions with his consultant who had been in the room too, reviewing the cost of his adherence to his particular positions and passions. I left it with them.

We are all part of history that carries big and complex legacies: our colonial and industrial past, slavery, communism, two world wars. The relevant history, the bigger truths, emerge in constellations. Then representatives can subject themselves to the natural forces in the situation that lead, however slowly, towards peace and reconciliation. They demonstrate the power of respect and inclusion. Simple words but very demanding feelings. But the representatives show us the way.

(Last year I also worked with a group of primary school teachers in Wiltshire as part of a research project run by the *nowhere* foundation on the value of the systemic approach in the classroom. We introduced the basic philosophy and gave them some experience of resolving issues using constellations, and they took the ideas back and developed them with their children, using support from us at the foundation. Here is a little quote from the final report of this project, also relating to a Muslim question.

> Child A, a Muslim girl aged 11, was struggling with aspects of socialising and learning in school. She had not been allowed to take part in the year six residential trip to Cornwall — the only child not allowed to go. In addition there were several parts of the curriculum not available to her on grounds of her religious beliefs. The teacher carried sadness and frustration that this child could not take a full part in the classroom activities.
> But when the teacher considered this child's conscience group she could see that her primary loyalty was to her family and culture and that the child could understand and accept the situation. The teacher was able to honour her cultural attachment and support her to uphold them.
> At the end of term performance, the child sang an unaccompanied song beautifully. Her father, who hardly

ever visits the school because of time pressures at work, had slipped into the hall to hear her. She saw him and turned to her teacher to ask if she could sing an extra song just for her father. Again unaccompanied, she sang a Turkish song exquisitely to her father. The whole row of parents were moved and touched by her powerful performance, which was a public declaration of her culture, language and loyalty.)

I have watched Bert Hellinger bring simplicity and wisdom to people who can't see their way forward, whether they are suffering from physical, psychological, spiritual or organisational symptoms. His approach has captured a generation, and his work keeps evolving. I would like to indicate some of the distinctive qualities of the approach, because I have found in them a 'bigger' framework — ordinary truths but with an affinity, as in Gestalt, to many spiritual paths. The approach actively emphasises respect, acknowledgement, gratitude, and agreement with fate — that which has happened and can't be changed, but which can be a source of strength if seen and honoured.

It sees love as a central motivating force. Perhaps all therapy deals with love, but here it is seen as the only leverage for change.

All therapy deals with the tension between the individual and the collective, between civilisation and its discontents. Systemic work emphasises our biological prioritising of the collective. The group comes before the individual.

Many spiritual paths see sex as problematic. Hellinger described it once as the highest spiritual act, since nothing more serves life nor establishes a bond.

All therapy helps people get to know and express their feelings and fantasies, but this work focuses more strongly on actions and their consequences.

Postmodernism stresses that what we see is as much a function of the way we have created our lenses as to do with anything 'out there' we could call 'reality', but this work rests on features of life, of Being even, that are far bigger than what we have the freedom to create and change. They are what Hellinger calls 'the orders of love', those universal forces that can bring joy and peace when we align ourselves to them. It took a while to engage with this perspective, brought up as I was in that thought-world where it seemed we were able to make things the way we wanted to see them. I understood about some orders like gravity, or even the law of gestalt, that universal tendency to move towards completion. It takes energy to oppose these orders that both enable and limit our freedom, and often someone else pays for what we deny. At their simplest, the orders of love show us that everyone in a system has an equal right to belong, and that love is served when those who come before give to those who come after. They sound simple but their ramifications are immense. It means that we can't sustain any solution that harms others within our system. And we can only deal with issues that are ours, not take on those that belong to those who came before us.

I always thought of health, in Gestalt terms, as to do with flow and energy and creativity. I now think of it also as to do with being in one's right place and at the right time. From that, all the rest flows and follows. It sounds rather conservative. But somehow it frames everything properly.

From having now done thousands of constellations I have a changed view about what it means to be an individual, and where memory and knowledge must be stored — certainly not in the individual brain. How is it that my experience can surface in the body of another representative? And change as something else in the field shifts? How do we know what we don't know that we know? We truly are connected by countless invisible threads, and belong together. Scientific knowledge may help us answer this question eventually but for now it remains mysterious.

And it isn't just people that are connected — the fact is that you can constellate anything and everything. You can include the component aspects of a homeopathic remedy, the stock exchange, the spirit of a nation, dogs and horses, or the supply chain of a global corporation. If your need for knowledge and insight is real, representatives can embody what is relevant. It seems that whatever exists in space or time can take form.

Doing systemic work I also have a different way of experimenting if I compare it to how I have worked as a Gestalt therapist. Using representatives, and guided by their responses, it feels more like the setting up of a kind of field conversation, between the many voices of the wider system. The therapist can offer hypotheses, establish more reality or use the orders, but the forces of the field carry an imperative. Dialogue that heals is with the key people from the system, not with the therapist alone. It is a different style of connecting, one that needs more distance from my clients so that I can speak freely with them about what I see. It has made me wary about doing long-term therapy, where these practices are almost impossible to maintain. Over time, we all lose our distance, we get drawn into the system, and we learn what we must not say. A more detached stance could feel hard for clients, but it is countered by the deep intimacy that the constellations generate, the heart opening energies that emerge from seeing people in a bigger context.

I am left with a very big question, which is, what supports the movement — any movement — that would help us identify with a larger group, the one that also includes our enemy? Can anything make the idea of humanity, or the world, carry the sort of sacrificial energy as does a family or a religion? What would give us a connection with this kind of vertical movement of identification, one that included the other? Are there experiences and rituals that would make a difference? Rupert Sheldrake thinks of this shift more in terms of spirit than soul, because soul takes us back to past patterns whereas spirit, our innate creativity, takes us beyond and into something larger. If soul brings us order and form, then spirit goes into the realm of the unpredictable, the new, and the mysterious. It is not so easy any more for us humans to be following old patterns in the modern world. Many old patterns have been disrupted, huge forces of change are at work, and so the creative role of spirit may be all the more pressing. Perhaps we will find new levels of creativity in the great world emergencies of life today. Hellinger says, 'don't look for completion. Be happy if things are unfinished. Everything creative never comes to an end. There is never a final truth or achievement. It's always new and changing'.

I believe that the strengths we need come from such openness of soul and spirit. Marianne was open in this way. She never stuck to the usual boundaries. And as I hold these different perspectives within me, I wonder whether any boundaries have more than a specific and temporary reality. The self, the other, the field — they are indivisible. But at any moment we shine a light on only parts. I look forward to hearing how the discussants here will respond and add to this unfinished journey between Gestalt, the systemic and the spiritual that I have begun.

10

A Part of the Whole, A Part to Play

Malcolm Parlett

This chapter is based on a lecture given in July 2007 at the annual conference of the Gestalt Psychotherapy and Training Institute (GPTI) held near Bristol, England. The lecture has been edited and expanded, not least to include points from two other lectures, one for the European Association of Gestalt Therapy conference in Prague in the Czech Republic in 2004; the other for the Esalen conference on the Future of Gestalt Therapy in Big Sur, California, in 2005. Both of these other lectures dealt with similar issues to those I address here.

The theme of the 2007 GPTI conference was "The Social, Political, and Ecological Field: Facing the Future." The address opened the conference and deliberately I chose a wide angle lens, taking in a large and diverse territory, rather than exploring one area in close-up. This chapter follows the same structure and purpose, and is written in the same "voice" as in the lecture. I am presenting a series of reflections about living in a stressed, uncertain world, living on the edge of possibly calamitous planetary change, with pervasive political problems existing globally, and embracing us all and affecting us all — albeit most of the time as part of the ground of our lived experience rather than what is immediately figural. Specialists in the Gestalt approach, while living with the seriousness of the world situation, are also embracing a fundamentally optimistic perspective, at least regarding the potential for human learning, change, and transformation. This contrast is always in the background, as we ask the questions of ourselves: "What can I do? What is my (our) part of the whole, the part that I (we) play? And what can the Gestalt approach itself achieve, contribute, even pioneer?"

I begin with exploring our personal connection to the present global situation and its related crises and challenges. I then discuss how Gestalt therapy was influenced by its founders' life experiences and how political thinking underpins Gestalt therapy practice itself. I suggest that Gestalt needs to look at its own political position within psychotherapy, and can embrace some routine research without danger. I voice concern about whether Gestalt therapy and its associated practices can have the impact it should have, if it remains outside major emerging developments, for instance with mindfulness. Staying with the readiness of the Gestalt community to engage more in the world, I raise the issue of how hidden divisions between us in our community may replicate wider social or cultural tensions. I speak of the sensitivity needed, both for minority positions and also the majority as it copes with "bewilderment" as described by McConville and Jacobs in articles cited. I also suggest that the contrast, perhaps conflict, between "spiritual" and "secular/ therapeutic" needs to be a matter for ongoing dialogue within the Gestalt community, with the middle ground needing to be explored. I end by advocating that all Gestaltists have the potential to become "citizen practitioners," drawing on known and tried principles of Gestalt methods.

Welcome, fellow readers, specialists and enthusiasts for the Gestalt approach.

Welcome also to all of you, a group of people, like me, whose material affluence and level of physical comfort is probably greater than that of the vast majority of people in the present world, and certainly greater than almost all people who have ever lived since the beginning of civilisation.

Welcome, fortunate readers who, like me, are not living in a war zone — at least in this place and at the present time, (and at the time of writing) — and thus are not living with daily threats of being bombed, shelled, or shot at, blown to pieces or subjected to extreme physical danger through armed conflict going on around us.

Welcome, readers who are members of various minorities and various majorities, ethnic, religious, sexual, political, and social, remembering that at one moment we can be amongst a majority grouping and the next moment find ourselves in a group that is a minority.

Welcome, fellow users of energy coming to terms with how much we are in excess of what our global ration should be. Welcome, fellow consumers, like me, largely oblivious of the circumstances in which the produce we consume has been created.

Welcome, fellow members of the dominant species of animal on this planet, often forgetful of our species being responsible for the extinction of thousands of other species of animal and for destruction of habitats.

If I read to you a list of some of the matters that are spoken of in our social, political and ecological fields, you will have some bodily felt reactions. I would like you to notice your bodily changes as I list some of the issues that preoccupy many of us today:

Climate change and its consequences, the accelerating rates of melting ice in the two polar regions; the melting of the permafrost in sub-arctic regions that leads to the release of methane into the atmosphere (with methane itself a potent greenhouse gas); and the indications of these changes happening more quickly than earlier predicted.

The recognition of higher and higher levels of toxicity in our atmosphere, soil, and water.

The demands of people in rich countries for every kind of food and produce, including flowers, all round the year, with consequent needs for refrigeration, and huge numbers of aircraft and container ships taking all this round the world.

Nuclear rearmament and proliferation, militarism and the obscene levels of military budgets, arms manufacturing and virtually uncontrolled distribution of guns.

The use of child soldiers, the deaths as well as the abuse of civilians in war zones across the Middle East and Africa; the unknown number of women who have been raped in war; the tens of thousands of wounded, disabled, and traumatised ex-combatants that result from armed conflict; and the millions of families affected by all of the above.

The vast growth in city life, the breakdown of social and family supports, the extent of loneliness, with depression as the fourth biggest health problem of the world.

International financial transactions that are so rapid, complex, huge, and interconnected, that the regulatory authorities claim that no longer are the checks and balances, in place for the last 50 years, anywhere near sufficient to maintain financial stability.

The rise of antibiotic resistant pathogens; the fact that more people are being infected every year by the HIV virus than are being treated for its effects.

I could go on. Of course, you are bombarded with this kind of information if you read newspapers or watch television or are at all attuned to the social, political and ecological questions that face us in the contemporary world.

I will stop for a moment or two. What do you experience in your body? Take a few moments simply to register what happens for you, at an embodied level. Notice any reluctance to do this...

As we know, often people feel so disheartened they turn away, they feel depressed, or they feel powerless. The sheer scale of the global problems, once confronted, can be overwhelming. We have all perhaps gotten used to having global issues and problems in our awareness, even if we shove them to the back of our minds in order to live with the immediate concerns of "everyday life." Yet these issues remain in the background and do not go away.

Not all is gloom and doom. There are other stories to be told, of course, that offset the huge hopelessness that can be engendered. Alternative narratives point out how scientific advances are accelerating incredibly; knowledge is ever more widely available; we are still only at the beginning of the computer age. Moreover, human beings are highly adaptable and resilient — witness what happens after great disasters, like tsunamis or earthquakes, have wiped out whole communities; people put their lives back together, they rebuild, they adapt, they live with the crisis, they may even become more inventive and responsible — when people have to adapt to survive, they can do so.

Another narrative is along the lines that we have huge untapped brain capacity, and unlimited potential for learning, and that some huge shift in global consciousness is not impossible, especially given the communications revolution and the ever-widening access to media of many varieties.

In short, some suggest, as did Jeffrey Sachs (2007), who this year delivered the BBC sponsored Reith Lectures that, even now, ways can be found through what is obviously an acutely critical period in the history of our species and of our planet. He insisted that we should not give up hope and that the massive changes necessary were possible to make, if the political elites would follow scientific advice, as they had sometimes done in the past (for instance about CFCs and the hole in the ozone layer, which has been repairing itself since international action was taken). Sachs — speaking as an eminent economist with a track record of turning around seemingly hopeless economic situations of devastated countries — articulated a positive and practical outlook that counters other more doom-laden scenarios.

Whatever our personal reactions to massive global events, we do all have some, even if these are for most of us mixed with desensitizing or denial, or some other protective or magical thinking against the fear or anxiety that arises. Having feelings and thoughts about enormous global issues that exist is obviously not confined to any particular group, such as psychotherapists. Of course, as Gestalt therapists we may approach them slightly differently. For instance, as holists we may be particularly drawn to patterns that connect, more at home with grasping interdependency and multiple causes than maybe others whose traditional focus is on viewing problems in isolation. We may instinctively grasp and picture, for instance, how global warming and shifts towards growing water-intensive crops such as sugar beet, lead to dramatic declines in the water tables, with the shortage of water having political fallout as well as economic and health consequences which, in turn, increase the likelihood of disputes with neighbouring states and may even lead to armed conflict. Making interconnections may be more natural for us to recognise than those viscerally opposed to holism, but don't let us kid ourselves — we're not fundamentally different from others who are awake and attending to what's happening around us, politically, socially, culturally, and ecologically.

My point is that as Gestaltists or psychotherapists we are not inoculated against fear and despair; nor are we likely to be any more super-consistent in, say, energy-saving practices. Also, if we have children and grandchildren, or personal connections with young people, we are likely to be just as concerned as any other adult person if we imagine their future in 20, 30, 40 years' time. We are Gestaltists and yet are also world citizens, Earth dwellers, polluters and consumers, concerned members of the public, generators of hopes and fears and confusions, just like everyone else. We may talk about others as "them"'but of course we ARE them.

At this point I would like to pause and give you a chance to explore what your reactions have been to what I have said, notably your bodily felt reactions as I read through the list of some global problems. I also invite you to look into something else. Given the huge range of themes and issues that we can be concerned about, which are the particular ones that affect you most in the world, as you encounter them or come across references to them in books and newspapers, or see them discussed on television? What are the things that "get" to you? That you cry over? Or that you want to turn the television off in order to avoid looking at, because you find it all so painful? Or want to have another gin and tonic to try and forget about? Or, if you are very indifferent towards a particular issue, or have absolutely no interest in it whatsoever, what specifically do you find yourself feeling indifferent towards? Do not go about this inquiry in a judgmental way but simply as part of becoming more aware of your pattern of interests. In the whole panoply of political, social, and ecological issues that there are, which are the ones that affect you most and least? [In my original lecture I suggested at this point that you find a partner, take five minutes, and reflect together on the above. You may want to stop and do that now, as you read.]

It is a fair guess that at this point we represent a wide range of concerns and kinds of feeling reaction. We have very individual reactions. We engage in different ways. Our roots in existential thinking are relevant here. As therapists, we become conscious of how each human person is born into or grows up in a particular family milieu, however fragmented, with its history, connections, narratives, its handed-down introjects, its modes of communication, and its intergenerational unfinished business. In the same way we are also born and grow up in a wider world, of locality and community, of nation state and language, and our portion of the global scene. We are here, we are in it, THIS is our world. We face the reality we encounter. Martin Heidegger was brilliant in his exposition of how we encounter the world and become part of it. He speaks of our "thrownness" and of our "being-in-the-world." "Being in" is unavoidable and implies more than just "being," (in Gestalt terms we are always in and part of a situation or field). Our "being in" is specific to us individually. Heidegger gives some examples of different ways of "being-in" that are applicable to our very participation in life, to how we exist, to our interest or concern: "having to do with something, producing something, attending to something and looking after it, making use of something, giving something up and letting it go, undertaking, accomplishing, evincing, interrogating, considering, discussing, determining. All these ways of being have concern as their kind of being." (Heidegger, 1967)

What I take from this, and I understand very little of Heidegger, is that each of us is bound to be affected in different ways by the trends and problems that we were talking about earlier, and to be concerned with them in distinctive, individual ways. We will differ in how we engage or disengage with them, approach or withdraw from them, follow them up or live with not doing so.

I had an interesting experience recently. I met an old friend – a retired priest – whom I hadn't seen for a good many years. Soon we were doing that kind of life review that you do when you haven't met an old friend for a long time – and I asked him: "What are you doing these days?" And he said that he was working a lot with supporting asylum seekers and campaigns to prevent refugees from Zimbabwe from being sent back there from Britain, and suddenly something clicked for me. I vaguely remembered that he'd come from another country early in his life. So I asked him about this. And he told me the story about how as a child he lived with his family in Switzerland and in 1940, when France was invaded, Switzerland basically became an island surrounded by hostile powers. And in Switzerland at that time they didn't believe that Hitler would honour their neutrality. And his parents made the decision that they would leave. And they left quite suddenly and came to Britain where they then stayed. And I said: "Oh that's interesting, I wonder whether in some sense your present interests connect to this life experience?" And he replied, "Yes, maybe." But clearly he had not made a strong connection between his present concern and his history.

Now I don't know how many of you, as you were reflecting about the things that affected you, were making similar kinds of connection between the topics that concerned you most and your own life story, particularly your early life. But one of the things that I'm proposing that we think about tonight is the relationship between the global and the deeply personal. As Gestaltists, approaching these global issues, one of the things we can do is to relate them to the wider narrative of our lives, the figure to the ground of our previous life experience. This is something that, as Gestalt therapists, we can bring to our own and others' experiences of great contemporary issues.

So I would like you just to return — for a few minutes with your partner [if you have found one for this exercise — or with your journal] — just to see whether, like the priest, you can make the connections that he hadn't appeared to make. Remember that we're talking about either turning towards a particular subject or problem or turning away from it, identifying with it or alienating it, in our terms. So I'll give you about 5 minutes. Just run a check.

Did you find some kind of connection between the things that you identified in the first round and your second? Whatever the particular connection, our personal "concern," there is likely to be a deep personal story involved, so that in a sense our construction of the state of the world is also part of our life narrative, it's linked into our history, and past experiences.

Sometimes psychotherapists, particularly from more interpretive traditions, appear to cast some doubt on the legitimacy of a strong impulse to do something, even if it is palpably beneficial, if they recognise, or the person recognises, that it's connected to a personal issue. Those following reductionism seek to "explain" a phenomenon in terms of its "origins." There is nothing wrong with this except that explaining an impulse can easily lead to devaluing it, regarding the action that flows from it as somehow suspect or irrational, as "less than..." even as something to be ashamed about. There are obvious examples where an impulse is destructive and selfdestructive, and investigation and even preventing the action may be called for. But many impulses are constructive or creative, and even "suspect" or destructive ones can be put to good use — someone fascinated by dead bodies may become a firstrate pathologist, for instance.

As a present-centred holist rather than a reductionist, I regard impulses, longings, and strong reactions as intrinsic parts of our overall response to world events and life issues. Instead of being detached and sceptical about them, we need to explore, honour their existence, maybe even cultivate them. As energizers they may fuel individual initiatives. Deep impulses to help, right the world, or do good for others can be precious gifts. Impulses and preferences provide us with the embodied knowing of where our attention needs to go, what is our experienced truth, what is calling us, what will satisfy us. They are not the whole, but part of the whole, and belong in our life-experience. They need investigating and honouring for part of "what is."

Applying Gestalt Knowledge

Well, this is one way of looking at us in the room today, as we face the world scene and are affected in unique ways. We are global participants in the drama that is unfolding. We are part of the whole and we have a part to play. For most of the time, as Gestalt practitioners, whether as therapists, counsellors, consultants, or coaches, we are dealing with the immediate issues of people's lives. At the same time, we can see that the way that people live is massively influenced by the economic, social, technological, and cultural patterns that exist in our society and in our time. Elsewhere (Parlett, 2000), I have argued that we need to consider so-called mental health problems in the greater context of the pressures and pulls, rewards and disincentives, inequalities and opportunities of the world as we know it. As many have now pointed out, our field orientation does not allow us to stay with an intrapsychic view of human beings and their experience.

So we might well, as Gestalt thinkers and practitioners, pay more attention to the background pathologies and processes which impact on the society and representations of "reality" that circulate and are reflected in mass media, especially by that potent modulator of experience in many people's lives — television. We may be able to bring greater focus, some heightened awareness, into a more public arena than we usually do. This was the task that Paul Goodman undertook. He was not interested in grandiose, centralised social movements but in direct interventions on the small or medium scale, getting people to think in new ways about the connections between their own experience — like loss of creative juice — and the social and political structures, such as hierarchical organisations, that help bring about a human loss of this kind. Among contemporary Gestaltists, Philip Lichtenberg (2006) is in the same tradition.

So we could, for instance, begin to think and write and talk more publicly about how so much of people's attitude to the world comes from "taking in uncritically" what is presented in simplified news reports, or by newspaper columnists, or by spin doctors, evangelists, the scientific establishment, propagandists of many persuasions, and above all by advertisers. Introjection is alive and well and living amongst us, big-time! There is a view that politically our society is becoming infantalised – that critical discussion is in decline, investigative reporting is less searching, dumbing down has become taken for granted as a commercial necessity, direct participation is regarded as unimportant (more and more people do not bother to vote), and policies are communicated as sound-bites.

We ourselves could take a more active stance in publicly speaking about the process of introjecting, of the avoidance of the chewing over of complexity, so either people swallow whole, or alternatively reject everything, becoming so sceptical and cynical that they turn their back and become altogether alienated.

And just as we have something to say, even perhaps to teach, about the "taking in" process at multiple levels of our society, so do we have things to contribute to the understandings of stereotyping, disowning aspects of experience, and the way that people find the devil is over there in other people rather than in themselves. Arguably, there is a growing public understanding of the processes of projection, for instance around prejudice against minorities. But it is only a beginning. The issues of polarisation and ethnic and religious identification and alienation are so prominent in the contemporary world that we need to be more assertive in talking about what we know — that they are universal human processes, that they can be pathological, and that through awareness training can be unlearned. (I shall come back to some majority-minority issues later in my talk.)

The greater point I want to make here is that our familiar dimensions of contact-modulating (some say interrupting) are applicable and recognisable within the contexts of general social experiencing. Projection — in the form of exporting problems of which we are ourselves part — is ever-present, as in statements such as: "It was so crowded in the — one couldn't move for people!" or "The traffic was terrible, that's why I am late driving here." But so are all the familiar contact disturbances — familiar, at least, to those with a Gestalt education. Thus, we can see evidence of mass desensitisation — as for instance in "compassion fatigue" — as well as its opposite, hypersensitivity and almost allergic reactions (for instance to noises coming through walls in semi-detached houses). Arguably, many of the non-stop activities and distractions of the affluent (like addictions to shopping, gadgets, and "entertainment") are also deflections — away from confronting solitude, silence, and perhaps despair.

This is a huge area, but surely one that deserves focused attention. Lichtenberg's (Lichtenberg et. al., 1997) exploration of how to confront prejudiced people in family or other intimate contexts is a model of what can be done, taking Gestalt sensibilities and insights and applying them to widespread social, public, collective phenomena and illuminating them, sparking new awareness and having a long-term educative function.

Gestalt Therapy Itself

Gestalt emphasizes thata we need, as part of considering our relationship to the greater world and planet, to consider ourselves. Several different themes arise for me, and I would like to think aloud about our approach today in the company of fellow specialists.

Bearing in mind the relationship between global and personal issues, we can see how Gestalt therapy itself was deeply affected by the experiences of our founders, particularly Laura and Fritz Perls. From the end of the First World War (in which, of course, Fritz was at the front and having a troubled and traumatic time...) through until 1933, was a momentous time for the young couple. This 19 year period coincided with a time of extraordinary historical events in Germany. By the time they fled from the Nazis and went to Holland in 1933, leaving behind virtually everything they possessed, they had experienced nearly two decades of political turbulence and passionate involvements in political, social, and cultural activity. It was a time of increasing anti-Semitism, hyper-inflation for a period, and ongoing political instability. The young Perlses must have seen at close hand violence in the streets, mobs attacking people, shop fronts smashed, and many insults delivered to Jewish people, including themselves. Sitting on the fence in cool detachment was not a serious option. They were implicated in so many ways in the turbulent changes, including by choosing to take an active part in socialist politics. It must have been an extraordinary and formative time — take a moment to imagine it... And the turbulence did not end with their escaping from the Nazis, possibly only a day or two before they would have been rounded up. They became refugees in Amsterdam, and then went to South Africa, and with the Nationalist Party about to gain power, with its intention of introducing apartheid, they left for America. So they knew at first hand what it meant to be uprooted from their homes, to be confused (as one is at first on moving countries), to be outsiders, to have been part of a despised minority, to have lost many supports and to survive on their own.

I think that some of the important values that came to be embedded in Gestalt therapy — even what you might call its ideology — reflect some of this history. For instance, the early emphases on self-reliance, self-support, self-responsibility, and self-help make sense given what they endured. Dependence on others must have seemed at best precarious and at worst dangerous in the extreme. They also must have derived from the years of growing Nazi power a visceral aversion to mass confluence, to dehumanisation, to the submergence of the individual, and the loss of capacity for independent thought.

Because that 19 year formative period also coincided with a time of avant garde artistic and cultural experimentation — it is not surprising that they shared disrespect for bourgeois values and trivial social niceties, and questioned conservative institutions and formal religions. They were for exploring and experimenting, pushing at boundaries rather than playing it safe, and always questioning the status quo. They would have learned to be contemptuous towards the kind of lies told by those in power, and to mistrust hierarchies, systems, and values that seemed to restrict individual freedom and sexual expression. They would have been a natural constituency for the writings and teachings of existentialists, libertarians, and those advocating freeing of the body from repressive social forces. Like many of the psychoanalysts and philosophers they were studying or training with, they would have come to value the ideals of living a full life, overcoming petty constraints and fearfulness, and recognising here and now urgency.

I suggest the deep foundations of Gestalt were laid in their circumstances and experience of that time and milieu. Attitudes to the world they were immersed in became shared attitudes of the Gestalt community. They were embodied and communicated. And implicit were a wholesale critique of major societal values and a bias favouring political, social, and personal innovation. Given their values and priorities, it is hardly a surprise that they saw therapy practice as itself a political activity. This was enunciated in the often quoted statement of Laura Perls (and with this, at least, I imagine Fritz agreed) when she said:

> I think the work that I am doing is political work. If you work with people to get them to the point where they can think on their own and sort themselves out from the majority confluences, it's political work and it radiates even if we can work only with a very limited number of people. (L.Perls, 1992, p.17)

At this point I want to talk about the experiment that you have already become part of when you arrived at the conference. You may not have thought of yourself as having a political function when you pursue Gestalt therapy, perhaps alone in your consulting room with a client or a couple. At any rate it may seem a very small-scale political field. But suppose we scale it up, and think of our collective impact, does this make a difference? Well, let's find out.

Ahead of this lecture the attenders were given a piece of paper, inviting them to think about how many people they have had contact with, professionally speaking, over the course of the last twelve months. They were invited to make the best estimate they could of the number of people whom they have given therapy to, or taught, or supervised, or worked with in some capacity as a Gestalt practitioner, in the course of the last twelve months. Having collected their rough and ready estimates, I was then in a position to announce the result. I received estimates of the number from 64 participants. Adding the numbers together, these 64 practitioners saw in total 7644 clients, trainees, supervisees, etc. (pause) I feel very moved by this thought — that 64 of us have impacted over seven and a half thousand people... to a greater or lesser extent. And, if that group of people has been in some way affected by what has happened in relation to us and our efforts, then also think of all the people they know, work with, live with, socialise with...who may also have been influenced indirectly.

Evidence for Gestalt Therapy's Effectiveness

If we talk about Gestalt therapists having influence in the world, and of Gestalt making an impact, we have to accept the fact that we don't live in a society which is greatly supportive of us as Gestalt specialists. In the psychotherapy world we have to fight for our corner, alongside all the other approaches which are making equally strong claims for their effectiveness and superiority. A lot of them make a better job of displaying their strengths than we do as a community. So I think that the intention today to look at one particular quantitative procedure to compare the "effectiveness" of Gestalt therapy with other forms of psychotherapy, IS worth following. The questionnaire research will produce comparative data that will either strengthen our approach in the eyes of the world, or of it appears that according to this research that we are not effective, well, we shall have some important questions to ask ourselves.

Of course, I am very conscious of the problems that this kind of exercise can cause us philosophically. As Gestaltists we may have a visceral dislike of quantitative data that subsumes singular and diverse situation-person events into some composite mass in which individuality is submerged, at least for statistical purposes. One can ask: "How can numbers and the dubious quantification of reported experiences *ever* be acceptable to us who value the idiosyncratic and changing nature of the field and the self?" In the 1970s I was someone who was developing alternative kinds of evaluation that did not rely on numerical questionnaire data, but on qualitative observational evidence and interviews. I argued then that the "numbers game" was inherently flawed (Parlett and Hamilton, 1972). Yet here I am today advocating that we collectively engage in these evaluation procedures. My reasons for a shift in position are pragmatic and political. Whatever we might think as Gestaltists of the methodology, there's no question, politically speaking, in today's competitive context, with Government regulation of therapy around the corner, that we acknowledge the "what is" of our present political field. Gestaltists in the past have sometimes taken a fundamentalist or "pure" stance, ignoring simple things that they could do to enhance their position in the world, and they usually suffer. A protest sometimes achieves nothing, and can appear quixotic, further diminishing the possibility of a cause being taken seriously. This is one of those occasions when we need to adjust creatively to the times, to the political climate, and to the fact that we stand to lose out significantly if we do not take part. We need to use whatever means we can to demonstrate our efficacy and thus to strengthen our position as a specialist integrative psychotherapy.

Insulated Thinking

I would like to suggest, in fact, that there is another, bigger reason why we as a community have made less collective impact than we might have done. I think we have largely lost touch with a view of what espousing a specialised integrative psychotherapy entails.

In the introduction to Perls Hefferline and Goodman (1951) the authors write:

> We believe that by assimilating whatever valuable substance the psychological sciences of our time have to offer we are now in a position to put forward the basis for a consistent and practical psychotherapy. (p.XX).

Notice the wording: "...assimilating whatever valuable substance the psychological sciences of our time have to offer." It is an active process of assimilating. We are integrative as well as specialised in that there is a synthesising and integrating task for us to do.

My sense is that in large measure the Gestalt community as a whole has insulated itself from many of the psychological developments that have occurred. In part this may be because we already have a very rich synthesis to hand: for most of us Gestalt is already a satisfying mix of different strands of practice and concept, theory and method, which works, and it also satisfies us. Why shop around when we already have a nourishing feast at hand?

The point, of course, is that if we do not carry on with the ongoing task of further integrating what is "valuable substance (in) the psychological sciences" we shall find ourselves backward, down a defunct and dried up tributary while the river of new thinking is nearly in flood and flowing past us.

I suggest, therefore, that as synthesisers and integrators, we need to go back to the position of the founders who were rabid stealers of other people's ideas. In the Gestalt community we often complain about others stealing "our" Gestalt ideas, but our founders were always doing that themselves from others, and we need to do it again.

Think about it. If Gestalt in its developed form, as it is thought about and practised now, were being put together as a synthesised approach for the first time in 2007 rather than in 1950, it would be combining elements from a whole variety of contemporary approaches. Let me list some: relational psychoanalysis, intersubjectivity theory, mindfulness-based cognitive therapy (MBCT), complexity theory, acceptance and commitment therapy (ACT), art therapy, psychodrama, focusing, dance and movement therapy, existential psychotherapy, core process therapy, and plenty of other fields, including work with children and family systems. So if Gestalt therapy was not yet an established integration, and we were starting now, fresh with a blank sheet, we would be looking around at all of these things and finding numerous ideas and discoveries, language and techniques, that we would want to incorporate in our new synthesis.

Of course, Gestalt is an already established integration and has had a major impact. Recognising similarities and overlaps with all these other approaches listed is in part because they have taken pieces of our integration and built on them. But they have built on them — that's the point. We may have been centrally interested in the present moment long before Daniel Stern got interested. But it is Daniel Stern who has taken the idea and written a book about the present moment (Stern 2003).

Recently I have been looking into some of the literature around mindfulness research and what I find is extraordinary; there is an enormous body of work that I did not know about, much of which is at the very forefront of brain research. Here is one area where for certain I need to learn more and maybe you do too. Mindfulness researchers, working with meditation, shifts in consciousness, and brain imaging techniques, are advancing at great speed into "our" area regarding awareness and awareness training, and going further. The research shifts us onto a new plane of sophistication (see, for instance, Siegel 2007), investigating meditation practices and linking them to brain mechanisms; describing phenomena in ways that bring fresh language and ways of looking, such as "mindfulness...as a form of intrapersonal attunement" (p.17) with its "capacity to disentangle oneself from the chatter of the mind, to discern that these are 'just activities of the mind'" (p.19). I particularly liked the attention to three new senses, after the five we know about, each of which can be developed further: the sixth being our bodily sense; the seventh being "mindsight" which refers to "metacognitive processes that enable both awareness of awareness and the focus of attention on the nature of the mind itself," and the eighth being a "relational sense" in use "when we attune with another person" and become aware of a "resonant state that is created within the relating" (pp122-123).

I maintain that if the Gestalt community ignores the reality of such developments, then we shall impoverish our discipline and reduce ourselves to being an isolated tribe far from the mainstream, insulated from the wider changes that others are responding to.

I would like you to imagine a picture. The existing area of Gestalt therapy is represented by a smallish circle. Surrounding it are all the adjacent fields of inquiry and practice, many of which overlap ours. And what I'm suggesting is that instead of Little Gestalt we need Big Gestalt – that is, that we need to extend our boundary outwards to incorporate more of these "other" areas of work. We need to steal more, in other words, to claim more for ourselves as a specialised integrative therapy, to be bolder in continuing the active work of integrating and synthesising that our founders began. This is not about losing or watering down what we already have – in fact it is the opposite. Simply by redefining the boundaries of our approach, extending them outwards into these (at present) "other" areas, we transform our approach into something more expansive, complex, inclusive, and up-to-date. Why not? Personally, I do not mind "claiming" pioneers like Stern and Siegel as Gestaltists, at least honorary ones. Margherita Spagnuolo Lobb has almost done that anyway in the case of Daniel Stern, and the collaboration benefits both parties. It requires a significant change in mindset, for sure, away from being exclusive to being much more inclusive; but surely we ourselves define the limits and parameters of the approach, the entry criteria and can set them wider than they have been if we choose to do so.

While my complaint is that we have been too exclusive and inward-looking, in another respect there has been a vast improvement. In recent years, there has been fantastic growth in communication between Gestalt institutes and between various schools or sub-schools in different countries. We really do find ourselves part of a great international community, with email networks and, increasingly, discussions and contact between people with divergent views and from differing Gestalt lineages. Gone are the times when every institute seemed to be running down the others, and snobbish and supercilious "my Gestalt is better than yours" type attitudes prevailed. Given our history, what has happened in recent years seems wholly good, something of a miracle even. I am excited by the range of international and local collaborations and convergences.

Old Language, New Language

Continuing to reflect on the Gestalt approach itself, I want to talk about how we communicate our perspective to others. Part of being a Gestalt specialist involves being able to talk and understand its specialised language. Sometimes trainees refer to "Gestalt-speak," a term that makes me wince. In mocking us a little, I think they are pointing to our use of jargon that those who have been around for longer barely notice, and our inability sometimes to speak our truths in language that others use. I am deeply divided here, in that I speak this specialist language and love it; it can help me to converse with others economically. I am comfortable with it, teach it, use it, yet I am also deeply suspicious of it.

First, I do not believe that everyone uses the terms to mean the same thing: try asking Gestaltists to define "contact boundary," say, or even "gestalt" and you will find immense variation. Frank Staemmler bravely tackled the definition of "field" as used by Gestalt writers and he described the journey he went on as "an exhausting tour de force through a thicket of theories and terminologies" (2006, p.76). The ways we label and argue about our theory and practice depend on the specialised terminology in use. Is this terminology, which holds together the experiences and ideas that characterise our approach, still fit for purpose? Some of it is — I think the term "field" may be, in part because of Frank's article — but I think some of our jargon may have rigidified. In this respect, we should be grateful to Lynne Jacobs for disputing the value of "projection" (Jacobs 2000) as a phenomenon and label, even if we do not agree with her. Other terms, deep in sediment, may have become stoppers rather than liberators of thought, and also need dredging up for fresh inspection.

A second worry is that through our specialist language we may actively drive non-Gestaltists away. Our jargon helps to define us as a Gestalt community and enhances a sense of allegiance to it. At the same time, our preciousness around language may be one of the reasons for people not persisting with the Gestalt approach, despite initial positive experiences. It may be another sort of insulation and inflicting damage on ourselves as an approach.

To offset disadvantages of relying on one Gestalt "official language," is there not the possibility of having supplementary ways of talking about what we do? In part, an urge to develop an alternative descriptive base for the Gestalt approach has fuelled my interest in what I have termed the "five abilities" that the Gestalt approach seeks to foster (Parlett, 2000). My ideas have grown, and been fed by others, (e.g. Spagnuolo Lobb, 2006, and Wheeler, 2006) and hospitality to the ideas in several quarters suggests that they can reach new constituencies of people, serving purposes that the usual Gestalt framework and language may not be able to.

I do not have the time to discuss them in detail, but I thought I could show how I might bring together five abilities thinking with our main theme today, the relationship between the personal realm we know so well, and the global issues around and within us. This is what I would say.

Human beings, in the world-as-it-is, face numerous challenges — personal, social, communal, political, environmental, organisational, and international. In each of these spheres, there exist examples of what we might call "good practice": well-working wholes, satisfying events, flowing processes, and creative solutions. Our world needs more of them, and fewer examples of situations that are destructive, inept, paralysed, or hopeless.

I am making strong value statements here, and make no apology for doing so.

The Gestalt approach has values embedded in it. And in my view what it values most are movements within people, and within systems, that indicate development towards wholeness, beauty, flow, health, authenticity, and creative action in the world in relation with others. Our principle base is our interest in fostering creative adjustment — not un-creative or destructive adjustment, and not mere adaptation or passive compliance with what we encounter in life, but the work of encountering the world as it is and engaging fully with it as an involved participant.

Describing the five abilities — Responding, Interrelating, Self-Recognising, Embodying, and Experimenting — provides a means for taking this line of thinking further. Thus, to participate fully in the world, a person or system has to respond to the totality of the present field, and to "self-organise," drawing on the supports available, experiencing the field and living as part of it and as an agent. There are numerous ways in which each of us fails to engage with "what is," preferring our fantasies, stale routines, or distractions, and as a consequence our capacity to respond effectively is limited.

Each of the abilities is necessary for the others to develop or to be manifested. Thus, we are also necessarily interrelating. We are interconnected beings, dependent on one another, and from our birth seeking to meet relational needs. Arguably, as a world community we cannot respond effectively to the overall world situation unless we undergo massive development of our ability to interrelate. Our Gestalt knowledge has a part to play in contributing to conflict resolution, peacemaking, new ways of collaborating, dealing with past grievances, and dissolving prejudice, all of which enhance people's capacity to interrelate on a small or medium scale.

At the same time as responding and interrelating, we also have a need to learn and manage ourselves as conscious, aware beings. To gain more facility with any of the other abilities, human beings need to self-recognise what they are doing, to wake up, to know themselves, to register their situation, and to find or make meaning of it. Human systems (such as international organisations) need to do the equivalents of these — to recognise the role they have, to "get what is happening," to "know what they are about," and what their vision is and their effect is upon the world.

Embodying, as Gestalt practitioners in particular well know, is a critical part in any process of development or learning, and it is the ability most under threat. Human beings are bodily creatures, with senses, feeling states, and physical needs. Gestalt specialists believe that life is less satisfactory if it is "virtual," or "mechanistic," or "lived without feeling or emotion." In fact, we would say that separation from our lived bodies and our physicality and sensate life is impossible. Embodied existence is part of being alive; but many might be considered only "half-alive." As greater embodying becomes present, people react more as whole beings, with feelings from the heart and gut also playing their part – incorporating a different wisdom from that of "rational objectivity."

The fifth area of interlinked inquiry, is the necessity for humanity to be more open to experimenting. There is any amount of novelty and technology-led change, yet most human beings and institutions make conservative rather than creative adjustments — seeking to prolong the status quo until forced to change. Gestalt practice is based, not least, on the invitation to try things out, to be open to the possibilities of living and acting in a different way. This invites us into the present, for it is only by focusing on "now," "here," and "next" that we can make conscious and actual change. As with each of the five abilities, experimenting is a necessary support for enhancing all the others, just as the others are all entailed in supporting the development of this ability. The five are mutually necessary, as dimensions of a holistic overview of human functioning in the world.

I am not suggesting that the five abilities could or should supplant our usual ways of describing the Gestalt approach, but they offer an alternative way of talking about what matters to us as Gestalt practitioners.

Minorities and Majorities

As we continue this thinking about our part in the political and social arena, I think we should look at some general issues in our society that may be played out in our own community, in our own back garden.

With more communication and goodwill, many of the divisions that used to exist within the Gestalt community have disappeared. However, other divisiveness is less visible but no less damaging. Some is present in our own community today, here in this room. The issues are elsewhere too, of course, but being closer to home heightens our attention. We have the opportunity to explore them at both levels, as issues local to us but which are also general to society at large.

In a recent communication on these themes, Anne Makin wonders aloud "about the issues of race, gender orientation, culture, religion etc. and what we don't do (or say)...about (these) in GPTI". She begins with her own (non-GPTI) past experience:

I remember angry black students whose cry to other students was, "Why do you leave it to us to be the ones who raise the issues? Why do we have to be the ones to teach you? Why won't you take responsibility for your own learning on the subject of racism?"

Anne Makin also remembers the fears expressed by other students who were in a majority at "the thought of raising questions of race, religion, sexual identity, and disability, for fear of offending in the manner of their questions...of being found and/or declared 'to be bad?'" Anne Makin points out that there is anger on both sides: first, "The anger of the culturally minoritised group at being treated as different in a less-than, not-as-good-as way," and, second, "the anger of the majority group for being held responsible for ... attitudes and actions within the (majority) culture – for somehow being held guilty despite having...(a) different approach" themselves.

Anne Makin cites a view of what is required, based on some teaching she received from Aileen Alleyne:

> ...that before we (can) begin the task of healing, each group (has) to let go of its attachment to anger, and the protective stance to the other (and to allow the experience of hurt, and vulnerability to further hurt...whilst, at the same time, being open to the possibility of hurt on the other side).

Anne Makin wonders aloud about how in GPTI the separate section for Lesbian, Gay, and Bisexual members was established recently. While understanding that it was to gain "support from each other in order to speak about your experience of the British GPTI" she also wondered "if the very formation of a group" might have made it less of a "safe-enough-emergency for the remainder" [of GPTI members outside the group]. She was making the point (personal communication) that an initiative like this requires extensive groundwork in the larger community, to provide the basis of support for a new enterprise in a way that allows energy for the venture to arise from within the whole community. She goes on:

> So how can we meet each other, with our shame and pain, and not be labelled bad?... Do we have enough ground...in GPTI to accommodate the mini-ruptures arising from pain, often arriving in the form of anger, without breaking the fabric of relationship? Is there enough to hold the projections and projections of other's projections? If not, how can we create this, so we have safe-enough-emergency conditions?

Anne's email invites us into a dialogue between, if you like, minority perspectives and majority perspectives where the majority become much more conscious of their under-acknowledged privilege, to borrow this idea from Lynne Jacobs. In fact I would like to quote a passage from a paper written by Jacobs (2006). (This is not the paper that was published in the British Gestalt Journal in 2000, titled "For Whites Only," which has already achieved deserved classic status – but another paper covering some of the same territory.) In this paper she writes:

> People who are identifiably "other" usually notice the signals of how they're being placed in the social location hierarchy, because they are not placed in the taken-for-granted centre but are always in relation to the centre – if you like, the straight or white location or able-bodied. We do not by any means live in a gay affirmative world or a black affirmative world. The gleam in the eye of the other is largely reserved for straight white able-bodied folk.

She goes on to quote some work by McConville (1997) who describes cross-race and cross-sexual orientation conversations where "bewilderment" arises:

> It is a dawning sense of my own ignorance and with that, a realisation that I'm not as innocent as my good intentions claim. Beyond my intentions, there is an impact of my behaviour on others, and an uncomfortable realisation that I'm not owning enough responsibility for that impact, and worse yet, that I'm not owning up to my responsibility for this ignorance.

These half-born awarenesses are fuelled by my knowledge that bigotry indeed exists, that it is all around us, that it permeates the air we breathe, even this air, right here, present in this room, as we speak. It is, in other words, the simultaneous prehension of my innocence and my guilt, my non-racist intentionality and my immersion in an atmosphere saturated with inequity and bias. This is bewilderment.

Whenever I find myself bewildered by someone's response to an action of mine, it is because I am blind to the ground of their experience. My advice to myself here is simple: get interested in the impact, particularly when it surprises me.

In short, those in majority groups have some self-recognising to do, (in the language I just introduced). We need to acknowledge, if holding a "majority" position in the relational field, that we have privileges that we are more than likely to take for granted. We can practise not taking them for granted. To help us do that, we can also remember other occasions when we have NOT been in a majority position, but (if only temporarily) in an uncomfortable minority position.

I suggest, as we go forward with the heightened consciousness of the issues highlighted by Makins, McConville, and

Jacobs, that we remain vigilant. And, equally, that we extrapolate from our experiences here to consider how they represent equivalent tensions and obligations in the world at large.

If we are to have an increased impact in the world, as a global Gestalt community, we need to be forever vigilant — so that we practise what we preach: namely (1) more aware consideration of the relational field, including its minorities and majorities, either of which can be hidden or missed or not acknowledged; (2) the importance of our readiness to self-disclose; (3) our staying with difficult contact rather than deflecting from it; (4) acknowledging the shame issues of all those who feel they have not been understood; and (5) the importance for I-Thou communicating with a commitment to courage and authenticity, and respect for others, whoever they are.

The Spiritual and the Secular

There's another conflict, in a sense another division, which exists within the Gestalt community that I want to mention because it is also likely to be present in the room. It is an ongoing divergence of views in the Gestalt community which we need to name and address. It is the question of whether we are amenable to, and sympathetic towards spirituality, or whether we are thoroughgoing secularists in our approach.

No less a figure than Bud Feder is quite clear where his views lie. He writes, in an article in the on-line journal Gestalt (20XX):

> Incorporating spirit, soul, "God," sacredness or religion into Gestalt therapy can only serve to blur our theory and inappropriately direct our practice, since our theory directs

us to pay attention to what is, and not to myths, stories and wishy-washy concepts which all of the above are.

He goes on, a bit later in the article, to give his reactions to an article by Ruth Wolfert (1996):

> Ruth talks of telling a client who suffered severe early traumas that she must "focus on the ultimate questions about the nature of reality and herself in order to heal her breached grounds of safety and find new connections to the universe..." Talk about introjects, give me a break!...In short, [Feder concludes] our profound theory gives us all the tools we need to help clients deal with the mysteries and ambiguities of life without resorting to vague ideas and concepts which do not harmonise with our own basic grounds.

Feder's strong position is in line with many people's within the Gestalt world. At the same time, among many (in fact most) of the people whom I know in the Gestalt world, there is a strong interest in the kind of making of meaning which takes us into the realm of what is called "spiritual." The word, of course, raises problems in and of itself. But if we think of spirituality as encompassing the wisdom traditions that are thousands of years old, does this change the picture? For me, I think it does. Consider these traditions, which are about the human state and how people can best live, what ultimately satisfies us most, how we can prepare for our death, and what is "right living," and then juxtapose these thousands of years of thinking and contemplation with our Gestalt discipline, all of sixty years old. I do not want to diminish Gestalt — I am an ardent enthusiast for our approach. But as exponents of a body of practice and understanding, we need to approach the wisdom traditions and a sense of the sacred with respect and curiosity. Also, surely we need to validate and not rubbish people's experiences — taking their spiritual interests seriously, if they have them.

Of course, the Perlses, as noted earlier, were sceptical towards any formal religion, or hierarchical institution that told people what to do. They would be considered similar to Freud in this regard. He was an avowed atheist too — wasn't he? Well, he may not have believed in a transcendental god, but his position seems to have been more complicated.

Mark Epstein's excellent book (2001), *Going On Being*, contains an intriguing anecdote about a conversation between Freud and

> Ludwig Binswanger, a Swiss psychiatrist and the founder of the existential movement in psychoanalysis...Binswanger felt there was something missing in Freud's approach to therapy. Too many patients simply did not get better. He raised the problem of the paralysis of analysis with Freud.
>
> "Might there not be a deficiency of spirit," asked Binswanger delicately, such that certain people were unable to raise themselves to a level of "spiritual communication" with their analysts? Could this lack of spiritual communication be the thing that stopped people from healing?
>
> To Binswanger's surprise, the old man readily acknowledged his point. "Yes," he said, "spirit is everything." "Binswanger thought that Freud must have misunderstood his use of the word spirit, perhaps thinking he meant something on (sic) the order of "intelligence." But Freud continued on. "Mankind has always known that it

possesses spirit," he said firmly. "I had to show that there are also instincts."

Epstein concludes: "When Freud sought to make room for instincts against the background of spirit, he did not anticipate a time when we would forget about spirit altogether. (pp 1-2) "

Let me be clear. I am not saying that we should set aside the emphasis that Bud Feder places on staying grounded in our particular field of expertise. Nor am I saying that an openness to spiritual phenomena and ways of describing experience means we have to sign up to a particular orthodoxy. Nor, of course, if you take a strong secular stance yourself, does it mean that you cannot work with someone very appropriately and responsibly who does have a spiritual perspective — in fact, Bud Feder at another point in his article, talks about being willing and able to do just that. But I do suggest that in terms of us as a school of thought, we might embrace a wider definition of our approach, to accommodate at least some features of what is deemed "spiritual."

I also believe that, as a way of thinking, as a practice, that one of the reasons why people may sometimes be put off Gestalt is that they want to go into the spiritual area, for want of a better term. They undertake a therapy journey and they want to go further, and it is in the spiritual and wisdom traditions that one finds serious attention being given to such notions as "higher levels of consciousness," or "learning to live in grace," or "being open to the numinous," or "preparing for one's death." Such statements need to be approached phenomenologically, not dogmatically, if we are true to Gestalt therapy practice. And there are many other terms (and phenomena) that belong in that border-zone between the two realms of discourse – for instance, the word and notion of "surrender" deserves inquiry, as do the many varieties of "love."

Again, lest I be misconstrued: I'm not saying that we should become a spiritual discipline, but rather that there exists in the space between the world of therapy and personal development on the one hand, and the world of spiritual experiencing on the other, a substantial middle ground. Traditionally, this has been occupied only by a few Gestaltists, perhaps for fear of being criticised by their professional peers for writing something "non-Gestalt." I think we have been polarised as a professional community around this subject, and perhaps hesitant to engage together about it, in case our discussions degenerated into something like the bickering between competing fundamentalists.

This "hands off" position has to change. The secular and spiritual poles of Gestalt therapy need to be articulated. I myself think that there is this big middle ground. There are experiences that most of would agree are profound in the extreme — call them spiritual, existential, mysterious, transpersonal, it may not matter too much — and which we encounter in the work we do. I think, for example, of the collective sense of great coherence and peace that can suddenly settle over a group that has been deeply exploring its differences for some time; or the extraordinary intimacy and dissolving of boundaries that can occur in I-Thou communicating; or the amazing synchronicities and intuitive leaps that come from nowhere when we are very embodied and present with ourselves; or the sense of the sacred that can suffuse a place or a meal or a meeting; or simply the overwhelming sense of presence and peace that can arise in silent contact-making or in meditation. There are many such phenomena, and for many people exploring their lives and seeking to live more in the present, they assume great significance. And, within the Gestalt approach, individuals and groups should be able to explore them, talk about them freely, and we need collectively to learn about them.

More and more people are turning in some way to spiritual movements or reverting to formal religions which they or their families left behind a generation ago. This may have to do with confronting the existential dilemma of what it means to live on a planet that may be uninhabitable in 100 years' time. Or it may be a swing of the pendulum, an antidote to the assertive atheism and hubris of some scientists. It may also be a function of survival needs being met and people having the time and security to engage in self-reflection more. Or it may be fear of the unknown or of future uncertainties. But we would be foolish to explain them away and to diminish people's longings for meaning-making, inner peace, and an alternative to a society based on alienating and trivialised values. The search for a spiritual home is a form of reaching for a better quality of life in a non-material sense of the term. We are in the same business, it seems to me, and we limit ourselves if we exclude the possibility of exploring this area because it is "not part of our tradition" when arguably it already is, even by default.

An additional small point, there was some laughter at the end of the quote I read from Bud Feder. I feel sensitive that if we are going to have more of an open and generous-minded dialogue, that we don't start from mocking someone else's position. We need to take care of minority (or majority) positions.

The Citizen-Practitioner

In my capacities as a co-founder of a training institute — and therefore one of those setting up the original training curriculum — and in my 15 years as editor of the *British Gestalt*

Journal, I was one of those promoting and wanting there to be a strong theoretical basis for Gestalt therapy. I thought we had no chance of surviving unless we could have a written as well as an oral tradition. And without question we have moved as a worldwide community towards being far more theoretically sophisticated than we were twenty years ago.

Now I think the time may have come when we need to redress the balance a bit. I think we have leant in the direction of becoming more academically respectable, more theoretically engaged, and that is very good overall. However, we are an approach to working with people, groups, and (some of us) organisations, which emphasises practice; ultimately it is what we do that counts, not what we theorise about. We are engaged in professional work which has art and craft in it as much as conceptual versatility. One thinks here of the tendency generally for abstraction and the written word to be elevated to a higher status than practical "know-how," as it is often termed. What actually happens with clients and in groups is what matters — more than writing research papers and books, as important as they are.

Rather than set up a new duality, opposing theorising with practising, I want to suggest a third position — namely that we attend more to our "theories of practice" (Schön 1983) — that is, to our assumptions, working principles, and rationale for our interventions, some of which we talk about, obviously, under the general heading of "theory," and a lot that perhaps we do not talk about very much because the methods and interventions have become so routine, so accepted as givens by practitioners that they no longer seem important enough to talk about. But in the passing on of skill and professional experience, more attention to theories of practice can only be a good thing.

I am thinking of an old article by Erving Polster, on "tight therapeutic sequences" (1991), an even older article by Stratford and Brallier (1979)and a very recent piece by Lynne Jacobs (2006) on support — all of which provide essential ideas based on long clinical experience that has been "digested" and then articulated for the benefit of others, who can make direct use of the know-how. These are examples of theories of practice, of HOW we do what we do.

More weight given to theories of practice would help bring about a rapprochement between the nuts and bolts of our practical methodology and the theoretical descriptions and justifications we have in our literature. They would avoid the impression growing that discussions about theoretical differences are played out in one space, while what people actually do is consigned to another space altogether.

This is a hobby-horse of mine, but it also serves to introduce the idea that there is, I believe, another way in which we can have a direct and useful impact on the wider world. And that's through all of us becoming what I call "citizen practitioners."

The two main areas of practice where Gestalt is currently applied — namely, in psychotherapy and in organisation development — are separated for good reasons. They are not identical; there are particular ways in which therapists and OD consultants work that are very different, despite a common allegiance to Gestalt thinking. The differences are important to understand and not ignore. However, I think that there are a number of "generic practice principles" which are shared as givens, that have been widely incorporated by different professionals. In short, I am suggesting that Gestaltists, whether they be teachers in the classroom, therapists with families, psychologists working with groups of depressed people, managers in large organisations, or trainers working with students in small training groups, actually share certain "theories of practice" which derive from their exposure and training in Gestalt, and which they incorporate, apply, adapt, and display in their various kinds of work.

I suggest that these generic practice principles can form the basis for our all becoming "citizen-practitioners." We have procedures that form our practice, that guide us in what we do and can do. And they may not be rocket science for us, and maybe not for some of those we work with, but they are rocket science for a great number of people, organisations, teams, and practical situations for whom they are novel.

This body of expertise needs to become more available for use. We need to bring it out more, to be bolder in using it, applying it more assiduously, demonstrating it with conviction. For example, one thing that every organisation, from the village hall committee to the school governors to the local political campaign to the environmental activist organisation on a national scale ALL have in common is that they have meetings, Lots of them. And we know a lot about meetings. We know a huge amount about how people work together and can stay energised or can tune out and feel their energy dropping. We know about reclaiming their interest and how to bring it back.

This is not the time to develop a whole action strategy, but I can point to some of the procedures and principles that I think we share as Gestalt practitioners — of all types and persuasions. Moreover, they are portable, have multiple possibilities for application, and can be infinitely adapted and experimented with. They represent modest, useful, and serviceable things which we can do and which make a difference.

Let me give you some examples of the kinds of intervention I am referring to.

The first one I wrote down was to prioritise the personal. In California recently, I heard about some research being done at Stanford University where they were getting people in organisations to describe the history (or "the narrative") of the organisation they were in. There would be certain reactions and a fair amount of interest. Then the organisers of the experiment invited the person who was telling the narrative of the organisation to tell their own story — the story of their personal journey and experience of the organisation. And, lo and behold, (surprise! surprise!) what happened was that the energy shot up, people remembered the story with the personal added much better, and they got more deeply involved and more deeply thoughtful. As we know, self-disclosure can enhance contact; we are moved when statements are more embodied and direct, and less interested with abstract statements delivered in a more detached and impersonal way. We know a lot about the value of I-statements and taking ownership of what we say, and bringing our personal experience into the public realm. In fact, it relates to the first exploration we did today, relating global concerns with personal biography.

The second area I want to mention is that we understand ways of managing stuckness. Practising, we all have experience of "stuck" situations, those kinds of complicated times when you cannot see a way through something, where a kind of awful pall descends, the conflict or the "not knowing" seems intractable, the problem unsolvable, the situation dire. At such times, there is sometimes a case for a break; sometimes a deflection is in order, like a shift in the physical arrangements, body position, or the atmospheric environment (open those windows, take a big breath or two). More often, though, we need to "stay with the process." We need to endure more stuckness than is comfortable. I think that all of us have learned to trust the process, to have faith that something else will happen if we hang in, if we stay in the difficult situation or collective feeling going nowhere. We know nine times out of ten (well maybe seven or eight!) that a reconfiguration will spontaneously come about, perhaps prompted by a question like "What is missing?" or "What is the polar opposite of what's happening at the moment?" These kinds of questions open up new dimensions of possibility. And we know it. We work with this kind of thing. And we know stuckness is a phase to go through, not the end of the road.

My third suggestion is around attending to completions – not accumulating more unfinished business than is necessary. Often there are all sorts of bits of business left over at a meeting when just a little tidying up of loose ends might make a big difference. We take it for granted if we're in the Gestalt context, but in most contexts elsewhere they don't take completions seriously enough. Perhaps you say: "OK can we just run over the arrangements to make sure everyone knows what is next?" or "I am aware that we never got around to Marjorie's point and I think we should come back to it at the next meeting..." or "We seem to have covered a lot today and I think the listing of topics on the flip chart was a very useful thing to do." These are so apparently commonplace and yet they derive from a sensitive appreciation of the need to finish, round off, or allow a closure of some kind. There are also times, I know, when it is very important that unfinishedness is preserved...but that's another story and another bit of "practice lore."

My fourth suggestion is that in remaining sensitive to the whole gestalt of the situation, and perhaps to some complex arrangement that has been proposed, we attend not just to "what is present" but also to what is "missing," (true to our Gestalt psychology roots). Often we identify this best by disengaging for a moment or two, allowing some "soft-focus" awareness at a felt-sense level. The observation: "What we haven't talked about here is...," especially if it relates to an energised but ignored theme, can change the course of a meeting. (It may not be popular with chairpersons, so it needs to be used with care!)

The fifth area refers to the need to try things out. The spirit of experiment, trying things out, bringing issues into the "laboratory space" of the meeting room is something that all Gestaltists know about. It is part of our way of doing things. "Let's stop talking about it and try it out here." People move, they get energised, perhaps they assume some "crazy" role (the management, last week, Cynthia in accounts) and they wake up, they see things differently; perhaps they then switch roles, take a different position from usual, exploring what would be different and doing it in the present, enjoy themselves and playing a little. A little outrageousness, well-timed, can lift a meeting from torpor or endemic gloom.

Sixth, we can be prepared to encourage people to question authority, not so much as an act of defiance or bloody-mindedness, but at least challenging the swallowing whole of expert pronouncements. Again, a healthy bit of unconventionality or ruffling feathers can be stimulating, especially if one is not always doing it (when it becomes far less experimental).

Another, my seventh, is related: giving everyone a voice. Now this is sometimes very difficult, as we know. But, reverting to the issue of minorities and majorities, clearly it is crucial that people participate, feel ownership in whatever is decided, and feel respected for their point of view, and for having a point of view. I am thinking of a famous Gestalt organisational consultant, Carolyn Luckensmeyer, who was interviewed in the British Gestalt Journal in 1997. She worked in the Clinton White House for several years. Carolyn now runs something called "America Speaks," an extraordinary enterprise where she gets together maybe several thousand people and they are grouped table by table in some huge space and each table has a facilitator with a laptop and each table is consulted about some big public issue that is being addressed by the whole meeting. Everyone has buttons to press so that the feeling of the whole meeting and people's views are assessed in several ways. Modern technology is incorporated , but the underlying value is in giving everybody in a community a voice. Philip Lichtenberg also highlights the necessity for this (Lichtenberg 2006). The principle is the same at whatever level of system you work with, in small group settings as much as in bigger, institutional ones. Many of us are committed to doing this as a matter of principle, and of course, sometimes we forget, but we come back to it again and again. We know that silencing people is to kill initiative-taking, it is to dull the momentum, and lessens the involvement of all.

My eighth point is that at times of crisis, with a rapidly evolving situation for which nobody has planned, there is a particular role for a Gestalt-trained practitioner. Gestalt comes into its own as a practice of staying with the unfolding present and doing what is required at the time. Those whose professional expertise has more to do with planning, pre-specification of objectives, and maintaining regulatory procedures, can be wrong-footed and stymied when an extraordinary situation arises which does not fit any preconceived model. Our Gestalt field orientation should predispose us to be constantly updating what is present in the moment, and to adjust accordingly. One can go a long way in extreme situations with questions like: "What's next?" and doing that, and asking the question again.

Lastly, think support — all the time. Support — i.e. "that which enables" (Jacobs 2006) — offers any number of possible interventions and possibilities. What are the factors which will sustain, reinforce, revitalise, or transform a particular proposal? And what are the converse forces at work — the energy-drainers, the impediments, things which distract or detract from what needs to happen? And are the latter acknowledged, addressed, and seen for what they could do? With too little support, leaders, projects, grand designs can all fail.

What is involved in being a citizen practitioner? Well, of course you will run up against the cultural momentum that takes people away from doing these things. So this is an invitation for us all, and a reminder to myself, to pick up the challenge and to learn more graciously to deal with difference, to learn to be subtle and skillful in advocating these kinds of small process innovations. As always, we need to get the timing right and have humility rather than hubris. For many of us it does take courage, and the capacity to support oneself, to speak up or to try and bring influence to bear upon a public process where we might not have a specific professional role to lean back into. Other kinds of support are feasible, notably building solidarity with others, forging alliances, or creating networks of the like-minded.

Finally...

In this long address I have wandered across a large landscape. It's been more of an informal ramble than a carefully planned walk. But certain core beliefs and values lie at the heart of it.

Inspired by Paul Goodman, Laura Perls, Philip Lichtenberg, and others, I regard the Gestalt approach as having a political as well as personal focus, to do with the nature of living, the quality of existence, people's lives in systems, and the interplay between the contextual and the individual realms. I am also convinced that Gestalt therapy, with its various derivatives and multiple fields of application, is a potent, lively, relevant, flexible, and serviceable approach to thinking about human beings and their lives, and comes as near as anything I know to being an appropriate outlook for our time.

Our Gestalt perspective and model survives, against the grain, against the flow of the dominant culture a lot of the time, because it is holistic; because it is an integrative as well as a specialised approach; because it does justice to and can handle complexity; because it satisfies many people who are put off by more formal or inflexible approaches; because its models of human being-in-the-world are congruent with experience; and because it "rings true."

It was good to be reminded of the huge direct impact we have collectively, in terms of numbers of people that we actually work with. I have wanted to ask hard questions of our own organisations as Gestalt specialists, because otherwise we could split between what we believe in and what we do. That would be a failure of authenticity. I have spoken for the need for new outlooks, and ways of talking about what we do. I have urged us all to be bolder, more daring, and to communicate what we find exciting about Gestalt.

Finally, in the discussion of becoming citizen-practitioners, I invited you to remember, as you go about your everyday business, attend meetings, work with varieties of colleagues, encounter your extended families, engage with neighbours and local communities, that you do not have to leave all your expertise locked up in your professional briefcases. Let us come back to our methodology and celebrate it. We have a wonderful theory and we need to remember what its purpose is – that is, to underpin and support the practice we do, and how we are and can be in the world that we live within. We are each a part of the whole and we each have a part to play.

References

Epstein, M. (2001). *Going on Being*. New York: Broadway Books.
Feder, B. (2001). On "spirituality" – a dissenting view, *Gestalt!* 5(3).
Heidegger, M. (1967). *Being and Time,* trans. J. Macquarrie and E. Robinson. Oxford, England: Blackwell.
Jacobs, L. (2000). For whites only. *British Gestalt Journal*, 9(1): 3-14.
Jacobs, L. (2006a). Racializing whiteness, queerifying straightness: contextualising the "normative" mind. Presentation, ICP Conference entitled, Encountering the mysterious other: Hidden obstacles to exploration of difference.
Jacobs, L. (2006b). That which enables: Support as complex and contextually emergent. *British Gestalt Journal*, 15(2), 10-19.
Lichtenberg, P. and Gray, C. (2006). Awareness, contacting, and the promotion of democratic-egalitarian social life., *British Gestalt Journal*, 15(2), 20-27.
Lichtenberg, P.,van Beusekom, J., and Gibbons, D. (1997). *Encountering Bigotry: Befriending Projecting Persons in Everyday Life*. Cambridge, Mass: GestaltPress.
Lukensmeyer, C. (1997). Power, change and authenticity: a political and gestalt perspective (interviewed by Malcolm Parlett), *British Gestalt Journal*, 6(1), 4-15.
Makin, A. (2007). Email Communication to members of the Gestalt Psychotherapy and Training Institute in the UK.
McConville, M. (1997). The gift. In T. Levine Bar-Yoseph (Ed.). *The Bridge* (pp. 173-182). New Orleans: Gestalt Institute Press.
Parlett, M. (2000). Creative adjustment and the global field, *British Gestalt Journal*, 9 (1), 15-27.
Parlett, M. (2003). Creative abilities and the art of living well. In M. Spagnuolo Lobb & N. Amendt-Lyon (Eds.). *Creative License: The Art of Gestalt Therapy*. Wien and New York: Springer.
Parlett, M. and Hamilton, D. (1972). Evaluation as illumination: A new approach to the study of innovatory programs, University of Edinburgh, Centre for Research in the Educational sciences, Occasional Paper No.9.

Perls, F., Hefferline, R. and Goodman, P. (1951). *Gestalt Therapy: Excitement and Growth in the Human Personality*. New York: Julian Press.

Perls, L. (1992). *Living at The Boundary: Collected works of Laura Perls* (edited by J. Wysong). Highland, New York: Gestalt Journal Press.

Polster, E. (1991) Tight therapeutic sequences. *British Gestalt Journal, 1* (2), 69-81.

Sachs, J. (2007). Bursting at the Seams, BBC Reith Lectures, 2007. www.bbc.co.uk/radio4/reith.

Schön, D.A. (1983). *The Reflective Practitioner: How Professionals Think in Practice*. New York: Basic Books.

Siegel, D.I (2007). *The Mindful Brain*. New York: Norton.

Spagnuolo Lobb, M. (2006). Malcolm Parlett's five abilities and their connection with contemporary scientific theories of human interconnectedness. *British Gestalt Journal, 15* (2),36-45.

Staemmler, F-M. (2006). A Babylonian confusion? : on the uses and meanings of the term 'field," *British Gestalt Journal, 15*(2): 64-83.

Stern, D. (2004). *The Present Moment in Psychotherapy and Everyday Life*. New York: Norton.

Stratford, C.D. & Brallier, L.W. (1979). Gestalt therapy with profoundly disturbed persons. *The Gestalt Journal,* 2 (1), 90-104.

Wheeler, G. (2006). Parlett's creative abilities model and the Esalen curriculum for the human potential: a comparative study, *British Gestalt Journal, 15*(2), 46-58.

Wolfert, R. (1996). The broken doll: a survivor's journey into life. In B. Feder and R. Ronall (Eds.). *A Living Legacy of Fritz and Laura Perls: Contemporary Case Studies*.

Afterword

••••••••••

Narrative and Evolution: The Human Adventure
Gordon Wheeler

Who are we? What is our situation? And then what are the tools we have at hand for putting those two things — our basic nature and our living evolutionary moment — together in a way that speaks to our deepest instincts for survival, connection, meaning, adventure, ongoing evolution and love? These are the crucial questions of our times, and the questions that this collection points itself toward: not to answer them completely by any means, but with the intention of joining and shifting an ongoing conversation — one which has not been going particularly well — for want, we would argue, of some of those tools.

And note how the second question — what is our situation? — follows from the first. Our understanding of our situation depends on who we think we are, as individuals and as a species among other living forms. We are integrally part of our own "environment:" to fail to realize this is yet another instance of the "individualist fallacy," the idea that "I" am "here" and "my environment" is "around me" or "over there," — and that there's some essential difference between "me" and "it" (what philosophy calls an ontological difference — and Goodman treated as a "false dichotomy"). We're "in" a different situation, depending on who and what we are, as dynamic constituents in it and of it. (In evolutionary perspective this is known as "Baldwinian" thinking — the reminder that "the environment" is a different dynamic "place," once you factor in the existence and reciprocal effects of the evolving organisms themselves who populate and co-constitute that "environment," modifying it as we go. There is no "natural environment," apart from the species constituting it. The environment we've got is the environment we've got, with us in it. Whether that whole system is viable or not depends of course on us — our nature, our potential, and our creative choices).

Who we are changes utterly the character of the situation we are "in." In other words, story at the most basic level — our assumptive narrative of who and what and where we are — is not just a reflection of our situation and our possibilities: it is the vital constituting dynamic of that situation and our possibilities in it.

Insights like these are generated and supported by a field/relational reading of the Gestalt model, a qualitative leap in complexity, over other models of human behavior and experience, in how we understand the individual, the group, and the wider field. When we are supported to move beyond a static, two-dimensional picture (and a one- or two-person psychology) to a dynamic field view, we access a complexity of vision that is itself an evolutionary step in our own consciousness — a crucial one, enabling us to deal with the degrees of systemic complexity we see in us and around us and among us today. And for that, we need Gestalt.

This is what this book is "about," in the sense of what all the pieces here point to. Each is a perspective on this most key question: who are we? what is our nature, our human potential? And each chapter is a different refraction of the beginnings at least of a set of answers: we're not who we think we are. We are not, "in fact" isolated individuals, devoid of any prosocial "instincts," forced by the demands of "ego" (in either the Freudian or the pop-spiritual sense) or "being-in-the-world" to compromise our essential self in the messy mudbath of politics and human relations. Rather, we are complex political animals through and through, social before we are individual (and social pervading individual, as ground infuses figure), challenged with constantly shifting "boundaries" (always provisional and situational, never ontologically final, as in older, more static models). Complex social animals, and by virtue of that, gifted with an enlarged cortex evolved for solving social problems of unimaginable everyday complexity — and thereby able to create novel solutions to other novel challenges, because of our evolved social capacity and nature.

Thus, among implications of this kind of thinking, we begin to see that we do not "create our own experience," in the rigid sense of the old shibboleth of high Modernism and high mid-Century Exisentialism. Rather, we and others cocreate a field, in dynamic interaction with the "found parameters," — and that cocreated field gives rise, with us actively at play in the process, to those interpretive wholes of meaning we call "experience." And yes, that experience can be influenced and changed by a change in connectivity of patterns — ideas — active in my brain (otherwise why write books, and why read them?). That's one way my experience changes. Another way is by you undergoing a change in your pattern connectivity, which likewise changes "the field," — thereby affecting my "inner thinking" as well, by the shift in the climate of discourse I live and think in.

Your "inner experience" affects mine, is part of mine — part of the experienced and neurochemical context in which "my" patterning arises — including my sense of "me" and "mine," which are not objectively fixed either, but are themselves cultural, interpersonal cocreations. This kind of insight is a radical departure from the one-person psychologies of the past in the West — including those echoes and holdovers of older models that found their way, inevitably into earlier readings of Gestalt.

"The personal is the political," went the saying of a generation ago, as we woke up to the perspectives of Feminism, which began the slow halting work of liberating men and women, boys and girls, from some of the rigid cultural strictures of the past. To this we can now add: "the interpersonal is the intrapersonal." The "individual" and the social, "inner" and "outer" worlds, interpenetrate. We cocreate each other's "private" worlds of experience — in a felt way that is also now measurable in the brain, laying down pathways and patternings that can persist, and enter into "my" future thinking. We're doing that right now, you and I — not just me to you in some way, to some degree with these words, but reciprocally, as my past and imagined experience of your reception, your response, enters into and coshapes the words "I" select and string together. It's no accident, as developmentalist Alan Fogel (1993) put it, that thought " has the form of conversation."

Today, more and more, we are getting to be at home with these paradigm-busting ideas, and others like them. This means it is now time, as Deborah Ullman suggests in the Foreword to this collection, to begin weaving these new ideas together into a new gestalt, a new human story, as a living ground for new understandings and actions. Each chapter in this book offers a contribution to this process — a report from the edge, if you will, of the kind of thinking that was derrogated as "soft" (meaning impotent, dangerously unaggressive), or "idealistic" (meaning counterfactual), or worst of all, "feminine" (meaning emotional, not rational — at best decorative, something like the silver service at some rapacious power lunch) only a generation or less ago. Today, with our cultures, our economies and other interests, our experiential worlds careening and crashing chaotically and ever more desperately into each other, we are waking to the idea that these new perspectives are not only hard empirical realities that can no longer be dismissed: — more than that, they are in a real sense our only hope. In the end, our evolved ability to see into each other's worlds of experience, to dialogue and be influenced by that dialogue, are where that hope lies and grows. Each of these chapters, again, speaks to one or more sets of those tools we spoke of above, for actualizing that hope.

Our "species default," our set-point that we naturally tend to revert to, is not normally the murder of the fathers, the rape of the mothers and neighbors, the slaughter of our own sons, all of it out of sheer loneliness, aggression, and greed, as our culture has often taught us — and enacted, — from Homer through Abraham down to Nietzsche, Freud, and Ayn Rand. This is all part of that new story, which supports and empowers us to see dynamics that were out of focus in the old, individualistic paradigm — and to take new creative action based on that new vision. Our human set-point is prosocial, relational, and altruistic across a wide group of identification — with competition, acquisitiveness, and dominance, even murder, always basically contextualized in this prosocial background (even the successful dominant leader draws heavily on intersubjective or "mind-reading" capacities). Humans would never have survived and thrived without this amazing capacity for creative social complexity; here lies all our progress in the past, and all our bright hope for survival and continued evolution as a species today and in the future.

But is there really hope for us, in a time of unparalleled dangers, even with this new story and these newly-owned (or re-owned) tools? Is it really as simple-sounding as that — we're prosocial, therefore now we can all just get along? Here's where the picture darkens, and grows even more complex. For if our basic evolved nature, our fundamental self-story, is steeped in belonging, altruism, even love across a wide identified group of belonging, at the same time that very idea of an "identified group of belonging" also contains seeds of our own potential destruction. For if we are evolved and born for complexifying relationship and intersubjectivity, we also contain, deep in our evolved history and nature, an inherent reductive default, a sort of tripwire or prepotent stress-point, which can limit and undercut those same essential capacities. Under stress and trauma, in place of building and organizing an increasingly complex social view, we may suddenly flip, drop from higher cortical processing down to "reptilian brain," and suddenly, discontinuously, and radically simplify the social field by re-solving complexity into a dichotomous us-them boundary. This is so universal a tendency, across millennia and situations, that plainly it has the same kind of "basic human story" character as our prosocial drive and capacity themselves. We see this sudden collapse of social complexity not merely in cases of distant conquest and war, among peoples who don't know each other — but at least as often among neighbors, trading partners, even deeply integrated populations. At times, seemingly out of nowhere, groups that have lived side by side or even interpenetrated for generations, even centuries, can suddenly flip, lose much or all sense of the others as fellow beings within the scope of our identification and care, and regard them instead as "not us" — meaning not just "not our crowd," but not human, not part of the circle of belonging that follows from or activates our prosocial nature itself. Suddenly they are "beyond the pale" of shared humanity — a term which is itself associated with persecution and pogrom.

Thus our creative sociality suffers from an inborn fragility, a tendency to instability under stress. And from the outside of a given situation at least, it doesn't appear to take much stress, at times, to trigger the collapse to a comforting oversimplification, a drastic collapse of complexity in our story of ourselves and our worlds. The Holocaust in Europe of course comes to mind — an event which Jung claimed had put a final end, once and for all, to "the projective theory of evil." Alas, nothing could possibly be further from the case. "Holocausts" — known today as "ethnic cleansing" continue to be the way of history, just as they always seem to have been. If anything, with increasing density in the world's population and resource use, they seem to be picking up speed.

Now these paroxysms and collapses, when they happen, are never total by any means. Dissent, courage, altruism persist, sporadically anyway. Heroes and heroines seem always to arise, sometimes as martyrs and sometimes with full effectiveness, sometimes even breaking the "us-them" trance that can fall over us so quickly — and then, at times, disappear again almost as rapidly. Those who actually commit atrocities are often, maybe nearly always plagued with anxiety reactions and other PTSD symptomatology, frequently for the rest of their lives (thereby visiting the after effects of trauma, whether suffered or committed, on subsequent generations of children). It's heartening in a way to know just how deeply these acts of atrocity clearly do violate our deeply-embedded, evolved prosocial nature.

But that of course doesn't stop these things from happening, again and again and again. Clearly then we are dealing with something as deep in our bones as loving and nurturing "our" children (including the biological children of others), caring for the needy and vulnerable, building bonds of exchange, alliance, and trust.

Ironically, tragically, our approach to these two levels of conflict, the interpersonal and the intergroup, may at times seem to be exactly backwards. In one-on-one or small group conflicts, our individualistic biases can lead us to overemphasize the role of interests and positions, to the neglect of the natural power of intercourse and dialogue. Gestalt teaches us about the transformative power of living contact: when we touch the humanity of our "adversary," directly and personally, we are both changed in the process; this after all is why "fraternizing with the enemy" is commonly seen as risky and subversive: because we know where it can lead.

On the other hand, when it comes to conflict across an active, highly charged intergroup "boundary," we often fail to take into account that we're not dealing with fully available human individuals, with their creative, complexifying cortices and their empathic, mirroring social "mammalian brains" fully on line. Now the same kinds of "contact" (as for example in some poorly-planned programs of forced integration) may boomerang, causing an intensification of the hostilities they were designed to alleviate. This is because of the radically simplified nature of the projective interpretations flying back and forth across the "boundary," which have the effect of undercutting and reinterpreting the most seemingly positive gestures and strategies (because, hey, with "people like that," all those things might be tricks). It's a bit as if we were to try to approach and "fix" a "PTSD" pattern (which is similarly a kind of "short-circuiting" of higher, more relational cortical functioning under drastic stress) by assuming that the person in the grips of a panic reaction still has the support at that moment for full, creative, prosocial problem-solving).

All this has to be reimagined and replanned, if our ever more crowded world is to survive at all, much less thrive. And to do that, we need the tools and perspectives of a fully developed, field/relational Gestalt model, which can handle dynamic complexity and shifting "rules of the game" at these levels. All that too has to be incorporated in our new human story.

Can we make it? On a rational level, the most optimistic answer is, it's touch-and-go. Which will win out — our immense capacity, often underappreciated and underutilized, for creative prosocial problem-solving? Or our equally deep tendencies, under certain kinds of stress conditions, to drop down to "trauma-brain," leaving all that evolved capacity for creativity, growth and love "offline," so to speak, not available when we most need it? (Even worse — these tendencies are not underappreciated and underutilized; rather, they are fanned and cultivated actively by those who would exploit them for short-run selfish gain — no matter how short-sighted that may be even to themselves and their own interests. And in a sad further irony, these people themselves are always trauma survivors, in one way or another, and thus without benefit of the stable neurocircuitry and integral social resonance that a robust prosocial environment would have given them, innoculating against their own worst fears and most destructive reactions, at least to some degree).

Thus again, the personal is the political, the "inner" is the "outer," and vice versa. Particularly in Gestalt we've always maintained that individual therapy is a subversive social act, in the most positive sense. My own work today, after a lifetime of individual and group work, is focused more on direct organizational and larger-system transformation; but that gearshift never means that I fail to appreciate the social impact of personal transformation, much of it facilitated in live psychotherapy, one-on-one or small-group, with influential leaders of business or politics (or teaching, or family), either directly or close around them with members of their families and friends. Certainly today the fact that countless numbers of leaders in every field have had direct or nearly direct experiences of psychotherapy or counseling-like interventions, often in connection with their children, their marriages, even their worklives in complex organizations, is building a powerful constituency for the kinds of change and new story we are all writing about in this book. Each of us is called to do the work we have developed to do, and the work at hand, whatever and wherever that may be. And all of us are needed, if the shifts we are part of are to reach those crucial tipping points in our shared world, in time.

We're born alone and we die alone, goes another of those mantras of high midcentury Western Existentialism, each of us supposedly imprisoned in his/her own monadic experiential world. From attending the births of my five children, plus several others, I can attest that the first part of that is definitely untrue. From the moment of birth the neonate is reaching, nuzzling, looking to those around to cocreate her/his experience, looking instinctively for partners to stabilize his/her nervous system and shape and select the accumulating apperceptive ground, even at the most basic somatic level.

As for the second part of the slogan, there too I can tell you, at least from my own experiences of slipping in and out of that far country, that whatever that process and place were or are, they are definitely not solitary, on either side of that discontinuous divide. In this view, this experience, we are knots of complexity in a universal weaving, or "text," unique nodes of perspective and reflection in a vast sea of consciousness. That sea, that text is itself evolving, I believe, and us with it as the agents of that evolution. The next chapters in our story are not yet written: It is our actions here that will create them. That is adventure, and mystery, and spirituality enough for me.

Will we make it? That depends on who "we" are: both who we "really" are (in terms of our evolved capacities, as uniquely creative animals), and who we think we are (which goes to whether and how we make use of those capacities now). This much we know: we are a grand tale in the telling. We tell it first by living it, and then by getting together in deep conversation, as we do at Esalen and so many, many other creative venues, to review and revise and reinterpret that living. At times, such as here, we even try to write some of that conversation down. Whether that advances the story depends very much on you, your living and your responses. Please do respond, if you are moved to — at gestaltpress@comcast.net and/or gestaltpress@aol.com, — as we all go on telling and living together.

Welcome to us all, to the great adventure.

By which we mean, in this new view based in complexity and interpretation, not some final objective divine Truth, but rather our cultural interpretations of data which are themselves culturally generated. Our way of regarding "facts" in a contemporary, Gestalt-based approach is a qualitative leap in complexity over modernist epistemology, which essentially left no role for hermeneutics and deconstructive critical methods, or for felt experience in dialogue, which we understand in Gestalt as an essential check-point for current interpretations of data from empirical science. Still, we do not regard today's "facts" as "true" in the old sense of unalterably final. They are and always remain interpretations.

Personally I do experience certain truths as ultimate — truths which we might term "spiritual." Even there, however (or especially there), I have to keep in mind that my own way of languaging those experiences is culturally relative and interpersonally coconstructed in a particular situation and field. I'm happy to speak about these felt truths, but always with the reminder that that speech itself is always metaphorical and evolving, never concrete and final.

April 4, 2009   Gordon Wheeler
                                                 Big Sur, California

Selected Titles from GestaltPress

Organizational Consulting: A Gestalt Approach
Edwin C. Nevis

Gestalt Reconsidered: A New Approach to Contact and Resistance
Gordon Wheeler

Gestalt Therapy: Perspectives and Applications
Edwin C. Nevis, editor

The Collective Silence: German Identity and the Legacy of Shame
Barbara Heimannsberg Christopher J. Schmidt

Community and Confluence: Undoing the Clinch of Oppression
Philip Lichtenberg

Becoming a Stepfamily
Patricia Papernow

On Intimate Ground: A Gestalt Approach to Working With Couples
Gordon Wheeler Stephanie Backman, editors

Body Process: Working With the Body in Psychotherapy
James I. Kepner

Here, Now, Next: Paul Goodman and the Origins of Gestalt Therapy
Taylor Stoehr

Crazy Hope Finite Experience
Paul Goodman, edited by Taylor Stoehr

In Search of Good Form: Gestalt Therapy With Couples and Families
Joseph C. Zinker

The Voice of Shame: Silence and Connection in Psychotherapy
Robert G. Lee & Gordon Wheeler, editors

Healing Tasks: Psychotherapy With Adult Survivors of Childhood Abuse
James I. Kepner

Adolescence: Psychotherapy and the Emergent Self
Mark McConville

Getting Beyond Sobriety: Clinical Approaches to Long-Term Recovery
Michael Craig Clemmens

Back to the Beanstalk: Enchantment and Reality for Couples
Judith R. Brown

The Dreamer and the Dream: Essays and Reflections on Gestalt Therapy
Rainette Eden Fants, edited by Arthur Roberts

A Well-Lived Life: Essays in Gestalt Therapy
 Sylvia Fleming Crocker

From the Radical Center: The Heart of Gestalt Therapy
 Irving and Miriam Polster

The Gendered Field: Gestalt Perspectives and Readings
 Deborah Ullman & Gordon Wheeler, editors

Beyond Individualism: Toward a New Understanding of Self, Relationship, and Experience
 Gordon Wheeler

Sketches: An Anthology of Essays, Art, and Poetry
 Joseph C. Zinker

The Heart of Development: Gestalt Approaches to Working with Children, Adolescents, and Their Worlds (2 Volumes)
 Mark McConville Gordon Wheeler, editors

Body of Awareness: A Somatic Developmental Approach to Psychotherapy
 Ruella Frank

The Unfolding Self: Essays of Jean-Marie Robine
 Jean-Marie Robine; edited and translated by Gordon Wheeler

Encountering Bigotry: Befriending Projecting Persons in Everyday Life
 Philip Lichtenberg, Janneke van Beusekom Dorothy Gibbons

Reading Paul Goodman
 Gordon Wheeler, editor

The Values of Connection: A Relational Approach to Ethics
 Robert G. Lee, editor

WindowFrames:Learning the Art of Gestalt Play Therapy the Oaklander Way
 Peter Mortola

Gestalt Therapy: Living Creatively Today
 Gonzague Masquelier

The Secret Language of Intimacy: Releasing the Hidden Power in Couple Relationships
 Robert G. Lee

CoCreating the Field:Intention & Practice in the Age of Complexity
 Deborah Ullman & Gordon Wheeler, editors

Transforming the way we live and work in the world

Gestalt International Study Center

GISC is a diverse worldwide learning community based on trust, optimism and generosity. We study and teach skills that energize human interaction and lead to action, change and growth, and we create powerful learning experiences for individuals and organizations.

- **Leadership Development**
    - **Leadership in the 21st Century**
    - **Leading Nonprofit Organizations**
    - **Graduate Leadership Forum**
- **Professional Skill Development**
    - **Cape Cod Training Program**
    - **Introduction to the Cape Cod Model**
    - **Executive Personality Dynamics for Coaches**
    - **Applying the Cape Cod Model to Coaching**
    - **Applying the Cape Cod Model in Organizations**
    - **Finding Your Developmental Edge**
    - **Women in the Working World**
    - **Advanced Supervision**
- **Personal Development**
    - **The Next Phase: A Program for Transition & Renewal**
    - **Optimism & Awareness Essential Skills for Living**
    - **Couples Workshop**
    - **Building Blocks of Creativity**
    - **Nature & Transitions**
- *Gestalt Review*

Launched in 1977, Gestalt Review focuses on the Gestalt approach at all systems levels, ranging from the individual, through couples, families and groups, to organizations, educational settings and the community at large. To read sample articles, or to subscribe, visit:

www.gestaltreview.com

For more information about any of GISC's offerings or to read our newsletter, visit:

www.gisc.com